The Cultural Theory *of* Matthew Arnold

The Cultural Theory *of* Matthew Arnold

Joseph Carroll

UNIVERSITY OF CALIFORNIA PRESS
Berkeley • Los Angeles • London

University of California Press
Berkeley and Los Angeles, California

University of California Press, Ltd.
London, England

Library of Congress Cataloging in Publication Data

Carroll, Joseph.
The cultural theory of Matthew Arnold.
Bibliography: p.
Includes index.
1. Arnold, Matthew, 1822–1888—Philosophy. 2. Arnold, Matthew, 1822–1888—Religion and ethics. 3. Culture. 4. Social evolution. I. Title.
PR4024.C37 821'.8 81-23996
ISBN 0-520-04616-1 AACR2

Printed in the United States of America

1 2 3 4 5 6 7 8 9

To Paula,
whose good judgment forestalled many a false step

Contents

Note on Sources and Abbreviations

All quotations of Arnold's prose works are taken from R. H. Super's edition of *The Complete Prose Works of Matthew Arnold* (Ann Arbor: University of Michigan Press, 1962–77); quotations will be cited parenthetically in the text by volume and page number.

All quotations of Arnold's poetry are taken from *The Poetical Works of Matthew Arnold*, ed. C. B. Tinker and H. F. Lowry (London: Oxford University Press, 1950).

The following abbreviations will be used in citing Arnold's notebooks and letters:

NB *The Note-Books of Matthew Arnold*, ed. Howard Foster Lowry, Karl Young, and Waldo Hilary Dunn (London: Oxford University Press, 1952).

LETTERS 1 or 2 *Letters of Matthew Arnold*, ed. George W. E. Russell (New York: Macmillan, 1895).

LC *The Letters of Matthew Arnold to Arthur Hugh Clough*, ed. H. F. Lowry (Oxford: Oxford University Press, 1932).

Introduction

There has been a great deal of scholarly and critical work done on the poetry and prose of Matthew Arnold, much of it very good, some of it thoroughly distinguished. Arnold's rank as one of the better poets and as the most important critic of his period seems firmly established.[1] Nonetheless, the shape of his intellectual development, the import of his ideas, and the exact nature of his affinities with classical, European, and English literature remain issues subject to widely divergent and often conflicting interpretations. One of the few points on which there seems to be something approaching a critical consensus is that Arnold is not to be regarded as a systematic thinker. The supposedly unsystematic character of Arnold's thought has been taken variously as a simple defect of logical power or as evidence of that "flexibility" Arnold himself urged as a primary intellectual virtue. T. S. Eliot, in a well-known essay, gives us the negative side of this reading. "Arnold had little gift for consistency or for definition. Nor had he the power of connected reasoning at any length: his flights are either short flights or circular flights. Nothing in his prose work, therefore, will stand very close analysis, and we may well feel that the positive content of many words is very small."[2] F. R. Leavis, in his

1. Basil Willey made this claim in 1949, and nothing in the last three decades has gone to discountenance it. *Nineteenth Century Studies: Coleridge to Matthew Arnold* (New York: Columbia University Press, 1949), p. 251.

2. T. S. Eliot, "Arnold and Pater," *Selected Essays*, 3d ed. (London: Faber and Faber, 1951), p. 431. See also *The Use of Poetry and the Use of Criticism*

response to Eliot's evaluation, concedes the justice of this judgment but seeks nonetheless to explain why Arnold remains "one of the most lively and profitable of the accepted critics."[3] In his solution to this problem Leavis defines the sort of intelligence he sees as characteristic of literary criticism: "an intelligence that, even if not trained to some kinds of rigour, had its own discipline, an intelligence that is informed by a mature and delicate sense of the humane values and can manifest itself directly as a fine sensibility."[4]

The defense of Arnold formulated by Leavis has set the pattern for the greater part of later criticism. In an influential essay John Holloway argues that Arnold "inculcates not a set of ultimate beliefs—a 'Life-Philosophy'—but simply certain habits and a certain temper of mind."[5] David DeLaura, who has done much excellent work in Arnold scholarship, maintains a similar thesis and specifies that it was to "the Oxford Movement, and above all to Newman," that "Arnold was to look for that temper of mind which he was to recommend as perhaps the chief substance of his critical and social essays."[6] William Madden, emphasizing Arnold's poetic

(Cambridge, Mass.: Harvard University Press, 1933), p. 114. Eliot's remarks are echoed by Leon Gottfried in *Matthew Arnold and the Romantics* (London: Routledge and Kegan Paul, 1963), p. 210, and by Warren D. Anderson in *Matthew Arnold and the Classical Tradition* (1965; reprint ed., Ann Arbor: University of Michigan Press, 1971), p. 45. Geoffrey Tillotson, taking a slightly different tack, criticizes Arnold's prose not so much for its lack of logical rigor as for its "lack of knowledge and grasp." *Mid-Victorian Studies* (London: Athlone Press, 1965), p. 155.

3. F. R. Leavis, "Arnold as Critic," *Scrutiny* 7 (1938), reprinted in *A Selection from Scrutiny*, ed. F. R. Leavis, 2 vols. (Cambridge: Cambridge University Press, 1968), 1:259.

4. Ibid., p. 261.

5. John Holloway, *The Victorian Sage: Studies in Argument* (1953; reprint ed., London: Macmillan, 1962), p. 203. In a later essay Holloway seems to have modified this view. He declares that the "willingness to speak out, and with decision, is the best thing in Arnold." "Matthew Arnold and the Modern Dilemma," *The Charted Mirror: Literary and Critical Essays* (London: Routledge and Kegan Paul, 1960), p. 162. Holloway's earlier thesis, that Arnold's message is contained more in his style than in what he says, remains prevalent. J. Hillis Miller offers a rather sinister inversion of this earlier thesis. In Miller's treatment Arnold is emptied of doctrinal content, and the message of his style becomes one of emptiness and futility. "Arnold resigns himself to being nothing. . . . He is condemned to be inwardly a void, to be always in motion, always an unsatisfied desire." *The Disappearance of God: Five Nineteenth-Century Writers* (Cambridge, Mass.: Harvard University Press, 1963), p. 262.

6. David J. DeLaura, *Hebrew and Hellene in Victorian England: Newman, Arnold, and Pater* (Austin: University of Texas Press, 1969), p. 8.

preoccupations, argues that "the main burden of Arnold's criticism is not a particular intellectual or moral gospel, but the exhibition and defense of this poetic temper and attitude."[7] Taking a wider focus, William Robbins declares that Arnold offers "not a rounded and coherent philosophy, but rather a set of humanistic ideals which stress the need for balance and a sane perspective."[8] In one of the most recent attempts to analyze Arnold's historical thought, Peter Dale continues to segregate the exercise of critical sensibility from definite doctrinal propositions. "His affectivist approach seeks to place value in the emotional and moral experience of the perceiver rather than in the object itself because he has ceased to believe that the truths of religion or metaphysics are anything but relative and has come instead to believe that the only truths one can be sure of are deep emotional reactions within oneself."[9]

In this study I shall argue that Arnold's great distinction as a critic, that which yields to his critical judgments their singular power and enduring interest, is something more than a fine sensibility, an urbane manner, or even the wisdom and dignity of his humanistic ideals. The fundamental source of Arnold's critical importance is his own sense that literary theory must not be isolated from other types of knowledge, that it must take its place within a comprehensive vision of man's place in nature and in history. His individual perceptions and judgments have weight precisely because they are not merely the expression of an amorphous sensibility, but rather formulations within a continuous effort to give shape and definition to the whole range of human experience. When Arnold comments on Keats, Goethe, or Voltaire, or when he judges Pope, Wordsworth, or Heine, he does not merely

7. William Madden, *Matthew Arnold: A Study of the Aesthetic Temperament in Victorian England* (Bloomington: Indiana University Press, 1967), p. 130. Madden maintains that Arnold's temperament was fixed early in his life, so that there is no real development in his thought. A similar opinion, though with different views on the nature of Arnold's temperament, is urged by R. H. Super in *The Time-Spirit of Matthew Arnold* (Ann Arbor: University of Michigan Press, 1970), p. 90, and by Kenneth Allott in *Matthew Arnold* (London: Longmans, Green, 1962), p. 13, and in "Matthew Arnold's Reading-Lists in Three Early Diaries," *Victorian Studies* 2 (1959): 266.

8. William Robbins, *The Ethical Idealism of Matthew Arnold* (London: William Heinemann, 1959), p. ix.

9. Peter Dale, *The Victorian Critic and the Idea of History: Carlyle, Arnold, Pater* (Cambridge, Mass.: Harvard University Press, 1977), p. 163.

note qualities of style and character or merely set them within a hierarchy of literary excellence. His overriding concern is to situate them within a complete cultural system.[10]

There are four distinct phases in Arnold's career: the period of discontent represented by the early poetry; the modernist Hellenism culminating in *Culture and Anarchy*; the eight-year period of Biblical studies; and a final decade in which Arnold returns to his modernism but attempts to integrate the doctrines of critical reason with the reverential imagination of Romantic poetry. Arnold's early poetry establishes the problems to which all of his later, critical work responds. The two basic problems, explored most thoroughly in "Empedocles on Etna," are the alienation of mind from nature and the sense of futility inherent in a cyclical conception of history. In poetry Arnold could not create a new "order of ideas" that would resolve these problems. Therefore, in "On the Modern Element in Literature," Arnold announces his critical mission, to find an "intellectual deliverance" from spiritual distress. As I shall seek to demonstrate, the modernist Hellenism of *Culture and Anarchy* represents the apex of Arnold's theoretical development, for it is in the cultural system worked out in this phase that Arnold succeeds in resolving the problems he has explored in his poetry. Arnold bases his system of culture on two assumptions that most of us no longer make. He comes to believe in the existence of objective, universally valid moral and aesthetic laws, and to believe that these laws have been progressively revealing and developing themselves throughout the history of Western culture.[11] Accordingly, Arnold fashions a comprehensive theory of

10. Lionel Trilling speaks of "the complex unity of Arnold's thought," but he also declares that "Arnold had a passionate dislike of system." *Matthew Arnold* (1939; reprint ed., Cleveland, Ohio: World Publishing, 1955), pp. 9 and 10. Trilling's book remains one of the most readable works on Arnold, but he makes too light of the systematic elements in Arnold's thought. Hellenism and Hebraism, for example, are facetiously compared with "buckets in a well," and the differences between them are said to be the same as those "between Square and Thwackum" (pp. 234 and 235). Vincent Buckley, in *Poetry and Morality: Studies on the Criticism of Matthew Arnold, T. S. Eliot, and F. R. Leavis* (London: Chatto and Windus, 1959), states that Arnold is "a systematiser, a synthetic thinker" (p. 25), but by emphasizing the "weakness in Arnold's grasp" (p. 76), he loses sight of this thesis and sometimes argues just the opposite (see pp. 54 and 57). Buckley is mainly concerned with Arnold's theory of poetry.

11. Raymond Williams, who gives an acute and sympathetic appraisal of Arnold's social views, maintains that in the conflict between the admission of

cultural progress, and he establishes a necessary correspondence between the shape of history and the structure of the enlightened individual mind. It is the formation of this theory that enables Arnold to satisfy his deepest and most abiding intellectual need—the need for wholeness, that is, unity and completeness.[12]

In order to grasp the difference in Arnold's outlook between the period of his poetic creativity and the writing of *Culture and Anarchy*, we may compare two poems, "Stanzas in Memory of the Author of 'Obermann' " (1849) and "Obermann Once More" (1867). At the time of writing the first elegy to Senancour, Arnold was twenty-five years old, in full poetic productivity, and struggling desperately to free himself from "the hopeless tangle of our age" (line 83). Senancour epitomizes for Arnold the extreme realization of one of his own strongest impulses, the simple urge to withdraw from the spiritual chaos of the nineteenth century: "this strange disease of modern life, / With its sick hurry, its divided aims, / Its heads o'ertax'd, its palsied hearts" ("The Scholar-Gipsy," 1853). Retreating to an Alpine solitude, Senancour manages to remain one of the "Children of the Second Birth," an innocent, "unspotted by the world," whose chief consolation for the loss of traditional Christian belief is a natural mysticism. He "heard accents of the eternal tongue / Through the pine branches play." Although it expresses a deep sympathy for Senancour, Arnold's elegy ends on a note of condescension and dismissal. "O unstrung will! O broken heart!" Like Arnold's youthful friend Arthur Hugh Clough, me-

---

cultural relativism and the grasping for "an absolute" there is a "final breakdown" in Arnold's thinking. *Culture and Society: 1780–1950* (New York: Columbia University Press, 1960), pp. 127–28. Williams is right in defining this issue as the theoretical crux of Arnold's work, but as I shall try to show in chapter 2 of this study, Arnold does in fact succeed in synthesizing these elements within his cultural dialectic.

12. Gaylord C. LeRoy's essay on Arnold in *Perplexed Prophets: Six Nineteenth-Century British Authors* (Philadelphia: University of Pennsylvania Press, 1953), provides one of the best brief accounts of Arnold's theory of history, which LeRoy praises for its "comprehensiveness and inner consistency" (p. 50). Since, however, LeRoy concentrates his analysis on the conflict between elitism and democratic sentiment in Arnold's political thought, he denies that Arnold achieves any adequate synthesis (p. 73). This conflict seems to me to be a peripheral issue. Fraser Neiman quotes and takes issue with LeRoy's eulogy of Arnold's historical thought. "The Zeitgeist of Matthew Arnold," *PMLA* 72 (1957): 979. Because Neiman's article concentrates on Arnold's use of the term *Zeitgeist*, he is thus led to emphasize the early poetry and the religious works, to skim over the early essays, and to skip *Culture and Anarchy* altogether.

morialized in "Thyrsis," Senancour is sensitive enough to recognize the spiritual malady of his time, but not strong enough to resist and overcome it. As Arnold explains in his essay "Obermann" (1869), there was "in the constitution of Senancour's own nature" a "root of failure, powerlessness and ennui" (V, 300).

In "Obermann Once More," published eighteen years later in Arnold's last volume of poetry, Arnold returns to Senancour's Swiss village. The ghost of Senancour, appearing to Arnold in a vision, announces the dawning of a new age and exhorts Arnold to return to the world with renewed hope and strength. The main body of the poem consists of Senancour's impassioned synopsis of the spiritual progression of Western culture. He begins with "that hard Pagan world" and proceeds through the Christian interregnum and its gradual dissolution, the slow recession of "that tide of common thought," and finally the shattering by the French Revolution of "the worn-out world we knew." What was left for Senancour—and for the early Arnold—were "poor fragments of a broken world." Senancour declares that he did not himself despair of some new hope that "must dawn at last," but that he had been born too early to take part in it:

'The day I lived in was not mine,
Man gets no second day.
In dreams I saw the future shine—
But ah! I could not stay!'

He maintains that Arnold himself has been more fortunate in his historical situation:

Despair not thou as I despair'd,
Nor be cold gloom thy prison!
Forward the gracious hours have fared,
And see! the sun is risen!

. . . .

The world's great order dawns in sheen,
After long darkness rude,
Divinelier imaged, clearer seen,
With happier zeal pursued.

Arnold recognizes that his own "youthful prime" is past. He has been shorn of his own personal "joy," that is, his youthful spirits, "the bloom, the power" that "best befits" the "bard" of a "world new-made." Even so, there is another kind of joy: the general possession of a spiritually and intellectually healthy epoch, "*One common wave of thought and joy / Lifting mankind again!*" It is still within Arnold's power to contribute to this.

Arnold's entire career, and the historical significance he attributed to it, must be seen within the context that Senancour's ghost establishes in this poem. Many of Arnold's most famous poems fall within the phase, chronological and ideational, of the first "Obermann." In the period between the two elegies Arnold developed a cultural theory that he felt would bridge the gulf between the old world and the new, that would preserve the spiritual heritage of the past and use it to unify and elevate the modern world. It is by his own critical effort that the world is "divinelier imaged, clearer seen." In a letter to his mother, written in 1869, Arnold says that "my poems represent, on the whole, the main movement of mind of the last quarter of a century."[13] Neither in "Obermann Once More" nor in the thematically similar "Thyrsis" does Arnold say specifically how and why the world has changed. Although the other poems of 1867 offer images of Arnold as a soldier in the war of intellectual liberation ("The Last Word") and give strong hints about his theoretical preoccupations ("Heine's Grave" and "Epilogue to Lessing's Laocoön"), they are generally more limited in range and depth than the early poems. The current of Arnold's intellectual life has by this time turned from poetry to prose. To understand, then, the world-transformation that Arnold announces in his poems, and his own role in that transformation, we must turn to the prose.

Arnold's initial critical doctrine, that of the 1853 Preface, is one of an aesthetic withdrawal from the modern world. Four years later, in "On the Modern Element in Literature" (his inaugural lecture as professor of poetry at Oxford), he redefines "modern" in a way that enables him to project a critical salvation, a "true point of view" from which to contemplate the entire spectacle of the past and present. My topic in this study will be the nature and development of this point of view. I shall, furthermore, attempt to situate Arnold within the modern critical and theoretical traditions from which he derives and to which he contributes. In his cultural theory Arnold's avowed affiliation is to the German line that extends from Lessing through Goethe to Heine. His nearest native English affinity, as I shall argue, is to the rationalist

13. *Letters* 2:10 (June 5, 1869).

neoclassicism of the eighteenth century. There is some overlapping of the two traditions, but the Augustans—chiefly Dryden, Pope, Swift, and Johnson—are preeminently characterized by an ahistorical rationalism, the faith in right reason. Two of the German writers on whom Arnold draws most heavily, Lessing and Heine, are useful to Arnold primarily for their orientation toward the reality of historical change.

In the first two chapters of this study I shall try to demonstrate that Arnold succeeds in establishing a coherent cultural theory. In chapter 3 I shall examine the personal, social, and intellectual reasons for Arnold's absorption in religious topics, and I shall analyze the way in which his religious thought ultimately negates itself, modulating into an advocacy of poetry as the spiritual foundation of modern life. In chapter 4 I shall be concerned to establish the doctrinal parallelism between Arnold and the English neoclassicists and to show that much of Arnold's practical criticism derives from that of his predecessors. In chapter 5 I shall consider how Arnold situates himself as heir to the tradition of German cultural theory. Arnold singles out Goethe as the greatest modern man and the greatest critic of all time, but Goethe's critical vision is largely ahistorical. The structure of history in Arnold's own work appears as a synthesis between the progressivism of Lessing and the dichotomy of Hellenism and Hebraism formulated by Heine. I have chosen to segregate the two comparative chapters from the initial exposition of Arnold's theory so that the systematic unity of that theory may be the more clearly delineated. I have placed them after the exposition so that Arnold's responses to the Augustans and Germans may be discussed in the light of his progressive intellectual development.

The religious phase of Arnold's career seems to be a period of regression.[14] It is equivalent to the dialectically necessary epochs of moral "concentration" in Arnold's historical scheme, but its Hebraic nature makes it rather narrow and exclusive. The Hellenic Arnold makes a provision for the Hebraic, but the Hebraic Arnold remains somewhat hostile to the sympathetic flexibility of the

14. For arguments to the contrary, see Basil Willey's *Nineteenth Century Studies*, p. 252. Willey locates Arnold's "centre of gravity" in his religious writings. In similar fashion, David J. DeLaura argues that it is only in the religious writing that Arnold managed to "work out with authority the conditions of 'the joy whose grounds are true.'" *Matthew Arnold: A Collection of Critical Essays* (Englewood Cliffs, N.J.: Prentice-Hall, 1973), p. 5.

Hellenic.[15] When Arnold returns in his last decade to his Hellenic doctrine, this doctrine is qualified by a lingering concern for moral salvation. Consequently, Arnold displays in this period a certain ambivalence with respect to the conflicting claims of the critical reason and the Romantic imagination. Although he succeeds in creating a coherent cultural theory, his victory retains a measure of anxious willfulness. The insecurity of his solutions to the problems he has explored in his early poetry reveals itself most clearly in his ambivalent judgments on the writers who most profoundly influence his own work: the German cultural theorists, the English neoclassicists, and the Romantics. By examining his struggle to mediate between Augustan rationalism and the Romantic imagination, between the critical and poetic aspects of Goethe's work, and between Heine's critical license and the reverential humanism of Lessing, we should gain a more vivid sense of the vital tensions beneath the surface of his discursive coherence.

Since the positive boundaries of Arnold's theoretical vision are, on the one hand, his faith in right reason and, on the other, his faith in a historical teleology, and since both of these faiths are now more or less obsolete, many of Arnold's ideas must appear today unintelligible or fantastic. Arnold himself, however, was thoroughly imbued with the spirit of empirical inquiry, and he seeks at all points to ground his idealism in the observed facts of cultural history. Arnold's doctrine of culture as the means and end of human perfection rests securely on a legitimate principle of self-validation; his ideal of human perfection still has cogency, and his theoretical system has a practical value for the criticism of literature and culture. My purpose will be to render that system more intelligible both in its own right and as a conscious contribution to the main currents of eighteenth- and nineteenth-century criticism.

15. It is for this reason that I disagree with William Robbins's contention that there is no conflict between the Hellenism of *Culture and Anarchy* and the Hebraism of the religious books. *Ethical Idealism*, p. 41.

1

1 *Aesthetic Compromises*

Arnold's early poems establish the spiritual plight to which all of his later, prose work responds. The Preface to his 1853 collection of poems represents his first prose attempt to cope with the problems articulated by the poems. Though perhaps his best-known essay, the 1853 Preface is not a success. In effect it repudiates the entire intellectual struggle that forms the substance of his poetry. The explicit purpose of the Preface is to explain Arnold's reasons for excluding "Empedocles on Etna" from the 1853 collection. Since "Empedocles" is a dramatic poem, and since Arnold's Preface, drawing heavily on Aristotle and the English neoclassicists, concentrates on the structure of dramatic and epic literature, it is possible to argue that Arnold's strictures against "Empedocles" do not apply to his lyric and meditative poetry. Consequently, contrary to the opinions of contemporary reviewers, there is no essential conflict between his theory and his own poetic practice.[1] In the Preface to the second edition of his *Poems* (1854)

1. Alba H. Warren, Jr., maintains that "what makes the Preface unique" in the nineteenth century "is the completeness and consistency with which it restates Aristotle." *English Poetic Theory: 1825–1865* (Princeton, N.J.: Princeton University Press, 1950), p. 169. Henry Ebel harshly, but more accurately, characterizes Arnold's use of Aristotle as "an often dishonest medley of straight paraphrase, loose recapitulation, and outright but unacknowledged embroidery." "Matthew Arnold and Classical Culture," *Arion* 4 (1965): 198. The charge of dishonesty rests on an unfounded assumption that Arnold presents himself as strictly and exclusively an adherent of Aristotle. For a discussion of the neoclassical influences on the 1853 Preface, see chapter 4 of the present study.

Arnold remarks that the first Preface leaves "untouched the question, how far and in what manner the opinions there expressed respecting the choice of subjects apply to lyric poetry,—that region of the poetical field which is chiefly cultivated at present" (I, 16). This defense will not stand inspection. The generic distinctions on which it relies are superficial. In the first Preface Arnold represents the "choice of subject" as in itself determining the structure of a dramatic work, and his structural criticisms of "Empedocles" irresistibly convert themselves into thematic criticism that extends itself to the greatest part of his poetry.

"Empedocles" is Arnold's most thorough exploration of the spiritual malaise of his own times. The problems it describes and the various solutions or alternatives it proposes subsume those of the shorter poems and, by subsuming them, implicate them in the final, suicidal frustration of Empedocles himself. Arnold repudiates this poem because it has no resolution; the suffering of Empedocles "finds no vent in action" (I, 2). His "continuous state of mental distress is prolonged, unrelieved by incident, hope, or resistance." His condition is "morbid" and peculiarly "modern." For Arnold at this point, *modern* is synonymous with *declining*, and the age of Empedocles, the declining period of Greece, serves as a prototype for post-Christian Europe. Like the age of Empedocles, Arnold's own modern age is marked by the doubt, discouragement, and self-involved intellectuality of Hamlet and Faust. In the Preface Arnold's proposal for dealing with this situation is that poets should withdraw from modern life altogether and turn to "the contemplation of some noble action of a heroic time" (I, 14). The Empedocles of Arnold's poem has already foreseen this tactic of evasion and has recognized its futility:

> And we shall struggle awhile, gasp and rebel—
> And we shall fly for refuge to past times,
> Their soul of unworn youth, their breath of greatness;
> And the reality will pluck us back,
> Knead us in its hot hand, and change our nature
> And we shall feel our powers of effort flag,
> And rally them for one last fight—and fail;
> And we shall sink in the impossible strife,
> And be astray for ever.
>
> (ACT 2, LINES 382–90)

The classical withdrawal of the Preface is a holding action. Arnold's delineation of the aesthetic qualities of classical literature —its detachment, objectivity, and unity—provides him with an aesthetic standard against which to measure the quality of his own experience, but it does not provide a cure for that experience. In "Dover Beach" and "Stanzas from the Grande Chartreuse" Arnold attempts to escape the morbid despair of Empedocles by transforming it into, or at least associating it with, the classical aesthetic standards of the Preface. However successful as lyric artifacts these poems may be, they do not provide an intellectual resolution, a guide for life, or a basis for a continuing poetic production. They are, as it were, sterile hybrids. In the development of his cultural theory Arnold will manage to transcend the doctrine of the Preface and to integrate his classicism into a modernist ethos, but to do so he will have to confront the intellectual sources of Empedocles' plight and construct an intellectual answer to them. In order to grasp the significance of his answer we shall first need to examine "Empedocles" and its relation to the other poems of this period.

In the 1853 Preface Arnold says that in the extant fragments of the historical Empedocles the characteristics of the early Greek genius, "the calm, the cheerfulness, the disinterested objectivity have disappeared" (I, 1). What Arnold does not here remark, but nonetheless implies by his reprinting of Callicles' songs as separate lyrics, is that these characteristics are not absent from his own poem.[2] Callicles, the young musician whose songs drift up to Empedocles from lower down on Mount Etna, represents the innocent freshness of an undisturbed traditional culture, and from this vantage ground he criticizes Empedocles in terms similar to those Arnold uses in the Preface. Since Callicles is himself insensible to the incipient decline of Greek culture, he does not, like Arnold, attribute Empedocles' distress to this historical situation. He does see that Empedocles is "too high-wrought," that "there is some root of suffering in himself," and that his mind is "preying on itself." Both Callicles and Pausanias, to whom he makes these remarks, are friends of Empedocles, but neither of them is a philosopher, and they are incapable of a sympathetic participation in his intel-

2. The publication information is given by C. B. Tinker and H. F. Lowry in *The Poetry of Matthew Arnold: A Commentary* (New York: Oxford University Press, 1940), pp. 286–87.

lectual trouble. The lyric harmony of Callicles' singing depends upon a harmonious world view, a mythic and ethical framework in which everything—man, nature, and the gods—has its proper place:

In such a glen, on such a day,
On Pelion, on the grassy ground,
Chiron, the aged Centaur lay,
The young Achilles standing by.
. . . .
He told him of the Gods, the stars,
The tides;—and then of mortal wars,
And of the life which heroes lead
Before they reach the Elysian place
And rest in the immortal mead;
And all the wisdom of his race.
(ACT 1, SCENE 2, LINES 57–60, 71–76)

For Empedocles "the wisdom of his race" has ceased to have any cogency. Consequently, he is cast back on the light of the independent intelligence. He counsels Pausanias against a superstitious credulity in the gods and urges on him the practical necessity of intellectual responsibility. "Mind is the spell which governs earth and heaven" (Act 1, scene 2, line 27). Yet he knows—and this is the essential source of his grief—that the mind can attain to no complete and certain knowledge:

Hither and thither spins
The wind-borne, mirroring soul,
A thousand glimpses wins,
And never sees a whole;
Looks once, and drives elsewhere, and leaves its last employ.

The Gods laugh in their sleeve
To watch man doubt and fear,
Who knows not what to believe
Since he sees nothing clear,
And dares stamp nothing false where he finds nothing sure.
(ACT 1, SCENE 2, LINES 82–91)

Empedocles' skepticism has become so complete that he refuses even to affirm his own uncertainty. "Is this, Pausanias, so? . . . I will not judge." Ultimately, "a slave of thought," he cannot resist judging, but in the long central section of the poem he suspends his intellectual despair in order to give to Pausanias advice whereby he "may bravelier front his life, and in himself / Find henceforth energy and heart" (Act 2, lines 9–10).

The advice that Empedocles urges on Pausanias is to turn skepticism into moral pragmatism. "Ask what most helps when known." The substance of his moral doctrine is not, however, simply to believe whatever seems most pleasant and gratifying. As he assures himself later, after Pausanias has left and he is alone, "I have loved no darkness, / Sophisticated no truth, / Nursed no delusion" (Act 2, lines 400–02). The doctrine he presents to Pausanias is severe in its delineation of the inevitable miseries and frustrations of life and in its rejection of false hopes and factitious consolations. He declares that man's folly, the source of both his discontent and his delusions, is his bent to make his desires the measure of his expectations. The "thirst for bliss" cannot, in the nature of things, be wholly quenched. The wise man is he who recognizes his limitations within a world order that has no special care for human happiness or human justice.

> Streams will not curb their pride
> The just man not to entomb,
> Nor lightnings go aside
> To give his virtues room;
> Nor is that wind less rough which blows a good man's barge.
>
> Nature, with equal mind,
> Sees all her sons at play;
> Sees man control the wind,
> The wind sweep man away;
> Allows the proudly-riding and the foundering bark.
>
> (ACT 1, SCENE 2, LINES 252–61)

With prudence, self-restraint, and renunciation, man may achieve, at best, "*moderate* bliss." It is, Empedocles maintains, the refusal to accept this brute fact that has impelled men to create the gods, "peopling the void air," so that the frustrations of worldly desire may be resolved in an afterlife and so that man's hopeless craving for intellectual fulfillment, to "mete the immeasurable All," may be vicariously enjoyed in the divine omniscience. For men of intellectual integrity like Empedocles, this sort of "resolution" renders all experience a sham. His conclusion for Pausanias contains an unequivocal injunction, "thou must not dream," coupled with a much less emphatic counsel of cheer, "thou need'st not then despair!" The good that Empedocles holds out to Pausanias as still possible consists of the common things in life, those pleasures that "the village-churl" is more likely than the philosopher to recognize and cling to: "To have enjoy'd the sun, / To have lived light in the spring, / To have loved, to have thought, to have done" (Act 1, scene 2, lines 398–400). These pleasures, however, are no longer accessible to Empedocles himself. He feels in himself a "weariness no energy can reach" and a "hurt" for which "courage," such as that which he urges on Pausanias, "is not the cure."

In the remaining part of the poem Empedocles attempts to define precisely what it is that has weakened his spirit and "dried its self-sufficing fount of joy." His answers to this question provide the starting point for Arnold's theoretical mission, but they transcend his own intentions in writing the poem. The final soliloquy of Empedocles gets away from Arnold and poses problems he is not willing to pose to himself at this time in the sobriety of prose. Tinker and Lowry, in their *Commentary* on Arnold's poems, publish his "prose outline and summary of the poem he wanted to create."[3] In this outline Arnold attributes Empedocles' spiritual condition solely to the misfortune of his personal and historical circumstances. Arnold says that Empedocles "sees things as they are—the world as it is—God as he is: in their stern simplicity" but that this vision is not itself the cause of his despair. On the contrary, "he does not deny that the sight is capable of affording rapture and the purest peace." His problem is, rather, that "his friends are dead" and that he is unable "to hold fast so great and severe a truth in solitude."

In Arnold's account in his prose outline Empedocles objectively recognizes a cosmic grandeur to which, because he has lost his "spring and elasticity of mind," he is no longer equal. "Before he becomes the victim of depression and overtension of mind, to the utter deadness to joy, grandeur, spirit, and animated life, he desires to die; to be reunited with the universe, before by exaggerating his human side he has become utterly estranged from it." This statement corresponds to only part of Empedocles' own analysis of his condition. As Arnold says, his intention is to die "before the soul lose all her solemn joys" and before man and the world "be dis-

3. Ibid., pp. 291–92.

array'd of their divinity" (Act 2, lines 33, 32). The exaggeration of "his human side" is the unbalanced emphasis on "words," an intellectual busyness that disturbs the simple pleasures of nature, and for this he blames the Sophists. As his soliloquy progresses, however, it becomes ever more apparent that he does not suffer merely from an imbalance in his own powers of feeling and thinking. Such an imbalance might be righted as, for instance, Wordsworth righted it in himself. The conflict is more fundamental, an irreconcilable division between "life" and "mind." Contrary to Arnold's statement in the prose outline and to Empedocles' own initial statement of his situation, he is already "dead to life and joy." It is already too late to forestall this form of despair through suicide.

> But no, this heart will glow no more; thou art
> A living man no more, Empedocles!
> Nothing but a devouring flame of thought—
> But a naked, eternally restless mind!
> (ACT 2, LINES 327–30)

As Arnold says, Empedocles does still recognize "animated life" in nature—the stars and elements—and to this he would return his body: "Our blood to water, / Heat to fire, / Breath to air" (Act 2, lines 334–36). However, he cannot find any relation between these elements of life and the activity of mind. At first he prays to the elements to "take me home!" But then he recognizes that mind and thought have no "home," no "parent element"; they are "the strangers of the world." There is no possibility of union between the animated life of nature and the divisive, intrusive, and distorting character of the intellect. This conclusion comes near the end of the poem, and it reveals to us, beyond the scope of Arnold's intentions, the real source of Empedocles' despair.

Since mentality is the defining quality of humanity, our "human side," spiritual frustration appears as the culmination of all human experience, and from this human condition there is no escape. Once the intellect becomes "the master part of us," once we have identified ourselves with our own conscious recognitions, we must then remain "prisoners of our consciousness," unable ever to "clasp and feel the All" but through the "forms, and modes, and stifling veils" of thought. After he reaches this conclusion, Empedocles recognizes that death cannot provide the resolution he seeks. Mind remains an alien element, and death only gives the stamp of finality to spiritual futility: "the ineffable longing for the life of life / Baffled for ever."

Carried to its logical extreme, Empedocles' problem is not merely personal and social but epistemological and metaphysical. The problem is not his alone and is not limited to one anomalous phase of history, the accident of decline in the Greek world. It appears to him rather as an inevitable and recurrent progression of intellectual alienation that provides a prototype for all of cultural history.[4] For Empedocles, standing at the apex of the intellectual progression, the cyclical view of history presents itself in the guise of individual reincarnation. This idea opens to him the prospect of a perpetual renewal of "impossible strife" and a futile struggle to achieve a state of poise in which "we are one with the whole world." Each succeeding age of experience changes only in the intensity and hopelessness of the struggle:

> And each succeeding age in which we are born
> Will have more peril for us than the last;
> Will goad our senses with a sharper spur,
> Will fret our minds to an intenser play,
> Will make ourselves harder to be discern'd.
>
> (ACT 2, LINES 377–81)

The last, useless tactic in this struggle is, as we have already seen, the attempt to revert to a simpler, more innocent age. Even if this were possible, it would provide no exit from the cycles of "sad probation" that always end in failure and despair. The only consolation that Empedocles can offer himself derives from his intellectual integrity. The fact that he has "nursed no delusion" allows him to think "but for a moment" that he has not been "all enslaved" and so permits him to die with a last, brief surge of hope

4. R. A. Forsyth has attempted to situate Arnold's Empedocles in the framework of Vico's cyclical conception of history. " 'The Buried Life'—The Contrasting Views of Arnold and Clough in the Context of Dr. Arnold's Historiography," *ELH* 35 (1968): 230. Also see Peter Dale, *The Victorian Critic and the Idea of History: Carlyle, Arnold, Pater* (Cambridge, Mass.: Harvard University Press, 1977), p. 97. Vico heavily influenced Arnold's father, but Arnold himself mentions Vico only once (IV, 145), and it seems to me that there is no very precise congruence between their ideas of history. Whereas Arnold's Empedocles regards reason as destructive of poetic myth, Vico believed the main function of reason to be the rediscovery and validation of ancient poetic wisdom.

for deliverance. He leaps into the crater before the hope can, as it must, die away.

In a letter written in 1867 Arnold objects to the common assumption that "I merely use Empedocles and Obermann as mouthpieces through which to vent my own opinions."[5] He concedes a certain "sympathy with the figure Empedocles presents to the imagination" but denies that his own "creed, if I wished or were able to draw it out in black and white," would "be by any means identical with that contained in the preachment of Empedocles."[6] Since Empedocles commits suicide, "his creed can hardly be meant to be one to live by." Arnold's presentation of his case begs the question of his own intentions. It implies that if Arnold were to voice his own opinions these would necessarily take the form of a positive moral doctrine, or a creed to live by. The advice that Empedocles gives to Pausanias is in fact a creed to live by, but what he says to himself when he is alone is not a creed but a probing exploration of spiritual distress. Arnold not only sympathizes with this distress but in a letter to Clough identifies it as his own: "yes—*congestion of the brain* is what we suffer from—I always feel it and say it—and cry for air like my own Empedocles."[7] By 1867 the terms in which Arnold actually does draw out his own creed in black and white imply philosophical assumptions fundamentally different from those of Empedocles, but in the early 1850s both the terms in which Arnold states his plight and the kinds of resistance he op-

5. Tinker and Lowry, *Commentary*, p. 287; this letter is not included in the standard collection of Arnold's letters.

6. Walter E. Houghton takes Arnold's protestations at face value and interprets the poem, in accord with Arnold's prose outline, "as a psychological and not a philosophical poem." "Arnold's 'Empedocles on Etna,'" *Victorian Studies* 1 (1958): 318. Louis Bonnerot and E. D. H. Johnson both argue that Arnold is in fact to be identified with Empedocles, but like Houghton, they both maintain that Empedocles' problem is not metaphysical but psychological—essentially a conflict between the need for society and the need for solitude. Louis Bonnerot, *Empedocles sur L'Etna* (Paris: Aubier, 1947), pp. 43 and 55. E. D. H. Johnson, *The Alien Vision of Victorian Poetry: Sources of the Poetic Imagination in Tennyson, Browning, and Arnold* (1952; reprint ed., Hamden, Conn.: Archon Books, 1963), p. 172. For a convincing evocation of Arnold's philosophical identification with Empedocles, see Kenneth Allott, "A Background for 'Empedocles on Etna,'" in *Essays and Studies 1968*, ed. Simeon Potter (London: John Murray, 1968), reprinted in *Matthew Arnold: A Collection of Critical Essays*, ed. David J. DeLaura (Englewood Cliffs, N.J.: Prentice-Hall, 1973).

7. *LC*, p. 130.

poses to despair are very much the same as those of Empedocles.

In the first three stanzas of an 1852 poem, "The Second Best," Arnold remarks that he has already lost the simple and coherent life that would be "best." The temperate mode of life that Empedocles urges on Pausanias is no longer possible for Arnold himself.

> MODERATE tasks and moderate leisure,
> Quiet living, strict-kept measure
> Both in suffering and in pleasure—
>   'Tis for this thy nature yearns.
>
> But so many books thou readest,
> But so many schemes thou breedest,
> But so many wishes feedest,
>   That thy poor head almost turns.
>
> And (the world's so madly jangled,
> Human things so fast entangled)
> Nature's wish must now be strangled
>   For that best which she discerns.

The "second best," Arnold's own alternative, is to "reject what cannot clear him" and to "cling to what can truly cheer him." His watchwords are "Hope, Light, Persistence," but these moral and intellectual standards are in themselves no resolution. They only provide a frame within which some possible resolution may be attained. If there is to be a resolution, it can come only through a critical effort that responds to the metaphysical and cultural malaise of which Empedocles gives the most complete expression.

In the 1853 Preface Arnold responds to the plight of Empedocles by adopting a creed of classical aesthetic unity and by insisting that literature concern itself exclusively with what is great and permanent in human experience, that is, actions that "most powerfully appeal to the great primary human affections: to those elementary feelings which subsist permanently in the race, and which are independent of time" (I, 4). With the aesthetic doctrine Arnold attempts to circumvent the two basic problems articulated by Empedocles: the problem of mind in its relation to nature and the problem of historical change. The "elementary part of our nature," Arnold maintains, is "our passions," and they are supposedly unaffected by the historical vagaries of belief. "The modernness or antiquity of an action, therefore, has nothing to do with its fitness for poetical representation: this depends upon its inherent qualities" (I, 4). Emotions, then, are permanent and inherent, and they are set in contrast to what is transient and accidental—the "dialogue of the mind with itself" and the recognition of cultural change (I, 1). Since, for Arnold, the natural modes of representing the "elementary feelings" are drama and the heroic epic, the subjective lyric and the meditative poem are necessarily inferior genres unless they too concentrate on the elementary and permanent. Accordingly, Arnold directs much of his own poetic activity at this time to pseudoclassical narratives like "Sohrab and Rustum" and "Balder Dead" (an unhappy mingling of the Nordic and the Homeric), and he makes as his most persistent lyric theme the affirmation of what is great and constant in nature.

One may measure the seriousness with which Arnold embraces his classical standards by noting that in judging his own poetry he elevates "Sohrab and Rustum" above "The Scholar-Gipsy."[8] This ranking, with which very few readers would agree, gives evidence of how far spiritual anxiety could impel Arnold into aesthetic moralism. In this letter of 1853 he is judging poetry almost entirely through the moral quality of its supposed effect. "Sohrab and Rustum" pleases him because it has the power "to *animate* and *ennoble*" men. "The Scholar-Gipsy," in contrast, "at best awakens a pleasing melancholy." Whereas "Sohrab and Rustum" occupies itself only with unambiguous passions, "The Scholar-Gipsy" is a modern poem, a meditation concerned with the pursuit of an intellectual ideal and aware of cultural change.

Arnold's classicist affirmations are themselves part of the internal dialogue that he was to carry on with himself for the rest of his life. They represent, however, only one voice in this dialogue. The other voice concedes that "*what you have to say* depends on your age," so that the quality of experience to be interpreted by poetry is radically altered by one's place in a cultural progression.[9] In "Empedocles" this recognition appears as a regret for the lost innocence of his own youth, a cultural phase that we may best regard as corresponding to Arnold's own immediate literary past, the Romantic prime.

8. *LC*, p. 146.
9. *LC*, p. 65.

And yet what days were those, Parmenides!
When we were young, . . .

. . . .

Then we could still enjoy, then neither thought
Nor outward things were closed and dead to us;
But we received the shock of mighty thoughts
On simple minds with a pure natural joy;

. . . .

We had not lost our balance then, nor grown
Thought's slaves, and dead to every natural joy.

(ACT 2, LINES 235–49)

These are the "prosperous days" that both Empedocles and Arnold have "outliv'd." In the first "Obermann" Arnold says that the two chief poets of his own literary youth, Goethe and Wordsworth, were able both "to see their way" but that both came to maturity in a world more peaceful and coherent than Arnold's own. Wordsworth was still able to evoke "the freshness of the early world" ("Memorial Verses"), and Goethe passed his youth "in a tranquil world" (first "Obermann"). Arnold's own time, like that of Empedocles' later life, has changed and has rendered impossible any harmonious simplicity and unity of vision:

But we, brought forth and rear'd in hours
Of change, alarm, surprise—
What shelter to grow ripe is ours?
What leisure to grow wise?

. . . .

Too fast we live, too much are tried,
Too harass'd, to attain
Wordsworth's sweet calm, or Goethe's wide
And luminous view to gain.

(FIRST "OBERMANN")

In "The Scholar-Gipsy" Arnold regards his own age, like the old age of Empedocles, as a phase of corruption within a cultural progression beginning in an earlier age of freshness and innocence:

O born in days when wits were fresh and clear,
And life ran gaily as the sparkling Thames;
Before this strange disease of modern life,
With its sick hurry, its divided aims,
Its heads o'ertax'd, its palsied hearts, was rife—

In his early lyric poetry Arnold responds to this situation, as does Empedocles, by fleeing from the world and seeking refuge in the grandeur, permanence, and vitality of nature. In "Quiet Work" (1849) he asks, "ONE lesson, Nature, let me learn of thee, / . . . / Of toil unsever'd from tranquility." In "Resignation" (1849) he admonishes his sister: "This world in which we draw our breath, / In some sense, Fausta, outlasts death." In "The Youth of Nature," another elegy for Wordsworth, he asks if the beauty of nature is something real in itself or if it exists only for the eyes of a poet gifted with a special vision. His answer is that "loveliness, magic, and grace, / They are here! They are set in the world, / They abide." A companion piece, "The Youth of Man," serves as a vehicle for the same theme: Nature is greater than any individual in it, and man's pleasures and accomplishments are not of his own making. This lesson is learned by a couple who in the folly of their youth claim that nature itself is empty and dumb and that all "glory" comes from man:

'We are young, and the world is ours;
Man, man is the king of the world!
Fools that these mystics are
Who prate of Nature! for she
Hath neither beauty, nor warmth,
Nor life, nor emotion, nor power.
But man has a thousand gifts,
And the generous dreamer invests
The senseless world with them all.'

Arnold presents this view as an error. As the couple begins "to grow old in darkness and pain," they recognize their folly and repent. In the apodictic conclusion to this poem, where Arnold draws his moral from the story, he sums up the two constant lines of exhortation in the early poems: "Yearn to the greatness of Nature; / Rally the good in the depths of thyself!" These are the twin counsels Empedocles gives to Pausanias: "Once read thy own breast right, / . . . / Sink in thyself! there ask what ails thee, at that shrine!" (Act 1, scene 2, lines 141–46). The shrine is not an altar for the self; the answer that is given through introspection to the question "What ails thee?" is that man has falsely taken himself to be a king to whom nature brings tribute. Though within the self, the shrine must be dedicated to something greater than man, to a nature that though itself regardless of man's welfare "proves the terms / On which man wins content." The lesson one learns by sinking into oneself is to yearn beyond the self to the greatness of nature.

Empedocles, though maintaining that there is an antinomy between the intellect and the elements of nature, concedes that these elements themselves possess "life and joy" and an "immortal vigour." By pursuing the life of the mind he has become detached from the life of nature, but he still feels a wistful reverence for the vitality that is beyond him:

> Oh, that I could glow like this mountain!
> Oh, that my heart bounded with the swell of the sea!
> Oh, that my soul were full of light as the stars!
> Oh, that it brooded over the world like the air!
>
> (ACT 2, LINES 323–26)

Throughout his life Arnold himself continues to draw strength and consolation from the idea that human sensation and sentiment derive from a nature greater and more permanent than the individual self. In "A Wish" (1867) he asks that on his deathbed he may be placed by a window where he may view "the world which was ere I was born, / The world which lasts when I am dead." This confidence in the permanence of nature sometimes offers Arnold a genuine sense of peace. At other times, however, his exhortations to emulate nature seem like ineffectual and anxiously repetitive moral injunctions against his own intellectual trouble. It is as if he were trying to cure "this strange disease of modern life" by the power of verbal command: "Be thou whole!"

Arnold's self-exhortations directly parallel the commands that Empedocles gives to Pausanias. The stoic recognition of man's dependent mortality has not, however, been sufficient to preserve Empedocles from despair. Nor is it, ultimately, what preserves Arnold. By the time of "Obermann Once More" Arnold has lost the spontaneous enthusiasm of youth, but he can nonetheless proclaim a world new-made. Arnold does not merely persist with more fortitude than Empedocles or sink into the contentment of respectable middle age. He overcomes despair by overcoming the causes of Empedocles' plight—the division of mind and nature and the consequent sense of futility in the cultural progression. In the critical effort that culminates in *Culture and Anarchy* Arnold will profess a creed that synthesizes the rationalist ideal of a complete and unified consciousness with a progressivist scheme of historical development. Rather than denouncing, as Empedocles does, the "lonely, imperious thinking power" for having deprived him of his early Wordsworthian joy, he will declare that the fault of English Romantic poetry is that it was intellectually premature, that it lacked "ideas." In the first "Obermann," while Arnold complains that his own age precludes wisdom like that of Wordsworth, he also declares that this wisdom was itself incomplete. "But Wordsworth's eyes avert their ken / From half of human fate." Arnold does not here say what it is that Wordsworth's vision lacked, but we know from Wordsworth's own testimony in the *Prelude* that his spiritual crisis was precipitated by an overbalance of the thinking power, and that in order to preserve himself and his poetry he reverted to a reliance on instinctive and traditional sympathies. Since for Arnold, as for Empedocles, this is not a sufficient basis for spiritual fulfillment, he will seek through his later cultural theory to provide a new ideational base that will replace the inadequate intellectual foundations of English Romanticism.[10]

Arnold's Empedocles found himself in a world where traditional beliefs in the relation of men to personal deities were rapidly disintegrating. The natural mysticism with which he tried to replace these beliefs was not adequate to sustain him. In 1853 this was Arnold's own situation, and rather than accede to Empedocles' despair, he denies that this cultural progression has any intrinsic or inherent significance. His own best poems of the period, however, derive from his unwilling but inescapable recognition of the reality of his historically conditioned situation. At the same time, such poems as "Dover Beach" and "Stanzas from the Grande Chartreuse" reflect Arnold's concern that poetry yield some form of resolution, some vent for distress, or some appeal to elementary passions that transcend the modern condition and that animate

10. A. Dwight Culler, objecting to the thesis (represented most prominently by D. G. James) that Arnold lost the Romantic faith, admonishes us that "we must remember that this faith had already been lost by the very men who created it." Their "vision of life had something fragile and precarious about it which led it to crumble almost as soon as it was produced." *Imaginative Reason: The Poetry of Matthew Arnold* (New Haven, Conn.: Yale University Press, 1966), p. 24. Culler's book is the most sensitive, witty, and astute treatment of Arnold's early poetic career. Culler's interpretation differs from mine in that he regards the poetry as providing not merely the starting point but the prototype of Arnold's thought. He reads the poetry as operating within a stable framework of mythic resolution.

and ennoble the reader. These poems are, in effect, compromises between his a priori aesthetic criteria and the actual experience given to him in his historical situation.

In "Dover Beach" Arnold stands, like "Sophocles long ago," listening to the sound of waves at the beach. To both Sophocles and Arnold the waves bring "a thought," and these two different thoughts mingle in the aesthetic impact of the poem. Arnold hears in the sound of the waves a reminder of the decline of Christianity, "its melancholy, long, withdrawing roar." At the same time, however, what he hears is "the eternal note of sadness," not just the sadness of a single historical epoch. The wave imagery implies that the retreating of faith is itself only a phase of what Sophocles heard—a "turbid ebb and flow / Of human misery." From the time of Arnold's early sonnet "To a Friend" (1849), Sophocles remains to him emblematic of a healthy tragic vision aesthetically antithetical to the morbid distress of Empedocles. The misery of Empedocles fails of tragic grandeur because his view of life fails of certainty and wholeness. Sophocles, however, "saw life steadily, and saw it whole" ("To a Friend"). In "Dover Beach," then, the association of a historically determined spiritual distress with all of human misery imbues Arnold's meditation with an elegiac dignity unattainable in the fretful lucubrations of Empedocles. Nonetheless, the association with Sophocles only partially and somewhat spuriously modifies Arnold's Empedoclean anguish. The closing stanza of the poem lists all the various lacks and frustrations that constitute the misery of a world not supported by faith in a personal deity and, by listing them, seems simply to lump them together as tragic topics:

> Ah, love, let us be true
> To one another! for the world, which seems
> To lie before us like a land of dreams,
> So various, so beautiful, so new,
> Hath really neither joy, nor love, nor light,
> Nor certitude, nor peace, nor help for pain;
> And we are here as on a darkling plain

In this list we find not only the typically tragic loss of peace and the inability to find a "help for pain" but also the lack of light and certitude—qualities essential for seeing life steadily and whole. It is, however, the dramatic poet's clarity and completeness of vision that renders tragic composition itself a help for pain. Without distorting or suppressing his own sense of things, Sophocles could represent "some noble action of a heroic time"—an action in which the struggle against fate, however terrible, found its aesthetic resolution in the affirmation of human grandeur. In a "modern" world like that of Arnold or Empedocles the predominant aesthetic quality is not tragic sorrow but "the doubts . . . the discouragement, of Hamlet and of Faust." For Empedocles the "ebb and flow" of individual and cultural experience is itself a misery precisely because it gets nowhere, achieves no resolution, and only repeats its routine of doubt and disillusionment.

In "Dover Beach" Arnold strikes a tonal balance between the "noble simplicity" and "calm pathos" of the "great classical works" (I, 12), and the morbid renunciations of Empedocles. However, in the last stanza the balance of discourse is thrown to a sweeping, indiscriminate negation of all human possibility. The "world" is not just the world of social action, as distinguished from the more emotionally reliable world of romantic devotion, but the whole world of appearances, everything that "seems." The implication here, as in other of Arnold's poems, is that the "dreams" of phenomenal perception can possess ontological validity only if the world, including man, has its origin in a divine mind. If things merely seem and are not supported in an omniscient unity, they exist only as delusion—what Empedocles calls the "forms, and modes, and stifling veils" of thought (Act 2, line 354).

These assumptions operate beneath the seemingly disjunctive rhetorical surface of the last two stanzas in "Dover Beach." In an 1849 poem, "In Utrumque Paratus," Arnold renders the assumptions explicit. The poem is structured on two metaphysical hypotheses:

> If, in the silent mind of One all-pure,
>   At first imagined lay
> The sacred world. . . .
>
> . . . .
>
> But, if the wild unfather'd mass no birth
>   In divine seats have known. . . .

The two alternatives are of fundamental importance. They determine the significance—the ontological quality and thus, for Arnold, the emotional and aesthetic quality—of all experience. The first alternative, that of a divine origin for the world, creates joy:

O waking on a world which thus-wise springs!
  Whether it needs thee count
Betwixt thy waking and the birth of things
Ages or hours—O waking on life's stream!
By lonely pureness to the all-pure fount
(Only by this thou canst) the colour'd dream
  Of life remount!

Within this cosmology "the colour'd dream of life" is something real and true. All of reality is bound up within the sentient unity of its origin. The alternative cosmology is materialist. The world does not proceed from a divine idea. Rather, "Earth, / Rocking her obscure body to and fro, / Ceases not from all time to heave and groan" and finally, in some fashion, brings forth man. Within this cosmology the "dream of life," human consciousness, both cuts man off from the "brother-world" of unconscious things and fails of itself to achieve ontological validity:

Oh when most self-exalted, most alone,
  Chief dreamer, own thy dream!
Thy brother-world stirs at thy feet unknown,
Who hath a monarch's hath no brother's part;
Yet doth thine inmost soul with yearning teem.
—Oh, what a spasm shakes the dreamer's heart!
  'I, too, but seem.'

This is the cosmology that Empedocles presents to Pausanias: a world that "hath toil perpetually, / And travails, pants, and moans" and that finally brings forth a human consciousness that "must not dream" of any truth beyond what "seems" (Act 1, scene 2, lines 294–95). It is also this cosmology that Arnold embraces in the first "Obermann" when he bids farewell to Senancour, who "heard accents of the eternal tongue / Through the pine branches play."

Away the dreams that but deceive
And thou, sad guide, adieu!

In "Obermann Once More," when Arnold announces a world where "joy" is again possible, he is not merely reverting to the nature enthusiasm of Empedocles' youth. A religious conception of the world order remains for him the source of spiritual fulfillment. In the prose outline for "Obermann Once More" he says that "feeling and the religious mood are eternally the deepest being of man, the ground of all joy and greatness for him."[11]

In the 1850s, although he believed that poetry must include religion, Arnold had not yet fashioned the complex cultural synthesis that would allow him to dream and find his dream to be truth.[12] The difference between Arnold's early and late religious views may be succinctly demonstrated through his 1867 revisions of the 1852 poem "Progress." Attempting to mediate between the profound but now obsolete faith of his Christian past, and the militant but shallow enlightenment of the post-Christian world, Arnold commands: "Leave then the Cross as ye have left carved gods, / But guard the fire within!" The inner fire, however, cannot burn within a vacuum. If not fed by some form of religious belief, it must become, as it does for Empedocles, "nothing but a devouring flame of thought." In the 1852 version of "Progress," although Arnold wishes to keep alive the fire within, he nonetheless confirms the universal significance of Empedocles' anguish:

> 'Children of men! the unseen Power, whose eye
> Ever accompanies the march of man,
> Hath without pain seen *no* religion die,
> Since first the world began.
>
> 'That man must still to some new worship press
> Hath in his eye ever but serv'd to show
> The depth of that consuming restlessness
> Which makes man's greatest woe.'

From this perspective the suffering caused by Empedocles' "eternally restless mind" appears as a representative case of the human predicament. Arnold and Empedocles have not only lost their faith in the relation of human and divine but have also attained to a critical perspective on the motives of religious belief. Although they have not extinguished the same motives in themselves, they have extinguished the credulity that would enable them to satisfy their needs. Consequently, the defense of religion in the following

11. Tinker and Lowry, *Commentary*, p. 270.
12. *LC*, p. 124.

stanza appears only as a counsel of piety toward the beneficent moral effects, in the past, of a religion that can no longer accomplish its purposes:

> 'Which has not taught weak wills how much they can?
> Which has not fall'n on the dry heart like rain?
> Which has not cried to sunk, self-weary man:
> *Thou must be born again!'*

For Empedocles, to be born again is merely to repeat the cycle of striving and despair through which he has already gone.

In the 1867 version of this poem religion ceases to appear as a symptom of a futile spiritual craving and becomes instead a constructive element in the education of humanity. Arnold alters the first stanza, which is quoted above, and drops the second:

> 'Children of men! the unseen Power, whose eye
> For ever doth accompany mankind,
> Hath looked on no religion scornfully
> That men did ever find.
>
> 'Which has not taught weak wills how much they can?'

In this version Providence, the "unseen Power," does not feel any loss for a religion that has died but rather respects all creeds for their contribution to the moral elevation of humanity. The implication seems to be that once a religion is "found," it does not wholly die but enters into the common heritage of mankind. This doctrinal implication is in keeping with the theoretical developments in Arnold's prose in the fifteen-year interval between the two versions of the poem. In this period Arnold constructs an organic, progressivist scheme of cultural history in which each historical phase is subsumed in the next. In 1852, however, history appears to him as a senseless jumble—a view he figures forth in the little fable of "Revolutions."

In "Revolutions" the elements of cultural order are represented as an alphabet, which man has been given to do with as he will: "God put a heap of letters in his hand, / And bade him make with them what word he would." Of the chief historical constructions that have resulted—"Greece, / Rome, England, France"—none has been right, and it has always been necessary to start all over again. The world is old and tired, but man is still obligated to resolve the puzzle that has been given to him, "since he has not yet found the word God would." Arnold does not deny outright that things may eventually fall into place, but any hope he feels seems to be submerged in exasperated disillusionment:

One day, thou say'st, there will at last appear
The word, the order, which God meant should be.
—Ah! we shall know *that* well when it comes near;
The band will quit man's heart, he will breathe free.

In most of the poems of this period Arnold resigns at the outset any hope of man's ever achieving an intellectual order for the world. Instead, he seeks peace for his own soul through the order of a nonhuman nature—the flow of time and its absorption in infinity. In "The Future" (1852) Arnold figures the world of human civilization as situated on the banks of "the river of Time," and he tries to find an escape from the noise and confusion of this world by following the course of the river beyond its temporal bounds:

And the width of the waters, the hush
Of the grey expanse where he floats,
Freshening its current and spotted with foam
As it draws to the Ocean, may strike
Peace to the soul of the man on its breast—
As the pale waste widens around him,
As the banks fade dimmer away,
As the stars come out, and the night-wind
Brings up the stream
Murmurs and scents of the infinite sea.

Arnold's use of the Wordsworthian "Intimations" mode achieves a certain freshness and delicacy of lyric naturalism, but the wistful subjunctive of the ruling verb, *may*, and the imagery of dissolving outlines create an impression of dreamy fatigue and a detachment from life that is like nothing so much as an evocation of peace before death. Empedocles, too, seeks a release from strife and confusion by returning himself to the elements of nature. If one is to live, however, there can be no resolution in an intellectual vanishing act. The problems of mind and of history remain.

In the poems that by theme and imagery group themselves around "Empedocles," the yearning for unity with nature appears as an emotional and subconscious impulse in conflict with the tendencies of the conscious intellect. For Empedocles the task imposed by each new incarnation is "to see if we will now at last be true /

To our own only true, deep-buried selves, / Being one with which we are one with the whole world." In "The Buried Life" (1852), as in "The Future," Arnold figures such unity through the image of a stream of life drawing toward an infinite sea. Here, however, romantic love takes the place of Romantic mysticism as the means for transcending the "distractions" of individual consciousness and achieving peace:

Yet still, from time to time, vague and forlorn,
From the soul's subterranean depth upborne
As from an infinitely distant land,
Come airs, and floating echoes, and convey
A melancholy into all our day.

Only—but this is rare—
When a belovéd hand is laid in ours,

. . . .

And a lost pulse of feeling stirs again.

. . . .

And there arrives a lull in the hot race
Wherein he doth for ever chase
That flying and elusive shadow, rest.
An air of coolness plays upon his face,
And an unwonted calm pervades his breast.
And then he thinks he knows
The hills where his life rose,
And the sea where it goes.

The "sea" is at once what Empedocles calls "the whole world" and at the same time "the soul's subterranean depth"; it is the subconscious union of the self and nature. As Arnold says, however, such moments of rest are rare, elusive, and brief. By situating the principle of union beneath the level of consciousness, Arnold only displaces the locus of conflict from metaphysics to psychology, from the relations between the self and nature to the relations between the conscious and subconscious parts of the self.

Arnold's early poetry, on the whole, establishes problems for which he can find no adequate solutions. What resolutions he does achieve to meet his immediate emotional and aesthetic needs are kept within the bounds set by "Empedocles" and the 1853 Preface. "Dover Beach" achieves an aesthetic compromise, but the thematic resolution Arnold proposes in this poem—domestic fidelity as a consolation for metaphysical anguish—is anomalous in the body of his work. At no other point, in poetry or prose, does Arnold profess that blind personal devotion must take the place of every other form of expectation or fulfillment. As its popularity attests, the poem has an effective rhetorical force, but it is not a fully coherent statement; a personal devotion devoid of "love," "joy," or "light" is scarcely imaginable. It is, at best, a bleakly subintellective form of mutual commiseration. If, as Arnold rather melodramatically declares, the world is so completely empty, individuals would possess very little to which others might be true.

In "Euphrosyne" (1852) Arnold describes a couple, similar to the one in "Dover Beach," who pledge to be true to one another. However, in this poem he does not contrast fidelity to all other human possibilities:

> Truth—what is truth? Two bleeding hearts,
> Wounded by men, by fortune tried,
> Outwearied with their lonely parts,
> Vow to beat henceforth side by side.
>
> The world to them was stern and drear
> Their lot was but to weep and moan.
> Ah, let them keep their faith sincere,
> For neither could subsist alone!

Arnold contrasts the "love and tears" that this couple may offer one another to the "light and warmth and joy" of those souls who are perfectly self-subsistent and who require no compassion and extend no love to others. The privileged beings of "Euphrosyne" are rather similar to those ideal entities, the stars, that Arnold takes in "Self-Dependence" and "A Summer Night" (both 1852) as emblems and models of self-sufficiency:

> For self-poised they live, nor pine with noting
> All the fever of some differing soul.
>
> . . . .
>
> O air-born voice! long since, severely clear,
> A cry like thine in mine own heart I hear:
> 'Resolve to be thyself; and know that he,
> Who finds himself, loses his misery!'
>
> ("SELF-DEPENDENCE")

In "A Summer Night" Arnold also denies that the stars contain even a "tinge" of futile human longing. In "Urania" (1852), however, the muse of astronomy, figuring as an ideal paramour, is invested with a reciprocal impulse of human passion. Still, she holds aloof, waiting for "one of some worthier race than ours":

His eyes be like the starry lights—
His voice like sounds of summer nights—
In all his lovely mien let pierce
The magic of the universe!

And she to him will reach her hand,
And gazing in his eyes will stand,
And know her friend, and weep for glee,
And cry: *Long, long I've look'd for thee.*

This sort of mystical mythology, though more smoothly coherent than "Dover Beach," is also anomalous in the body of Arnold's work. Nowhere else does he allude to or develop Urania as a poetic entity. She appears as but another symbolic variation on the theme of conflict between human yearnings and the dispassionate grandeur of nature. As such, she bears some resemblance both to the privileged beings of "Euphrosyne" and to the personified figure of "Nature" in "Morality" (1852), another poem in which Arnold attempts to figure an inaccessible, transcendental accord between nature and human nature.

In "Morality" Nature at first appears, like the stars in "Self-Dependence" and "A Summer Night," to be remote from human cares:

'There is no effort on *my* brow—
I do not strive, I do not weep;
I rush with the swift spheres and glow
In joy, and when I will, I sleep.'

Beneath this tranquil surface, however, there is as in "Urania" some deeper accord with human nature. Whereas in "Urania" the goddess awaits a companion equal to her own divine equanimity, in "Morality" Nature reapproaches man through a dim recollection of an affinity with his own moral character. The moral impulse is not, to be sure, an active force in the course of nonhuman nature. The affinity, such as it is, subsists in some precreation unity where all things have their origin:

'Yet that severe, that earnest air,
I saw, I felt it once—but where?

'I knew not yet the gauge of time,
Nor wore the manacles of space;
I felt it in some other clime,
I saw it in some other place.
'Twas when the heavenly house I trod,
And lay upon the breast of God.'

The "heavenly house" is closed to Arnold, and any validation of moral effort through this sort of religious proposition must be filtered through the forms and modes of thought. Thus Arnold's tone in this poem is less that of affirmation than of wistful questioning. By the time of *Culture and Anarchy* these limitations will have given way to a creed of a right reason that credits itself with a true perception of a "moral plan" in the natural order ("Pis-Aller," 1867). In his early work, however, Arnold follows Empedocles in asserting that morality is a human quality that transcends the natural order, so that "Nature and man can never be fast friends" ("In Harmony with Nature," 1849). The value of nature as a model is that it provides a standard of dispassionate and self-sufficient existence; by emulating nature, man may strengthen his power of stoic equanimity. Arnold's slight deviation from this line in "Urania" appears as only the poetic license of mythic fancy. The glossy surface and unruffled manner of the poem make it seem little more than an exercise, however deft, in aesthetic idealism. The seriousness of Arnold's spiritual struggle makes itself more strongly felt in those poems where he considers metaphysical problems from his own historical perspective.

"Dover Beach" attempts to synthesize the "eternal" tragic note with the subtragic distress of a lost faith. In "The Grande Chartreuse" (1855) Arnold depicts his own dramatic effort to overcome or mitigate his distress by transforming the faith he has lost into an object of aesthetic contemplation. In the first part of the poem Arnold narrates an actual journey to the Carthusian monastery near Grenoble and tells us that his purpose in making this journey is that he may "possess my soul again." The nature of the loss he hopes to recover is explained by the long middle section of the poem, where he describes the spiritual crisis of nineteenth-century Europe: "Wandering between two worlds, one dead, / The other powerless to be born."[13] Arnold escapes from this limbo by retreating into a setting from the old world. He has sought out the monastery so that he may use its atmosphere of penitential withdrawal to stimulate within himself a fantasy world of peaceful meditation. Instead of associating his Empedoclean distress with Sophoclean gravity, he associates it, paradoxically, with the religious gravity of the Carthusian monks.

"The Grande Chartreuse" might scarcely seem to contain any "excellent action" such as those that provided the Greeks with "a sufficiently grand, detached and self-subsistent object for a tragic poem" (I, 4 and 7). Like "Empedocles," "The Grande Chartreuse" is not so much an action as a dialogue of the mind with itself. It is possible, nonetheless, to regard Arnold's effort in the poem as at least partly in agreement with the advice he gives in the 1853 Preface, where the poet is urged to withdraw from the contemporary world "in order to delight himself with the contemplation of some noble action of a heroic time." To reconcile the poem with the doctrine, we must construe the words *noble* and *heroic* so as to include the moral heroism of religious renunciation. This reading, with its Christian transvaluation of values, finds support in the poem itself, for Arnold does find nobility in the spiritual travail of the monks. "The nobleness of grief is gone— / Ah, leave us not the fret alone!" The penitential exercises of the Carthusians may be seen as "actions" calculated to attain salvation. In going to the monastery, then, Arnold is attempting to cultivate in himself an aesthetic appreciation of a moral grandeur that can no longer be part of a living world for him. He accomplishes this purpose by merging in imagination the Carthusians' renunciation of the world of action with his own forced renunciation of the world of religious faith. Thus, his description of the monastery conspicuously employs gothic ghost imagery: "The silent courts / . . . / Where, ghostlike in the deepening night / Cowl'd forms brush by in gleaming white." It is a dead world, a "living tomb" both for the Carthusians, who have renounced life, and for Arnold, whose faith has died.

On the basis of this imaginative paradox Arnold creates for himself a mood of reverential meditation that culminates in the poi-

13. John P. Farrell argues that Arnold's protagonists are typically people—or gods—caught up in historical change. "Matthew Arnold's Tragic Vision," *PMLA* 85 (1970): 107–117.

gnant fantasy at the end of the poem: "We are like children rear'd in shade / Beneath some old-world abbey wall." This simile, extended through seven stanzas, fulfills Arnold's intentions in coming to the monastery. The achievement of resolution is signaled through the repetition in the last stanza of the imagery with which Arnold has declared his purpose in stanza 16:

> Take me, cowl'd forms, and fence me round,
> Till I possess my soul again;
> . . . .
> Fenced early in this cloistral round
> Of reverie, of shade, of prayer,
> How should we grow in other ground?

Arnold begins this fantasy by likening his retreat from the hardness and frivolity of the modern age to a medieval retreat into religion. As the image develops, however, he draws the world itself into his net of fancy. "The exulting thunder" of scientific and industrial triumph gives way to a world of "Gay dames"; "Laughter and cries"; and "Pennon, and plume, and flashing lance!" This world of medieval romance is more appealing to Arnold than the world he has actually left. Nonetheless, he still chooses not to heed the call to active heroism—"To life, to cities, and to war!"—but follows instead the call to introspective detachment:

> Banner by turns and bugle woo:
> *Ye shy recluses, follow too!*
>
> O children, what do ye reply?
> . . . .
> 'Long since we pace this shadow'd nave;
> We watch those yellow tapers shine,
> Emblems of hope over the grave,
> In the high altar's depth divine;
> The organ carries to our ear
> Its accents of another sphere.'

For the Carthusians the "other sphere" is something real. For Arnold, however, this sphere is itself inaccessible, and his closest approach to it is to situate himself fictively in a world where belief is still a vital power.

Arnold's fictive meditation serves to appease his regret for what has been lost, but earlier in the poem he has himself already passed judgment on the futility of his longing for the past:

> But—if you cannot give us ease—
> Last of the race of them who grieve
> Here leave us to die out with these
> Last of the people who believe!
> Silent, while years engrave the brow;
> Silent—the best are silent now.

The religious impulse, which in the Carthusians still stimulates an active struggle for salvation, persists in Arnold only as a lingering regret. The Carthusians must "die out" because their creed, regardless of their own conviction, is obsolete. By attaching himself emotionally to a dead past, Arnold both consigns himself to spiritual sterility and at the same time fails to attain any "nobleness of grief." His own grief, like that of his Romantic predecessors, appears to him as histrionic and ineffectual:

> What helps it now, that Byron bore,
> With haughty scorn which mock'd the smart,
> Through Europe to the Aetolian shore
> The pageant of his bleeding heart?
> That thousands counted every groan,
> And Europe made his woe her own?
>
> What boots it, Shelley! that the breeze
> Carried thy lovely wail away,
> Musical through Italian trees
> Which fringe thy soft blue Spezzian bay?
> Inheritors of thy distress
> Have restless hearts one throb the less?

Like Byron, Shelley, and Senancour, Arnold has taken as the subject of his poem his own emotional condition. When at the end of the poem Arnold attempts to transmute this condition into a dramatic representation of meditative retreat, he effects a compromise between the subjectivist mode of Romantic poetry and the classicist objectivism of the 1853 Preface. Insofar as his extended simile recreates a world of vital belief, he satisfies his own requirement that the poet choose as his subject a grand, detached, and self-sufficient object. Insofar, however, as this simile represents a romanticized fantasy of his own withdrawal from the modern world, it appears in conflict with the demands of his Preface as "an allegory of the state of one's own mind" (I, 8).

If Arnold has only ambiguously followed the precepts of the 1853 Preface in selecting a "noble action" for poetic representation, he does adhere to his formal standard requiring that verbal ornament, the "attractive accessories" of poetry, be restrained and subordinated to the "unity and profoundness of moral impression" a work is to create (I, 9 and 12). Up to the stanza on Shelley, Arnold's rhetoric has been, if not unmelodious, very plain. In this stanza, however, he skillfully imitates the musical expressiveness of the kind of poetry he describes. The alliteration of *w* in combination with the assonance of long *a*, the consonance of the liquids *l* and *r*, and the slurring of the sibilants *s* and *z*—all of this captures the "lovely wail" of Shelley's verse. At the same time, however, Arnold implies that such poeticizing is futile and insubstantial. Nonetheless, he himself employs all of his own considerable poetic resources to give imaginative substance to the scenes of medieval romance with which he closes the poem. This seven-stanza passage ranks with the best of Arnold's specifically lyrical poetry: "The Scholar-Gipsy," "Thyrsis," and the songs of Callicles. The unity of moral impression to which this lyricism is subordinated, however, subsists only as a fragile evocation of a world that itself no longer has any substantial reality. Arnold can associate his grief with a noble belief, but he cannot by the force of imagination alone transform this grief into belief.

The aesthetic compromise of "Dover Beach" concludes in an implicit repudiation of the possibility of tragic grandeur in the modern world. In "The Grande Chartreuse" Arnold's effort at an aesthetic compromise contains a conclusion that the rest must be silence. "The kings of modern thought are dumb." Arnold is himself not yet ready for the silence he requires, and it is against the severity of his own conclusions that he makes his plea: "Allow our tears." By speaking of himself in the first-person plural, as a representative of a cultural plight that transcends his personal distress, he reapproaches his classical ideal of detachment. He does not, like Byron, fill up the spiritual void with an image of the self inflated, if not ennobled, by passion. Even so, the very existence of his poem contradicts its call to silence. Expressive grief is fruitless, yet he must speak. "But we—we learnt your lore too well." The aesthetic reconstruction of the religious world effects a temporary reconciliation between Arnold's doctrine and his actual needs. Although this reconstruction can provide no permanent solution to the problem of a lost faith, it does enable Arnold in this poem to avoid the fault for which he repudiated "Empedocles"; it provides him with a "vent for suffering."

"The Grande Chartreuse" marks the apex of Arnold's effort to achieve a compromise between his cultural dilemma and his aesthetic standards. For H. F. Lowry it marks as well the apex of Arnold's entire literary production. "Closing the *Stanzas from the Grande Chartreuse* and feeling his power as an artist, we shall weep momentarily for the folly of the poet who left his vocation and went round begging the British Philistine to become urbane and civilized."[14] If, however, we take seriously what Arnold has to say in "The Grande Chartreuse," we must recognize that the folly for him would have been to continue dressing out the pageant of his own bleeding heart or to continue writing elegiac injunctions to stoical silence. Arnold's best poetry achieves its classical stature by struggling to attain "an Idea of the world."[15] The only alternatives to this sort of intellectualism appear to him to be either the confused "multitudinousness" of sensual impression with which he reproaches Keats and Browning, or the superficial prettiness of Tennyson's "dawdling" with the "painted shell" of the universe.[16] By the time of "The Grande Chartreuse" Arnold had largely exhausted the ideas of the world accessible to him in poetry, and they did not add up, in his own view, to that grand unity of vision he found in the best of ancient literature. In 1849 Arnold had written to his sister "K" (the Fausta of "Resignation") that it is impossible "to make my poems square in all their parts. . . . The true reason why parts suit you while others do not is that my poems are fragments—i.e. that I am fragments, while you are a whole; the whole effect of my poems is quite vague & indeterminate—this is their weakness."[17] Actually, the impression left by the poems is

14. *LC*, Introduction, p. 52. See also Kenneth Allott, *Matthew Arnold* (London: Longmans, Green, 1962), p. 21. "His vocation was to sing of melancholy and indecision, to express the sad confusion of desires which find no sufficient object."

15. *LC*, p. 97.

16. *LC*, pp. 97 and 63.

17. Arnold Whitridge, ed., *Unpublished Letters of Matthew Arnold* (New Haven, Conn.: Yale University Press, 1923), p. 18. The date given by Whitridge is incorrect. See Culler, *Imaginative Reason*, p. 267, and Arthur Kyle Davis,

quite clear and distinct, but it is a distinct impression of Arnold's own spiritual perplexity. This impression is only strengthened by his suppression of "Empedocles," the most complete representation of that perplexity.

If aesthetic compromise could provide no adequate rationale for a continuing poetic effort, there was still one poetic line open to Arnold. In *Merope* (1858) he strictly obeys the classicist prescriptions of the Preface and restricts himself to the dramatic depiction of an antique heroic action. Arnold's purpose in writing *Merope* was both therapeutic and didactic. In a letter of 1856, the year he began work on *Merope,* he remarks that "to make a habitual war on depression and low spirits, which in one's early youth one is apt to indulge and be somewhat interested in, is one of the things one learns as one gets older. They are noxious alike to body and mind, and already partake of the nature of death."[18] For Arnold the spirit of antique tragic grandeur serves as an antidote to introspective melancholy, and the preparation for writing *Merope* evidently had a salutary effect on him. "What I learn in studying Sophocles for my present purpose is, or seems to me, wonderful; so far exceeding all that one would learn in years' reading of him without such a purpose. And what a man! What works!"[19]

Arnold hoped that his own enthusiasm would carry over into his production and save it "from being entirely *ennuyeux,* professorial, and pedantic."[20] In this hope he was largely deceived. The success of his therapeutic purpose failed to transmit itself to his didactic purpose. He presented his work as a corrective influence for those staunch Romantics "who have been taught to consider classicalism as inseparable from coldness, and the antique as another phrase for the unreal" (I, 38), but the effect of *Merope* would tend rather to confirm than to modify these prejudices. Douglas Bush, one of Arnold's most sympathetic critics and no stranger to the genuine antique, sums up the majority judgment of both contemporary and later readers: "We are chilled by what seems a plaster reproduction of the antique."[21] Arnold's verse in *Merope*

Jr., *Matthew Arnold's Letters: A Descriptive Checklist* (Charlottesville: University of Virginia Press, 1968), p. 9.

18. *Letters* 1:60 (April 1856).

19. *Letters* 1:66 (July 25, 1857).

20. *Letters* 1:69 (February 9, 1858).

21. Douglas Bush, *Matthew Arnold: A Survey of His Poetry and Prose* (New York: Macmillan, 1971), p. 63.

is spare but stiff, his characters correct but lifeless. Throughout the play one has a tiring sensation of double vision. What we see is not, as Arnold hoped, "a specimen of the world created by the Greek imagination"[22] but a specimen of the Greek imagination recreated by an English gentleman. The most incisive criticism of the effect Arnold tries to achieve may be found in his own critique of modern Homeric imitations.

> Perfect simplicity can be obtained only by a genius of which perfect simplicity is an essential characteristic. So true is this that when a genius essentially subtle, or a genius which, from whatever cause, is in its essence not truly and broadly simple, determines to be perfectly plain, determines not to admit a shade of subtlety or curiosity into its expression, it cannot even then attain real simplicity; it can only attain a semblance of simplicity.
>
> (I, 205–206)

Regarded merely as an exercise, *Merope* is a remarkable performance. The dialogues between Merope and Polyphontes, though not animated with what Arnold calls dramatic "charm," display an acute analytical judgment about the conflict between pragmatic and absolutist ethical standards. In other words, what is best about *Merope* is its implicit criticism. If Arnold lacks the mimic faculty, he does have a strong and interesting voice of his own, and this voice is sufficiently audible behind the tonally undifferentiated speeches of his characters to make us impatient with all the dramatic paraphernalia that muffle it. Arnold himself, however, never conceded the failure of *Merope* as a drama. He vigorously defended it from what he took to be the obtuse public response, and he gratefully gathered in the few favorable comments on the work. Nonetheless, he had failed in his public purpose, and he pursued this line no further. For the next thirty years he deployed the chief strength of *Merope,* its critical intelligence, in a more direct and effective fashion. In 1863 Arnold remarks in a letter to his mother that "it is very animating to think that one at last has a chance of *getting at* the English public."[23] In his critical work, in contrast to his experience with *Merope,* Arnold's own sense of animation found a corresponding lively interest in his audience.

22. *Letters* 1:68 (February 3, 1858).
23. *Letters* 1:233–34 (October 29, 1863).

The problem presented by the gradual cessation of Arnold's poetic productivity has occupied a great deal of attention among his critics. There are three standard explanations for his abandonment of poetry. Tinker and Lowry, among others, detect the Coleridgean syndrome—the triumph of the discursive, analytical faculties over the expressive and imaginative.[24] The second explanation, embraced by Douglas Bush and again by Tinker and Lowry, is that Arnold's poetic vein just happened to be elegiac by nature, so that in abandoning his youthful melancholy and adopting a more positive attitude Arnold closed himself off from the source of his creativity.[25] The third explanation, which Trilling advances and to which Arnold himself gives countenance, takes a hint from Wordsworth's progress.[26] In a letter of 1851 to his sister, Arnold remarks that "the aimless and unsettled, but also open and liberal state of our youth we *must* perhaps all leave and take refuge in our morality and character; but with most of us it is a melancholy passage from which we emerge shorn of so many beams that we are almost tempted to quarrel with the law of nature which imposes it on us."[27] In context this statement refers more to the narrowing of personal relations than to the diminution of creative energy. The two tendencies seem to be related in Arnold's mind, however, for in "The Progress of Poesy: A Variation" (1867) Arnold employs a generalized, third-person viewpoint to declare that with advancing age the poetic spring has run dry:

YOUTH rambles on life's arid mount,
And strikes the rock, and finds the vein,
And brings the water from the fount,
The fount which shall not flow again.
. . . .

24. Tinker and Lowry, *Commentary*, p. 186.

25. Douglas Bush, *Mythology and the Romantic Tradition in English Poetry* (1937; reprint ed., New York: Pageant, 1957), p. 247. Bush argues that Arnold's unsuccessful struggle to gain serenity "made him a poet; in his later years he gained a partial victory and became a journalist and a classicist." See also Tinker and Lowry, *Commentary*, pp. 273–74. Frank Kermode asserts that the right answer for Arnold would have lain in "a series of Empedoclean victories, not in the carefully qualified betrayal, the compromise of life and art, action and inaction, which his Mask as Critic represents." *Romantic Image*, 2d ed. (London: Routledge and Kegan Paul, 1961), p. 19.

26. Trilling, *Matthew Arnold* (1939; reprint ed., Cleveland, Ohio: World Publishing, 1955), pp. 34–35.

27. *Letters* 1:17 (January 25, 1851).

And then the old man totters nigh,
And feebly rakes among the stones.
The mount is mute, the channel dry;
And down he lays his weary bones.

These three explanations are related one to another, and they all contain some measure of cogency, but they all need to be qualified. If it is true that Arnold was naturally inclined to elegy, it is also true that he later turned with equal success to wit and satire. If the poetic spring itself ceased to flow, there is nonetheless no feeling of aridity in the prose work. Indeed, Arnold was often compelled to defend the extreme "vivacity" of his criticism. It would seem, then, that the poetic stream did not so much dry up as become diverted into another channel; that is, the spring was not basically poetic but literary, and so convertible to Arnold's needs as he felt them change.

Throughout his career Arnold consistently maintains that poetry is the most complete and satisfying form of human utterance. With equal consistency, however, he maintains that poetry does not create the cultural context on which it depends. In his apology for criticism, "The Function of Criticism at the Present Time" (1864), Arnold concedes that "the critical power is of lower rank than the creative," but he qualifies this principle by remarking that criticism can be of a creative nature (III, 260). Furthermore, the cultural conditions necessary for high poetic creativity are of relatively rare occurrence, so that "labour may be vainly spent in attempting it, which might with more fruit be used in preparing for it, in rendering it possible." In a sense the critical function, in its broadest definition as cultural commentary, is more creative than imaginative literature, for "creative literary genius does not principally show itself in discovering new ideas, that is rather the business of the philosopher. The grand work of literary genius is a work of synthesis and exposition, not of analysis and discovery" (III, 260–61). In Arnold's thinking "philosophy" and "criticism" are closely related and often, as in the passage just quoted, virtually interchangeable terms. Philosophy proper (metaphysics and epistemology) occupies itself, within the sphere "of pure thought," with the relation of abstract ideas ("The Bishop and the Philosopher," III, 67). Insofar as philosophy is distinguished from criticism, it appears as a more narrowly focused study that comes under the ken of that critical inquiry that takes as its province "all branches of knowledge, theology, philosophy, history, art, science" (III, 261; quoted from the Homer lectures, I, 140). Unlike imaginative literature and like philosophy, criticism has a degree of control over the cultural situation on which it depends for its materials. The materials of the poet are his knowledge of life and the world, and no world is given unmediated by an "order of ideas"—an order that is "more within the control of the critical power" than of the imaginative. Through its effort of disinterested inquiry, criticism "tends, at last, to make an intellectual situation of which the creative power can profitably avail itself" (III, 261).

Arnold holds that poetry should, ideally, serve as the expression of a complete and harmonious spiritual existence. It is this standard to which Arnold appeals when he tells Clough that poetry must again become "a complete magister vitae as the poetry of the ancients did."[28] Seen in this light, Arnold's claim for the magisterial function of poetry does not, as it has sometimes been thought to do, stand in contradiction to his earlier remark to Clough that "the Muse willingly *accompanies* life but that in no wise does she understand to *guide* it."[29] The poetic "gift lies in the faculty of being happily inspired by a certain intellectual and spiritual atmosphere, by a certain order of ideas, when it finds itself in them; of dealing divinely with these ideas, presenting them in the most effective and attractive combinations,—making beautiful works with them, in short" (I, 261). Poetry ennobles and animates, but it does not undertake "to *solve* the Universe."[30] Arnold felt his own age "deeply *unpoetical*. . . . Not unprofound, not ungrand, not unmoving:—but *unpoetical*," for in his time the universe required to be solved once again; it required a critical theoretical effort for which poetry was unsuited.[31]

In certain ages, such as Arnold's own, criticism is an activity more essential and constructive than imaginative literature itself. Moreover, even in absolute terms, apart from all considerations of historical circumstances, Arnold holds that "excellent work in a lower kind counts in the long run above work which is short of excellence in a higher; first-rate criticism has a permanent value greater than that of any but first-rate works of poetry and art"

28. *LC*, p. 124.

29. *LC*, p. 84. For the charge of inconsistency see Bush, *Matthew Arnold*, pp. 23–24.

30. *LC*, pp. 146 and 63.

31. *LC*, p. 99.

("Sainte-Beuve," V, 306). Thus, if Sainte-Beuve does not rank above Milton and Molière, he does claim more intellectual glory than Lamartine, Hugo, or Chateaubriand. Johnson, as the author of the *Lives of the Poets,* ranks higher than the "creative" Johnson of *Irene*. Wordsworth's *Preface* is more valuable than his *Ecclesiastical Sonnets,* and Goethe, though "the greatest poet of modern times," is more important to Arnold as "the greatest critic of all times" (1853 Preface, I, 8). In defending Goethe from the precise and severe criticisms of the French critic Edmond Scherer, Arnold says that "it is by no means as the greatest of poets that Goethe deserves the pride and praise of his German countrymen. It is as the clearest, the largest, the most helpful thinker of modern times" (VIII, 274–75). Applying these distinctions to Arnold himself, we may say that, although he wrote a few poems that rank among the English classics, he produced a body of criticism second not even to that of Johnson in scope, depth, and definitive authority. By responding with originality and seriousness to the spiritual malaise of his age, he produced a highly respectable body of meditative and elegiac verse. By regarding with the same seriousness the consequences and implications of these poems, he produced a body of criticism superior, in its own field, to his poetry. In regretting that Wordsworth did not develop his intellect more fully, Arnold remarks, "I admire Wordsworth, as he is, so much that I cannot wish him different; and it is vain no doubt to imagine such a man different from what he is" (III, 262). One might give a similar response to those of Arnold's critics who lament his conversion from poetry to criticism; even more one should insist that a different Arnold would have been a worse Arnold, that the continued production of aesthetic compromises and imaginative paradoxes not only would have weakened his poetry but might, retroactively, have diminished the authentic power of the poetry he did write.

The parallel course of the careers of Arnold and Coleridge allows us to draw an instructive contrast between them, both in their motivation and in their achievement. Arnold valued Coleridge as a model of critical curiosity and intellectual integrity. Both Coleridge and Joubert, the French moralist to whom Arnold likens Coleridge, had a rare natural gift, "an ardent impulse for seeking the genuine truth on all matters they thought about," and rarer still, "a gift for finding it and recognizing it when it was found" ("Joubert," III, 189). Coleridge, even more than Joubert, provides

Arnold with an example from which he can draw support and consolation. Coleridge, like Arnold, worked in an age and a nation indifferent or hostile to true, disinterested criticism, "in a country where at that moment such an effort was almost unknown, where the most powerful minds threw themselves upon poetry, which conveys truth, indeed, but conveys it indirectly; and where ordinary minds were . . . habituated to do without thinking altogether" (III, 189).

Despite the excellence of his critical instincts, Coleridge's work suffered from despondency and an enfeebled sense of purpose. In "Dejection: An Ode" Coleridge, like Arnold's Empedocles, complains, "My genial spirits fail." Unspecified "afflictions" have impaired both his power of "joy" and his "shaping spirit of Imagination." His recourse from these afflictions has been to absorb himself in "abstruse research," but the medicine has ultimately become itself a part of the disease; what Empedocles calls "the lonely imperious thinking power" has in Coleridge robbed "from my own nature all the natural man— / . . . / Till that which suits a part infects the whole." Coleridge's abstruse research was undertaken not as a constructive program but as an escape. Whereas Arnold felt that his own age was incapable of producing great poetry but was ripe for criticism, Coleridge saw in Wordsworth a healthy poetic spirit. His own recourse to prose commentary seemed by its very nature to betray an inner weakness. The faulty character of Coleridge's motivation casts a blight on his actual production, which remained, as Arnold says, "desultory and incomplete" (III, 189). Coleridge's critical effort could not have been for Arnold the inspiration it was had it not been "crowned often with rich success" and imbued with sudden flashes of brilliant insight; nonetheless, his work as a whole is unsatisfactory. "How little either of his poetry, or of his criticism, or of his philosophy, can we expect permanently to stand!" In "On the Modern Element in Literature," when Arnold announces the beginning of his critical mission, he projects as its reward "that harmonious acquiescence of mind which we feel in contemplating a grand spectacle that is intelligible to us" (I, 20). Arnold enters on his critical career as a constructive response to the spiritual wants he has explored in his poetry, and the cultural solutions he offers work not to narrow and weaken his sensibility but to render him more whole.

2 *An Intellectual Deliverance*

The Modern Spirit

At the time of writing *Merope,* Arnold was composing the introductory lecture for his professorship of poetry at Oxford. "On the Modern Element in Literature" (1857) breaks radically with the doctrines of the 1853 Preface. By redefining the idea of the "modern" and associating it with "criticism," Arnold opens for himself a career of progressive intellectual effort. This essay looks both backward and forward. Through his analysis of "adequate" and "inadequate" literature Arnold implicitly passes judgment on his own youthful inadequacy in dealing with the problems of his age. In the presentation of two kinds of "deliverance," intellectual and moral, he foreshadows the first two phases of his critical career. In the first phase, comprising the early political and literary essays, the *Essays in Criticism,* and *Culture and Anarchy,* Arnold develops his doctrine of criticism as an intellectual deliverance from spiritual distress. In this phase he establishes the dominant line of his thinking and at the same time situates himself within the mainstream of European culture. As Arnold says in his essay on Heinrich Heine, "To ascertain the master-current in the literature of an epoch, and to distinguish this from all minor currents, is one of the critic's highest functions; in discharging it he shows how far he possesses the most indispensable quality of his office,—justness of spirit" (III, 107). Arnold's own contribution to this mainstream consists of a critical synthesis that draws its materials from his critiques of individual authors, nations, and cultural epochs. Through these criticisms Arnold works out for himself a scheme of intellectual faculties and aesthetic qualities, and he integrates this scheme with a theory of historical development.

In the second phase of his career Arnold occupies himself almost exclusively with reinterpreting the Bible and traditional religion in such a way as to preserve their moral and literary content while discarding their supernatural dogmas. Within the gradually formed dialectical historical scheme of the first phase, this second phase may be seen as a necessary contribution to Arnold's theory of culture. Though little read today except by specialists in Arnold scholarship, *Saint Paul and Protestantism, Literature and Dogma, God and the Bible*, and *Last Essays on Church and Religion* contain seminal ideas for all literary critics who concern themselves with a literature that espouses religious ideas they feel to be untrue. Nonetheless, this phase represents a marked departure from Arnold's own doctrine of criticism. The "free play of the mind on all subjects, for its own sake" (III, 268) gives way to a single-minded concentration on moral salvation. In his third phase, comprising the critical essays of his last decade, Arnold returns to the dominant, critical doctrine and struggles to integrate his own Hellenic and Christian epochs in a single point of view. Having already redefined religion as poetry, he now elevates poetry as the new, modern religion, and he seeks a principle of union between the ideals of intellectual "expansion" and moral "concentration" that he has designated as the primary forces in the history of civilization. (The terms "concentration" and "expansion" appear first in "The Function of Criticism" and then frequently thereafter.)

The triadic shape of Arnold's critical career recapitulates the structure of cultural history as he saw it. The disjunction between the critical doctrine of his first phase and the religious absorption of his second phase reflects in small scale the unresolved tensions in the main tendencies of Western cultural history. It does not, however, preclude for Arnold the possibility of a cultural synthesis and a continuous progress toward an ultimately inaccessible state of human perfection. Despite variations and reversals in his theoretical formulations, the consistency with which Arnold pursues this ideal of perfection gives unity to his whole body of thought. The coherence and cogency of his ideas are not dependent on a rigid, dogmatic consistency. Arnold himself found great amusement in the complaint of one of his critics, Frederic Harrison, that he had no "system of philosophy with principles coherent, interdependent, subordinate, and derivative" (*Friendship's Garland*, V, 76). Arnold made no pretense of building an abstract rational system on the basis of a priori principles. Nor did he feel that this method would have been appropriate to his task. He follows Heine in objecting to the repellent and delusory mathematical form in which Spinoza clothed his speculative insights (III, 159).[1] Arnold does, however, clearly signal and define what seem to him the crucial forces and elements of cultural history, and he validates his claims through extensive empirical analysis. In his handling, criticism remains a humanistic enterprise, where no absolute conclusiveness is possible, but where "justness of spirit" may operate freely and finally gain its proper recognition.

"The Modern Element" marks the beginning of Arnold's critical doctrine, but its definition of the "modern" and its presentation of criticism amount to a preliminary survey rather than a finished analysis. Arnold himself felt this to be so and left the essay unpublished for more than eleven years. When he finally did publish it, he appended a prefatory note deprecating both its content and manner. "No one feels the imperfection of this sketchy and generalizing mode of treatment more than I do; and not only is this mode of treatment less to my taste now than it was eleven years ago, but the style too, which is that of the doctor rather than the explorer, is a style which I have long since learnt to abandon" (I, 18). Whatever its imperfections as a finished statement, "The Modern Element" retains an important place in Arnold's canon and in the canon of English literature; it signals Arnold's entry into genuine cultural criticism on the continental, and especially German, model. The essay serves as a manifesto that repudiates the insular preoccupation with national literatures and the isolation of literature proper from the entire cultural complex of which it is a part.

1. In *History of Religion and Philosophy in Germany* Heine writes, "The mathematical form gives Spinoza a rough exterior, but this is like the rough shell of the almond; the kernel is that much the more delightful" [my translation]. *Sämtliche Schriften*, ed. Klaus Briegleb, 6 vols. in 7 (Munich: Karl Hanser, 1968–76), 3: 561.

> The spectacle, the facts, presented for the comprehension of the present age, are indeed immense. The facts consist of the events, the institutions, the sciences, the arts, the literatures, in which human life has manifested itself up to the present time: the spectacle is the collective life of humanity. And everywhere there is connexion, everywhere there is illustration: no single event, no single literature, is adequately comprehended except in its relation to other events, to other literatures.
>
> (I, 20–21)

The ostensible purpose of Arnold's essay, like that of the 1853 Preface, is to establish the importance of Periclean Athens as providing an intellectual and aesthetic ideal. In his conclusion Arnold suggests that "enough has at least been said, perhaps, to establish the absolute, the enduring interest of Greek literature, and, above all, of Greek poetry" (I, 37). What is most striking, however, in comparison with the Preface, is that enough has been said to establish the preeminent interest of Arnold's own epoch. Greece is no longer, as in the Preface, a satirical standard used to disparage the modern age, or a refuge from that age; it is an accessible model of a possible perfection. In a fashion that will become a characteristic feature of his theoretical work, Arnold validates this crucial shift in his outlook by associating it with a basic human instinct. "The human race has the strongest, the most invincible tendency to *live*, to *develop* itself" (I, 29–30). In a helpful article, "Matthew Arnold's 1853 Preface: Its Origin and Aftermath," Sidney M. B. Coulling describes "The Modern Element" as marking a significant turning point in Arnold's career, "the development of an affirmative response to life."[2] Coulling ascribes this change to Arnold's tacit acceptance of the contemporary critiques of the Preface, and Arnold does in fact now adopt the two main tenets required by his critics: a willingness to confront the contemporary world and to give moral guidance to it. It should be noted, however, that throughout his many polemical engagements Arnold never let himself be swayed by criticism that did not cor-

2. Sidney M. B. Coulling, "Matthew Arnold's 1853 Preface: Its Origin and Aftermath," *Victorian Studies* 7 (1964): 234. In partially incorporating his article into his book *Matthew Arnold and His Critics: A Study of Arnold's Controversies* (Athens, Ohio: Ohio University Press, 1974), Coulling has qualified his attribution of change to the influence of external critiques, but he has also softened and blurred his analysis of the change itself.

respond to his own attitudes, and that "The Modern Element" begins to answer the problems Arnold had already posed for himself in "Empedocles." Although it may have been stimulated by external criticism, his revision of the doctrines of the Preface should be traced ultimately to a deeper source—to his own need and power for growth. By retreating to an ideal past Arnold could only have survived in a state of suspended spiritual animation, the ghost world of "The Grande Chartreuse." In order to live and develop he redefines the turmoil of his age as a productive intellectual ferment, a challenge and an opportunity:

> An intellectual deliverance is the peculiar demand of those ages which are called modern; and those nations are said to be imbued with the modern spirit most eminently in which the demand for such a deliverance has been made with most zeal, and satisfied with most completeness. Such a deliverance is emphatically, whether we will or no, the demand of the age in which we ourselves live. . . . The demand arises, because our present age has around it a copious and complex present, and behind it a copious and complex past; it arises, because the present age exhibits to the individual man who contemplates it the spectacle of a vast multitude of facts awaiting and inviting his comprehension. The deliverance consists in man's comprehension of this present and past. It begins when our mind begins to enter into possession of the general ideas which are the law of this vast multitude of facts. It is perfect when we have acquired that harmonious acquiescence of mind which we feel in contemplating a grand spectacle that is intelligible to us; when we have lost that impatient irritation of mind which we feel in presence of an immense, moving, confused spectacle which, while it perpetually excites our curiosity, perpetually baffles our comprehension.
>
> (I, 19–20)

Arnold's declaration of a possible resolution to the "impatient irritation of mind" of which he has before so often complained depends on two assumptions of individual freedom: First, after recognizing the need for an adequate critical perspective, one may consciously and effectively set about satisfying that need; second, after recognizing the need for a moral fortitude sufficient to engage the pressure and complexity of a modern civilization, one may by choice assume the required strength. The querulous passivity of the letters to Clough and of "Empedocles" is suppressed through the assumption that the course of culture is in some measure subject to intelligent control. This is the central redefinition of "modern." A modern age is one in which the critical intelligence rises above the blind forces of history and by grasping them gains freedom over them. In *Culture and Anarchy* Arnold declares that "for more than two hundred years the main stream of man's advance has moved towards knowing himself and the world, seeing things as they are, spontaneity of consciousness" (V, 175). The resistance of the Puritan middle class in England to this main current has finally produced "a certain confusion and false movement." Responding to the need for "some sound order and authority," Arnold holds that "this we can only get by going back upon the actual instincts and forces which rule our life, seeing them as they really are, connecting them with other instincts and forces, and enlarging our whole view and rule of life." Already, in "The Modern Element," the fatalistic historical cyclism of "Empedocles" gives place to a more flexible scheme of conditions and circumstances that may be adjusted with regard to a given standard of excellence. Accordingly, Arnold resituates the point of comparison between the ancient and contemporary worlds. Focusing now on the flowering period of Athenian civilization as a "modern" age, he asserts that "this new world in its maturity of reason resembles our own" (I, 31).

Arnold lists the elements that seem to him the main characteristics of a sophisticated civilization, and by comparing them within three cultures—Periclean Athens, Elizabethan England, and late republican–early imperial Rome—he frees the concept of the modern from all chronological determinism.[3] His first requirement for

3. The inspiration for Arnold's redefinition of the "ancient" world as "modern" seems to have come to him most directly from the historical work of his father. In appendix 1 of his edition of Thucydides (also included in his *Miscellaneous Works* under the title "Essay on the Social Progress of States"), Dr. Thomas Arnold declares that "the largest portion of that history which we commonly call ancient is practically modern, as it describes society in a state analogous to that in which it now is" (London: James Parker, 1874), 1:522 (cited in Peter Dale, *The Victorian Critic and the Idea of History: Carlyle, Arnold, Pater* [Cambridge, Mass.: Harvard University Press, 1977], pp. 93–94). Some of the elements of social analysis in Matthew Arnold's work are similar to those in his father's, but the two men diverge widely in their exposition of the dynamics of social and cultural change. In the Thucydides appendix Dr. Arnold follows Vico in establishing a recurrent pattern of development through class conflict. In his *Introductory Lectures on Modern History,* Dr. Arnold assumes the more limited perspective of a practical historian. For his scheme of periodization, different in form and principle from that of his son, see

a modern world is civil peace. In this respect the Elizabethan habit of bearing arms marks it as a culture still semibarbarian. The second requirement is "the growth of a tolerant spirit; that spirit which is the offspring of an enlarged knowledge; a spirit patient of the diversities of habits and opinions" (I, 23). Arnold's evidence here against the Elizabethans is the flowering of Puritanism.

> Other characteristics are the multiplication of the conveniences of life, the formation of taste, the capacity for refined pursuits. And this leads us to the supreme characteristic of all: the intellectual maturity of man himself; the tendency to observe facts with a critical spirit; to search for their law, not to wander among them at random; to judge by the rule of reason, not by the impulse of prejudice or caprice.
>
> (I, 23–24)

In all of these respects Arnold finds the Elizabethans falling short. For the supreme characteristic, the critical spirit, Arnold dwells on a comparison between Thucydides' rational mode of historical composition and the fantastic vagaries of Sir Walter Raleigh. Arnold's case against the age of Shakespeare and Spenser is of course one-sided and slanted for the sake of his argument. He will himself later do more ample justice to the Elizabethans and find a parallel in them to the fresh and vital state of mind of the Athenians. However, his main point—the existence of a rational method of historical analysis in Athens and the relatively feeble development of this method in Elizabethan England—remains firm. And on this basis, his implicit contention that high culture is a complex of variable factors holds good.

Within his expanded concept of modernism Arnold still takes account of the intellectual neurasthenia he had previously marked as peculiarly modern.

> The predominance of thought, of reflection, in modern epochs is not without its penalties; in the unsound, in the over-tasked, in the over-sensitive, it has produced the most painful, the most lamentable results; it has produced a state of feeling unknown to less enlightened but perhaps healthier epochs—the feeling of depression, the feeling

---

lecture 5 (New York: D. Appleton, 1857), pp. 220–21. Duncan Forbes, in *The Liberal Anglican Idea of History* (Cambridge: Cambridge University Press, 1952), situates Dr. Arnold's historical ideas in their contemporary context.

> of *ennui.* Depression and *ennui;* these are the characteristics stamped on how many of the representative works of modern times! (I, 32)

It is in respect to this problem that Arnold introduces the distinction between "adequate" and "inadequate" literature. An adequate poet is one who represents a highly developed human nature with personal serenity. Sophocles is again the pattern, "a man who has mastered the problem of human life, who knows its gravity, and is therefore serious, but who knows that he comprehends it, and is therefore cheerful" (I, 35). An inadequate poet fails of this serene gravity and becomes frivolous (Horace), gloomy and morbid (Lucretius), or melancholy (Vergil). The distinction between adequate and inadequate was already at play beneath the surface in the 1853 Preface, but there Arnold attributed morbidity solely to the excess of intellectual activity. He now modifies this judgment and attributes morbidity to an inadequate intellectual or emotional power. Lucretius, he says, withdraws from "the wide spectacle of the Roman life of his day. . . . the world in its fulness and movement is too exciting a spectacle for his discomposed brain. He seems to feel the spectacle of it at once terrifying and alluring; and to deliver himself from it he has to keep perpetually repeating his formula of disenchantment and annihilation" (I, 33). The formula is *eadem sunt omnia semper,* "all things continue the same forever," and the whole passage reads like a critique of Arnold's own youthful self. In 1849 Arnold had written to Clough that "these are damned times—everything is against one—the height to which knowledge is come, the spread of luxury, our physical enervation, the absence of great *natures,* the unavoidable contact with millions of small ones, newspapers, cities, light profligate friends, moral desperadoes like Carlyle, our own selves, and the sickening consciousness of our own difficulties."[4] In 1851 he had written to his sister "K" that "I . . . retire more and more from the modern world and modern literature, which is all only what has been before and what will be again, and not bracing or edifying in the least."[5] Then, in 1852, again writing to Clough, he had complained of "the modern situation in its true *blankness* and *barrenness,* and *unpoetrylessness.*"[6] Arnold continues to feel that his own age is

4. *LC,* p. 111.
5. *Letters,* 1:118.
6. *LC,* p. 126.

not yet ripe for great poetry, but he ceases to call it blank and barren, and he diagnoses this attitude as an evasive ploy of a mind unwilling to face the challenge of critical comprehension. Arnold describes Vergil as weak and sensitive, "conscious, at heart, of his inadequacy for the thorough spiritual mastery" of the Roman world (I, 35). Two things, then, are necessary for an adequate literature: an age of high civilization and men with the power to interpret it. The moral and intellectual force of the individual becomes one more factor in the whole complex of culture.

Arnold found in the deficiencies of the ancient world—Greece in its decadence and Rome in its political prime—both of the seemingly contrary ills he has diagnosed in his own culture. In one of its aspects the Victorian age seemed to Arnold to be afflicted by spiritual impotence and aesthetic overrefinement. In another aspect it appeared, like Macedon and Rome, "a body without a soul," an adequate material basis without "an adequate intellect and soul to inform and inspire them" (I, 30). His task came to be the correction of both these tendencies, to give force and hope to the life of the mind, and to elevate the crude and brutal confidence of the materialist ethos by presenting it with an ideal of spiritual nobility.

The main achievement of "The Modern Element" is to have broadened the concept of modernism so as to include any brilliant, complex civilization and to have established for Arnold his own critical goal—the "comprehension of this present and past." Neither of these achievements is a solution so much as a problem that has been stated in such a way as to admit of some solution. The critical dissolution of the elements of culture entails a threat of historical anarchy and imposes on Arnold the task of reshaping history in some meaningful fashion, neither arbitrary and fantastic nor nihilistic and inhumane. His comparative critical method itself implies that there is some law of unity binding all the phases of "the collective life of humanity," and his dictum that humanity has an invincible tendency to develop implicitly presupposes a rationale for the course of civilization. Thus, from the beginning Arnold has precluded the point of view, taken by Voltaire, in which the entire Christian interregnum appears only as a grotesque mistake and as evidence of the folly and corruption of the human mind. Greece, while presenting itself as the finest pattern of cultural success, must still be situated theoretically in such a way as to generate dialectically its own principle of opposition (Hebraism) and yet retain its potential of ultimate synthesis. This will be the task to which Arnold will devote himself for the next decade and to which he will return after his period of religious preoccupation.

Already, at the beginning of "The Modern Element," Arnold briefly formulates the idea of a humane synthesis of the two main cultural tendencies. Both moral and intellectual deliverance are necessary, he says, "for in the enjoyment of both united consists man's true freedom" (I, 19). The ultimate good that Arnold here proposes for mankind, "freedom," answers to his own most immediate need, freedom from both social and historical determinism, freedom not to escape from but to gain mastery over the process of civilization. In the course of his theoretical development Arnold's concern for freedom will become subordinate, though not antithetical, to his concern for an intellectual and moral order that corresponds to an objectively given, natural good, or what he calls "reason and the will of God" (V, 92). In *Culture and Anarchy* the union of Hebraism and Hellenism will be described as resulting not in freedom but in "perfection." The free adjustment of tendencies given at random in various historical moments will be subordinated to the coherent ordering of these tendencies within the historical scheme. Man's own perfection will consist not only of a comprehension of present and past, as in "The Modern Element," but also in a right ordering of the individual mind that corresponds to the right ordering of history. Arnold is not a quietist. He consistently rejects the proposition that "whatever is, is right." Nonetheless he finally seeks and finds a rationale for every main historical phase within a scheme of progressive development.

Arnold's bold but "sketchy" formulations of doctrine in "The Modern Element" leave open the two central issues raised by his discussion: first, the nature of criticism as an intellectual deliverance and its relation to other modes of thought such as science and poetry; and second, the actual structure of his own modern culture and its place in the historical continuum. In the works that follow he addresses himself to both these issues as they arise in connection with his given topics. Before turning to the summation of Arnold's cultural dialectic in *Culture and Anarchy* I shall examine Arnold's exposition of the functions of criticism and the cultural situations to which he applies these functions. This should give us a basis from which to comprehend the modifications in Arnold's doctrine in the second and third phases of his career.

In "The Modern Element" Arnold considers criticism at two different levels, the analytical and the synthetic, which he does not himself clearly distinguish. The lower level, represented by Thucydides and Caesar, consists of "a rational arrangement and appreciation of facts," that is, a reasonable, naturalistic mode of historical analysis. The rational arrangement of facts is a necessary component of any culture that Arnold would call modern, but it may be present even though that culture has no "adequate" literature. In contrasting the imaginative, poetic literature of Athens and Rome, Arnold finds in the first a "noble serenity" that is lacking in the second, and this noble serenity is indistinguishable from "that harmonious acquiescence of mind" that he has defined as an intellectual deliverance. On the basis of his comparison of Rome and Athens, Arnold is led to a hasty generalization that he will soon have to modify: "It is to the poetical literature of an age that we must, in general, look for the most perfect, the most adequate interpretation of that age" (I, 22). In fact, although poetry may be "simply the most beautiful, impressive and widely effective mode of saying things" (III, 110), Arnold's initial definition of intellectual deliverance does not describe poetry; it describes cultural criticism—criticism on the higher, synthetic level. This is like criticism on the lower, analytical level in that "it begins when our mind begins to enter into possession of the general ideas which are the law of this vast multitude of facts," and it is like poetry in that it achieves by its very operation an intellectual resolution of conflict. Although still appealing to Sophocles as the standard of excellence, as in the 1853 Preface, Arnold has actually begun to establish a new, critical program. In his pursuit of this program Arnold will not resolve the ambiguity between criticism as rational analysis and as cultural synthesis, but he will approach a resolution in his concept of right reason.

If Athens is most adequately represented by its poetical literature, Europe of the eighteenth and nineteenth centuries is most adequately represented by its criticism. This is Arnold's own conclusion in his next critical work, the lectures *On Translating Homer* (1860–61):

> Our present literature, which is very far, certainly, from having the spirit and power of Elizabethan genius, yet has in its own way these faults, eccentricity and arbitrariness, quite as much as the Elizabethan literature ever had. They are the causes that, while upon none, perhaps, of the modern literatures has so great a sum of force been expended as upon the English literature, at the present hour this literature, regarded not as an object of mere literary interest but as a living intellectual instrument, ranks only third in European effect and importance among the literatures of Europe; it ranks after the literatures of France and Germany. Of these two literatures, as of the intellect of Europe in general, the main effort, for now many years, has been a *critical* effort; the endeavour, in all branches of knowledge,—theology, philosophy, history, art, science,—to see the object as in itself it really is. . . . almost the last thing for which one would come to English literature is just that very thing which now Europe most desires—*criticism.*
>
> (I, 140)

Arnold reserves for the English the honor of being among all modern nations the most poetical, but this very bent toward poetical expression at the cost of critical intelligence has rendered the English intellectually less influential than the Germans and the French. Arnold sees the English eighteenth century as a reaction of the critical intelligence against the vagaries of the poetic impulse (I, 140), but in the scope and profundity of its achievement he ranks the Augustan age beneath the ages both of Voltaire and of Lessing and Goethe. Nonetheless, in intellectual authority, modern English criticism also takes precedence over modern English poetry. "The chief sources of intellectual influence in Europe, during the last century and a half, have been its three chief critics —Voltaire, Lessing, Goethe. The chief sources of intellectual influence in England, during the same period, have been its chief organs of criticism—Addison, Johnson, the first Edinburgh Reviewers" ("The Bishop and the Philosopher," III, 41). In explaining why this is so Arnold gives a definition of criticism that clearly identifies it with his idea of intellectual deliverance:[7]

> "*Der Engländer ist eigentlich ohne Intelligenz,*" said Goethe; by which he meant, not that the Englishman was stupid, but that he

7. Arnold quotes this sentence again in "Ecce, Convertimur ad Gentes" (IX, 5).

> occupied himself little with the *rationale* of things. He meant that an Englishman held and uttered any given opinion as something isolated, without perceiving its relation to other ideas, or its due place in the general world of thought; without, therefore, having any notion of its absolute value. He meant, in short, that he was uncritical.
>
> (III, 40)

The ordering of the separate elements of knowledge is the work of the critical intelligence. It is not merely an arrangement of given facts but an evaluative assessment of the whole range of human experience. To judge of the rationale of things and to give them an "absolute value" is to interpret them. In this sense both poetry and criticism are contrasted to physical science (cf. III, 298 and VI, 13). They are contrasted to one another, however, in their modes of interpretation. Poetry interprets, Arnold says, by "so dealing with things as to awaken in us a wonderfully full, new, and intimate sense of them. . . . poetry interprets in two ways; it interprets by expressing with magical felicity the physiognomy and movement of the outward world, and it interprets by expressing, with inspired conviction, the ideas and laws of the inward world of man's moral and spiritual nature. . . . it reconciles him with himself and the universe" ("Maurice de Guérin," III, 13 and 33). Poetry is distinguished by its sensual, emotional, and moral intensity. Thus Arnold holds that "genius is mainly an affair of energy, and poetry is mainly an affair of genius" ("The Literary Influence of Academies," III, 238). In contrast, the "ruling divinity of prose" is "intelligence," that is, "quickness of mind" and "flexibility," and on intelligence depend "the form, the method of evolution, the precision, the proportions, the relations of the parts to the whole, in an intellectual work" (III, 246 and 238).

This dichotomy is not, of course, absolute. Genius could scarcely make itself effective without the controlling influence of intelligence, and the critical intelligence is capable of rising to the stature of genius. In "The Modern Element" Arnold takes from Johnson the definition of genius as that power "without which judgment is cold and knowledge is inert; that energy which collects, combines, amplifies, and animates" (I, 23, quoted from Johnson's "Life of Pope"). This power, he claims, "is in poetry at its highest stretch," but he also comes to allow for its operation in criticism:

> To have the sense of creative activity is the great happiness and the great proof of being alive, and it is not denied to criticism to have it; but then criticism must be sincere, simple, flexible, ardent, ever widening its knowledge. Then it may have, in no contemptible measure, a joyful sense of creative activity; a sense which a man of insight and conscience will prefer to what he might derive from a poor, starved, fragmentary, inadequate creation. And at some epochs no other creation is possible.
>
> ("THE FUNCTION OF CRITICISM," III, 285)

If poetry awakens in us a sense of the "magic" of nature, the critic, too, as he strives to be "scientific" and "to see and utter the real truth about his object," must accomplish his purpose by sensing "the soft play of life, following and rendering the thing's very form and pressure" ("A French Critic on Milton," VIII, 165–66). If great poetry is able to animate and ennoble, this power is not denied to higher, cultural criticism. "The human spirit finds animation and enlargement in having these *weltgeschichtliche Massen,* as Goethe calls them, presented to it—these broad masses of the world's main history" ("Edoardo Fusco," VIII, 8).

Taking into account these points of congruence between the poetic and critical faculties, Arnold adopts a synthetic term, "imaginative reason," and he maintains that it is "the element by which the modern spirit, if it would live right, has chiefly to live" ("Pagan and Mediaeval Religious Sentiment," III, 230). The ideal that this term signifies for Arnold is still that of Periclean Athens, and his chief exemplar is still Sophocles. The emphasis in the term itself and in Arnold's prescriptions for the modern spirit, however, is placed not on imagination but on reason. In the context in which Arnold first uses it ("Pagan and Mediaeval"), the term is set in contrast both to "the senses and understanding," which he takes to have been the dominant qualities of the late pagan world, and also to "the heart and imagination," the qualities that ruled in medieval poetry. In this essay Arnold does not define the imaginative reason. The only predicative term he gives to it is "well-balanced," and he seems to indicate that the balance intended is a satisfaction of both "the thinking-power" and "the religious sense" (III, 231). At first sight imaginative reason would seem to be merely the unification of these two contraries. Arnold concedes that "perhaps in Sophocles the thinking-power a little overbalances the religious sense, as in Dante the religious sense overbalances the thinking-power." Nonetheless, the quotation he gives from Sophocles as a perfect example of imaginative reason is a religious statement, a celebration of divinely ordered moral law: " 'Oh! that my lot may lead me in the path of holy innocence of word and deed, the path which august laws ordain. . . . The power of God is mighty in them, and groweth not old' " (III, 231). Despite this concluding emphasis on the religious sense, when Arnold next uses the term *imaginative reason,* he directly contrasts it to the religious sense (*On the Study of Celtic Literature,* III, 369). Relying on a principle of racial determinism, he calls for an abandonment of "Semitic" religiosity: "Whereas the Semitic genius placed its highest spiritual life in the religious sentiment, and made that the basis of its poetry, —the Indo-European genius places its highest spiritual life in the imaginative reason, and makes that the basis of its poetry."

If imaginative reason is set in contrast to religious sentiment and if religion is associated with the "heart and imagination," then the dominant quality of imaginative reason, even in its poetic mode, must be the critical intelligence. In "Democracy" (1861), the introductory essay to Arnold's official report *The Popular Education of France,* he declares that in the modern age "openness and flexibility of mind," the qualities of intelligence, are "the first of virtues" (II, 29). In "A French Eton" (1863–64) he says that "modern societies increasingly tend to find their best life in a free and heightened spiritual and intellectual activity" (II, 321). The "religious life," in contrast, "resides not in an incessant movement of ideas, but in a feeling which attaches itself to certain fixed objects" such as the stories, prophecies, and hymns of the Old Testament and the life of Christ (III, 67). The tendency of these ideas irresistibly draws Arnold to an elevation of intelligence as the master element of imaginative reason and the modern world.[8]

It is through these classifications of the mental faculties and aptitudes that Arnold organizes his historical scheme and situates his own age within it. The driving force of historical progress, "the modern spirit," is the critical intelligence. In "Pagan and Mediaeval" Arnold distinguishes Hellenism proper from the Hellenistic world ruled by "the senses and understanding," but he describes the Renaissance as "in part, a return towards the pagan spirit . . .

8. Frederic E. Faverty urges a similar thesis and supports it by reference to Arnold's theories on ethnic and national characteristics. *Matthew Arnold the Ethnologist* (Evanston, Ill.: Northwestern University Press, 1951), pp. 54, 59, 61.

a return towards the life of the senses and the understanding" (III, 226), and in *Culture and Anarchy* he describes the Renaissance as "that great re-awakening of Hellenism, that irresistible return of humanity to nature and to seeing things as they are" (V, 173). In "The Modern Element" Arnold says that if this critical spirit did not achieve a mature sense of rational order in the Renaissance, it nonetheless served as a source of stimulus and animation (I, 24). In "The Function of Criticism" Arnold significantly modifies his earlier, disparaging view of the Elizabethan world and brings it into partial parallel with Athens. "In the Greece of Pindar and Sophocles, in the England of Shakspeare, the poet lived in a current of ideas in the highest degree animating and nourishing to the creative power; society was, in the fullest measure, permeated by fresh thought, intelligent and alive" (III, 262–63). The modern element in Elizabethan England is the resurgence of the senses and the understanding, that is, a return to the "world" as it revealed itself to the human intelligence and not as it was created out of feeling and fancy. "Shakspeare's task was to set forth the spectacle of the world when man's spirit re-awoke to the possession of the world at the Renaissance" (III, 381). Nonetheless, the Renaissance did not consciously break itself off from its medieval, Christian past. It remained predominantly a "poetic" age, an age ruled by the heart and imagination.

The contemporary modern world, Arnold's own world, does not begin until after the death of Milton. The mainstream of modern culture, leading from Voltaire and Lessing through Goethe and Heine to Arnold himself, is marked by the reinstitution of the pagan spirit. "But the grand reaction against the rule of the heart and imagination, the strong return towards the rule of the senses and understanding, is in the eighteenth century. And this reaction has had no more brilliant champion than a man of the nineteenth, of whom I have already spoken; a man who . . . in his very last poem, divided the whole world into 'barbarians and Greeks,'—Heinrich Heine" (III, 226–27).

In a letter to Clough, Arnold had said that the Elizabethan world was simpler than the modern, that Shakespeare and Milton had not "the multitude of new thoughts and feelings to deal with a modern has."[9] In the 1853 Preface, however, comparing Shakespeare to the ancients, Arnold says that the English poet "has in-

9. *LC*, p. 65, written in 1847 or 1848.

deed a far wider range than they had, a far richer fertility of thought" (I, 11). Consequently, in *Celtic Literature*, Arnold decides that the real issue for the modern is not one of greater or lesser complexity but of a qualitative cosmological change. The Elizabethan world is premodern because it is still Christian. Arnold's own world is modern, like the world of Sophocles, because it is by necessity a new world.

> The basis of spiritual life is still at that time the traditional religion, reformed or unreformed, of Christendom, and Shakspeare has not to supply a new basis. But when Goethe came, Europe had lost her basis of spiritual life; she had to find it again; Goethe's task was,—the inevitable task for the modern poet henceforth is,—as it was for the Greek poet in the days of Pericles, not to preach a sublime sermon on a given text like Dante, not to exhibit all the kingdoms of human life and the glory of them like Shakspeare, but to interpret human life afresh, and to supply a new spiritual basis to it. This is not only a work for style, eloquence, charm, poetry; it is a work for science; and the scientific, serious German spirit, not carried away by this and that intoxication of ear, and eye, and self-will, has peculiar aptitudes for it.
>
> (III, 381)

By "science" Arnold does not, of course, mean versified physics or lyrical entomology. He means "patient fidelity to nature" and "knowing things as they are" (III, 381 and 298).[10] These are the same terms he has used to define criticism, so that insofar as poetry is to provide a new spiritual basis, it is to do so in large part through qualities not essentially poetic. Indeed, although Arnold maintains that "our great, our only first-rate body of contemporary poetry is the German" (III, 380), he also says that Goethe, the greatest of German poets, "owes his grandeur" to his "intellectual power" and that this power "hurt his poetical operations by its immense predominance."[11] Goethe's achievement is to have given "a moral interpretation, from an independent point of view, of man and the world" (III, 380). This is the same goal that Arnold begins to set for himself as a critic in "The Modern Element."

The English literature of the nineteenth century falls short of

10. Fred A. Dudley, in "Matthew Arnold and Science," *PMLA* 57 (1942): 275–94, gives a thorough exposition of the range of meanings in Arnold's use of the term "science."

11. *Letters* 1:147 (December 17, 1860).

Arnold's standard of imaginative reason. It cannot serve to give expression or guidance to the modern spirit, for it relies too exclusively on the heart and imagination. Byron and Shelley, alone among the English Romantics, made an effort "to apply the modern spirit in English literature," but they both failed (III, 121). Byron's poetry draws its force from his "Titanic personality," but like the other Romantics, he "did not know enough" (III, 380 and 262). Shelley had neither an adequate grasp of reality nor an adequate sense for intellectual order. "It always seems to me that the right sphere for Shelley's genius was the sphere of music, not of poetry; the medium of sounds he can master, but to master the more difficult medium of words he has neither intellectual force enough nor sanity enough" (III, 34). Both Byron and Shelley were hindered, Arnold says, by the want of sympathetic intelligence in the English public at large, and despite their deficiencies, he honors them for their effort "to flow in the main stream of modern literature" (III, 122).

The other English Romantics do not even make the attempt to give a comprehensive interpretation of the spectacle of the modern world:

> What, in fact, was the career of the chief English men of letters, their contemporaries? The greatest of them, Wordsworth, retired (in Middle-Age phrase) into a monastery. I mean, he plunged himself in the inward life, he voluntarily cut himself off from the modern spirit. Coleridge took to opium. Scott became the historiographer-royal of feudalism. Keats passionately gave himself up to a sensuous genius, to his faculty for interpreting nature; and he died of consumption at twenty-five. Wordsworth, Scott, and Keats have left admirable works; far more solid and complete works than those which Byron and Shelley have left. But their works have this defect,—they do not belong to that which is the main current of the literature of modern epochs, they do not apply modern ideas to life; they constitute, therefore, *minor currents.*
>
> (III, 121–22)

For Arnold this defect is not simply a matter of having a greater or lesser influence and prestige in the European community, though this also concerns him; to be outside the mainstream of culture impairs the absolute, intrinsic value of a literary work. An imaginative literature that does not take as its material "the best ideas, on every matter which literature touches, current at the time" cannot "be very important or fruitful" (III, 260). Ironically, by failing to enter the stream of historical change and to assimilate new ideas, modern literature fails to achieve permanence. A modern literature that has no "great critical effort behind it" is impoverished even of imaginative value. "It must be a comparatively poor, barren, and short-lived affair. This is why Byron's poetry had so little endurance in it, and Goethe's so much" (III, 261–62).

The decline in the significance of English literature is, Arnold thinks, parallel in origin to the decline of England as a political and social influence in Europe. Both sorts of decline are due to a defect of "intelligence," in the sense of understanding and sympathizing with "the way the world is going" (*Friendship's Garland,* V, 23) and in the sense of obtaining a coherent theoretical order for the world. The defect of the English is twofold: in the intellectual sphere they have thrown themselves on the vagaries of the individual genius and the subjectivism of poetic expressivism, and in the social sphere they have contented themselves with practical adjustments without regard to fundamental principles. Unlike the French, the English have managed to maintain, even through their revolutions, an unbroken connection with the traditional roots of their social order. Their greater political stability, however, has been purchased at the cost of an inadequate critical reason. Resting on custom and adaptation to local circumstances, the English system can have no universal appeal (III, 113). The French Revolution, in contrast, "found undoubtedly its motive-power in the intelligence of men, and not in their practical sense; this is what distinguishes it from the English Revolution of Charles the First's time. This is what makes it a more spiritual event than our Revolution, an event of much more powerful and world-wide interest, though practically less successful; it appeals to an order of ideas which are universal, certain, permanent" (III, 264). Because the French Revolution appeals not merely to law or to conscience but to reason, it appears to Arnold despite its "crimes and follies . . . the greatest, the most animating event in history" (III, 265). The extravagance and violence with which the French pressed the immediate application of their program, and the nationalist imperialism with which it became tainted, lend a color of justification to the English reaction against it (V, 13). However, the reaction itself served only to reinforce the native English resistance to rational order. The instinct for criticism is something "for which there is, I think, little original sympathy in the practical English nature, and what there was of it has undergone a long benumbing period of blight and suppression in the epoch of concentration which followed the French Revolution" (III, 268–69).

It is appropriate to Arnold's intellectual ethnography that within this epoch of resistance to the great movement of French "intelligence" there should arise in England a man of genius to lead the movement of resistance. Arnold was profoundly and permanently influenced by Burke's doctrine of the state as the nation in its collective and corporate character, and he exempts Burke from his general condemnation of English unintelligence. "Burke is so great because, almost alone in England, he brings thought to bear upon politics, he saturates politics with thought. It is his accident that his ideas were at the service of an epoch of concentration" (III, 266). This "accident" serves to demonstrate the power of genius to rise above the limiting influence of cultural circumstances, but it also demonstrates the pervasive influence of these circumstances on all intellectual labor undertaken within them. By deploying his native talents Burke arrived at a "profound, permanent, fruitful, philosophical truth," "the true philosophy of an epoch of concentration," but his efforts were directed toward preserving the sovereign authority of the British Constitution—an authority itself inimical to "philosophical truth" (III, 266). Arnold holds that "the British Constitution itself, which, seen from the practical side, looks such a magnificent organ of progress and virtue, seen from the speculative side,—with its compromises, its love of facts, its horror of theory, its studied avoidance of clear thoughts . . . sometimes looks . . . a colossal machine for the manufacture of Philistines" (III, 275). Because the English have had "neither the German wealth of ideas, nor the French enthusiasm for applying ideas," they have failed in criticism; despite their imaginative powers, social aptitudes, and individual genius, this failure excludes them from the mainstream of modern culture (III, 120). "We in England, in our great burst of literature during the first thirty years of the present century, had no manifestation of the modern spirit, as this spirit manifests itself in Goethe's works or Heine's."

In the first elegy for Senancour, Arnold had said that "Goethe's course few sons of men / May think to emulate." At the time of writing his critical essays Arnold has tacitly revoked this judgment.

By removing himself from the minor current of nineteenth-century English literature and entering the mainstream of European criticism, he has made it possible for himself "Goethe's wide / And luminous view to gain." This does not mean that Arnold simply adopts Goethe's views on particular topics. Although Goethe was certainly a far richer source for Arnold than Coleridge was, the main impact he has on Arnold comes not from the formulation of any single theory or matrix idea but, as with Coleridge, from "the stimulus of his continual effort . . . to get at and to lay bare the real truth of his matter in hand" (III, 189). From the example of Coleridge struggling alone in adverse conditions Arnold derives a certain moral support. In the earlier part of his career, before his work had begun to achieve general recognition and approbation, Arnold saw "the risk always before me, if I cannot charm the wild beast of Philistinism while I am trying to convert him, of being torn in pieces by him."[12] From the example of Goethe, however, he takes an ideal of world literature and the modern critical mission that lifts him above the confinement and dejection within which Coleridge worked:

> Let us conceive of the whole group of civilised nations as being, for intellectual and spiritual purposes, one great confederation, bound to a joint action and working towards a common result; a confederation whose members have a due knowledge both of the past, out of which they all proceed, and of one another. This was the ideal of Goethe, and it is an ideal which will impose itself upon the thoughts of our modern societies more and more.
>
> ("WORDSWORTH," IX, 38)

The same statement, with slightly different wording and without the attribution to Goethe, appears in "The Function of Criticism," where Arnold declares that it is this sort of criticism "which alone can much help us for the future" (III, 284). Progress, both for individuals and for nations, depends on the degree to which they adopt this program and submit themselves to "the critical spirit."

Critical judgment can operate only in complete freedom from prejudice and intellectual coercion. The most important factor in the influence exercised by Goethe is, Arnold says, his power of independent judgment:

12. *Letters* 1:240 (November 14, 1863).

> Goethe's profound, imperturbable naturalism is absolutely fatal to all routine thinking; he puts the standard, once for all, inside every man instead of outside him; when he is told, such a thing must be so, there is immense authority and custom in favour of its being so, it has been held to be so for a thousand years, he answers with Olympian politeness, "But *is* it so? is it so to *me*?" Nothing could be more really subversive of the foundations on which the old European order rested; and it may be remarked that no persons are so radically detached from this order, no persons so thoroughly modern, as those who have felt Goethe's influence most deeply.
>
> (III, 110)

Arnold was one of the people who felt this influence most deeply, and he applies it not only to the old European order but also to Goethe himself. On vital issues such as democracy, the French Revolution, the nature of historical change, and the religious function of literature, Arnold differs from Goethe. The significance of Goethe is that he successfully represents the modern Hellenic spirit, a willingness to live in a world of ideas and the ability to find complete spiritual fulfillment through them. "We are in an epoch of expansion; and the essence of an epoch of expansion is a movement of ideas, and the one salvation of an epoch of expansion is a harmony of ideas" (V, 126).

For Arnold, to live in a world of ideas is not to renounce the world of pleasure and activity but to assimilate it, to render it coherent and meaningful. In "The Modern Element," as we have seen, he disparages the hysterical detachment of Lucretius, and in his essay on Eugénie de Guérin (sister of the poet Maurice), he equally rejects an asceticism deriving from religious ardor.

> The insufficiency of her Catholicism comes from a doctrine . . . with a certain attraction for all noble natures, but, in the modern world at any rate, incurably sterile,—the doctrine of the emptiness and nothingness of human life, of the superiority of renouncement to activity, of quietism to energy; the doctrine which makes effort for things on this side of the grave a folly, and joy in things on this side of the grave a sin.
>
> (III, 98)

Arnold discerns this same tendency to "spiritualism" in Dante, and although he holds that Dante is "one of the greatest of artists," the emotional and moral foundations of Dante's achievement render him alien to the needs of the modern spirit. "The task Dante sets himself is not the task of reconciling poetry and reality, of giving to each its due part, of supplementing the one by the other; but the task of sacrificing the world to the spirit, of making the spirit all in all, of effacing the world in presence of the spirit" ("Dante and Beatrice," III, 4). Dante was "not complete in the life of the world," and the imaginative reason requires a human nature complete both in its inward qualities of heart and imagination and in its sensual and intellectual relations to the world. The poetry of Sophocles (and, we may add, of Goethe) is adequate, as Dante's is not, because "it represents the highly developed human nature of that age—human nature developed in a number of directions, politically, socially, religiously, morally developed—in its completest and most harmonious development in all these directions; while there is shed over this poetry the charm of that noble serenity which always accompanies true insight" (I, 28).

In "The Modern Element" Arnold has said that a modern epoch is simply an age that presents a grand spectacle requiring and inviting comprehension. In the essay on Heine, when Arnold addresses himself to the issue of contemporary modernism, the grand spectacle that he contemplates does not produce a "harmonious acquiescence of mind." Instead it produces a sense of radical disjunction between individual needs and perceptions, on the one hand, and the established modes of community experience, on the other:

> Modern times find themselves with an immense system of institutions, established facts, accredited dogmas, customs, rules, which have come to them from times not modern. In this system their life has to be carried forward; yet they have a sense that this system is not of their own creation, that it by no means corresponds exactly with the wants of their actual life, that, for them, it is customary, not rational. (III, 109)

Arnold here defines the modern spirit as precisely this recognition of a disjunction between the "new wine" of the eighteenth and nineteenth centuries and the "old bottles" of Christianity and feudalism. The purpose of the modern spirit is to achieve a harmony of ideas, but "ideas" (in the sense used by empirical philosophers such as Locke and Hume) consist not only of a priori concepts and their logical relations but also of "perceptions" given in experience. Thus, a "rational" order of ideas entails a reasonable ordering of empirical reality—an arrangement of institutions, social practices, and publicly established beliefs that corresponds to the needs given in individual experience. The task of the critic, as an exponent of "reason," is to free Europe from the bondage of an outmoded social and religious ethos and, at the same time, to fashion a new ethos that will nurture the instinct for development.[13]

At the time of writing "The Function of Criticism" Arnold's solution for this problem emphasizes the need for "curiosity," that is, for disinterested study. He declares that the business of criticism is "simply to know the best that is known and thought in the world, and by in its turn making this known, to create a current of true and fresh ideas" (III, 270). Arnold's intention in insisting on disinterested observation is to put a check to the English mania for "all questions of practical consequences and applications." Nonetheless, his formula for the dissemination of the best ideas contains an apostolic note, and this note becomes more pronounced when Arnold restates the formula later in the same essay.[14] "I am bound by my own definition of criticism: *a disinterested endeavour to learn and propagate the best that is known and thought in the world*" (III, 283). The best that is known and thought does not consist only of imaginative literature and philosophy but also of applied social theory. Thus, in *Friendship's Garland* Arnold's spokesman Arminius maintains that "France has 'Geist' in her democracy, and Prussia in her education" (V, 41). To propagate the best ideas, however free of personal interest one's motives may be, implies for Arnold a concern to make these ideas prevail in the contemporary world. This concern, however, cannot logically be derived from "curiosity." Recognizing this to be the case, Arnold

13. The supposed conflict in Arnold between disinterested observation and social involvement forms the substance of E. K. Brown's *Matthew Arnold: A Study in Conflict* (Chicago: University of Chicago Press, 1944). Henry Ebel, in "Matthew Arnold and Classical Culture," *Arion* 4 (1965): 209, follows Brown, but Brown's critique had already been adequately answered by Kenneth Allott in *Matthew Arnold* (London: Longmans, Green, 1962), p. 27, and by Gaylord C. LeRoy in *Perplexed Prophets: Six Nineteenth-Century British Authors* (Philadelphia: University of Pennsylvania Press, 1953), p. 80. More recently, Sidney Coulling, answering Brown, has placed this problem in a just perspective in *Matthew Arnold and His Critics*, p. 16.

14. This point is also made by David J. DeLaura, *Hebrew and Hellene in Victorian England: Newman, Arnold, and Pater* (Austin: University of Texas Press, 1969), p. 187.

redefines the nature of criticism in *Culture and Anarchy* so as to bring it more into accord with his actual purposes:

> But there is of culture another view, in which not solely the scientific passion, the sheer desire to see things as they are, natural and proper in an intelligent being, appears as the ground of it. There is a view in which all the love of our neighbour, the impulses towards action, help, and beneficence, the desire for removing human error, clearing human confusion, and diminishing human misery, the noble aspiration to leave the world better and happier than we found it,—motives eminently such as are called social,—come in as part of the grounds of culture, and the main and pre-eminent part. Culture is then properly described not as having its origin in curiosity, but as having its origin in the love of perfection; it is *a study of perfection.* (V, 91)

The shift in terms, from "criticism" to "culture," should not confuse us. Arnold is clearly not limiting the function of criticism to curiosity and yielding the constructive aspects of intellectual activity to something else he calls culture. He is broadening the idea of criticism to include the regulation and direction of the whole collective life of humanity according to the ideal of "perfection" that criticism itself establishes.[15] To be an agent of intellectual deliverance in the modern world, the critic must not only pursue knowledge as a good in itself, he must also seek to make the good that is revealed through knowledge the standard of life. It is on the basis of this requirement that Arnold denies to Sainte-Beuve a position in the first rank of criticism. He "stopped short at curiosity, at the desire to know things as they really are, and did not press on with faith and ardour to the various and immense applications of this knowledge which suggest themselves, and of which the accomplishment is reserved for the future" (V, 309). Sainte-Beuve's failure is not so much a failure of practical application—he was a senator—as rather a failure of evaluative synthesis. "Culture," when it enters the field of practice at all, does so only as a representative of the ideal of a completely and harmoniously developed human

15. Basil Willey points out that in "The Function of Criticism" Arnold defines criticism "in terms almost identical with those later applied to 'culture.'" *Nineteenth Century Studies: Coleridge to Matthew Arnold* (New York: Columbia University Press, 1949), p. 258. Douglas Bush also remarks that Arnold's "definition of culture is virtually identical with his earlier definition of criticism." *Matthew Arnold: A Survey of His Poetry and Prose* (New York: Macmillan, 1971), p. 147.

nature. Its criticisms of the existing order of things and its suggestions for their correction proceed invariably from a recognition of attitudes or material conditions that impede the realization of this ideal.

It is within Arnold's Hellenic ideal that we may find the theoretical link between the two seemingly divergent tendencies of his modernism, his democratic principles and his cultural elitism. Arnold's altruistic definition of culture proceeds, in part, from his belief that charity is a natural human propensity and that there can be no complete individual development outside of the common life of humanity. "Such is the sympathy which binds humanity together, that we are indeed, as our religion says, members of one body, and if one member suffer, all the members suffer with it. Individual perfection is impossible so long as the rest of mankind are not perfected along with us" (V, 215). In part, however, the social conscience of an advocate of culture derives from an enlightened self-interest. For a cultural elite to achieve its highest potential it requires, Arnold holds, the energy generated by a nationally diffused enthusiasm for the life of the mind:

> High culture or ardent intelligence, pervading a large body of the community, acquire a breadth of basis, a sum of force, an energy of central heat for radiating further, which they can never possess when they pervade a small upper class only. It is when such a broad basis is obtained, that individual genius gets its proper nutriment, and is animated to put forth its best powers; this is the secret of rich and beautiful epochs in national life; the epoch of Pericles in Greece, the epoch of Michael Angelo in Italy, the epoch of Shakspeare in England.
>
> ("A FRENCH ETON," II, 316)

The culture of Athens seems to Arnold the most successful of all "modern" epochs, not only because there the various elements of human development were most highly integrated in the individual, but also because this high standard was most widely diffused throughout the general population. "This is why the spectacle of Athens has such profound interest for a rational man; that it is the spectacle of the culture of a people. . . . it is the middle and lower classes in the highest development of their humanity that these classes have yet reached. It was the *many* who relished those arts, who were not satisfied with less than those monuments" and who "for the free yet refined discussion of ideas have set the tone for the whole cultivated world" ("Democracy," II, 25).

This concept of the importance of a nationally diffused intellectual enthusiasm enables Arnold finally to make sense of the "unique greatness in English literature of Shakspeare and his contemporaries" (III, 121). In a letter to his brother Thomas, written about the time of "The Modern Element," Arnold's historical theory had concentrated on the critical spirit as "a rational arrangement of facts" and had been unable to account for Shakespeare except through the miracle of genius. "The eternal greatness of the literature of the Greece of Pericles is that it is the *adequate* expression of a first-class epoch. Shakespeare again, is the infinitely *more than adequate* expression of a *second class* epoch. It is the immense distinction of Voltaire and Goethe, with all their shortcomings, that they approach *near* to being adequate exponents of first-class epochs."[16] In the essay on Heine, Arnold modifies this earlier judgment on the Elizabethan age by redefining the critical spirit so that it appears not as a finished, scientific order but as a vital movement of ideas. "In our greatest literary epoch, that of the Elizabethan age, English society at large was accessible to ideas, was permeated by them, was vivified by them, to a degree which has never been reached in England since" (III, 121). This implicit redefinition is made explicit in "The Function of Criticism," where Arnold declares that "the elements with which the creative power works are ideas; the best ideas, on every matter which literature touches, current at the time" (III, 260). The purpose of criticism is "to establish an order of ideas, if not absolutely true, yet true by comparison with that which it displaces, to make the best ideas prevail" (III, 261). This intellectual relativism does not, of course, free Arnold from the need for rational validity in his own ideas. What might have been relatively true for Spenser and the Cambridge Platonists no longer carries conviction for the modern age, and the growth of the scientific mentality has not only altered the substance of belief but also rendered more complex and rigorous the means by which conviction might be attained. "What distinguishes culture [from religion] is, that it is possessed by the scientific passion" (V, 92). For the eighteen centuries that Christianity had been the mainstream

16. Robert Liddell Lowe, "Two Arnold Letters," *Modern Philology* 52 (1955): 263.

of human development it was an advantage for a man to be a Christian, because "being in contact with the main stream of human life is of more moment for a man's total spiritual growth . . . than any speculative opinion which he may hold or think he holds" (V, 251). The mainstream now, however, is not Christian but pagan and scientific. Consequently, "the best ideas current" with which literature must work are the ideas produced by or in concordance with the spirit of naturalistic inquiry. If individual genius finds its inspiration in the collective life of humanity, a poet of the Middle Ages—and to a lesser degree, of the Renaissance—was of necessity bound to the dominant Christian ethos. In the modern age the man of literature is of a like necessity bound to the critical spirit.

In the England of his own time Arnold feels that there is no "national glow of life and thought," but he maintains that it is still possible, through study, for a man to construct "a world of knowledge and intelligence in which he may live and work" (III, 263). Arnold's own situation might have forced this conclusion on him, but he also finds historical evidence for it both in the great creative period of German letters and in the French Enlightenment. In Germany the collective efforts of a large intellectual elite had provided "a sort of equivalent" for "the nationally diffused life and thought" that were lacking to them. The main thing is for the individual to live in "a quickening and sustaining atmosphere," and "such an atmosphere the many-sided learning and the long and widely-combined critical effort of Germany formed for Goethe, when he lived and worked";[17] we may add that this German critical effort continued to form such an atmosphere for Arnold, when he lived and worked. In France under the old regime, a similar atmosphere of intellectual purpose animated the community of philosophes so that even without the support of a national intellectual life "the France of Voltaire and Rousseau told far more powerfully upon the mind of Europe than the France of the Revolution" (III, 264).

17. Arnold's contention may be verified by reference to Goethe's description of the remarkably animated intellectual milieu of his young manhood in his autobiography, *Dichtung und Wahrheit (Poetry and Truth)*, especially pt. 3, *Goethes sämtliche Werke. Jubiläums-Ausgabe in 40 Bänden*, ed. Eduard von der Hellen (Stuttgart: J. G. Cotta, 1902–1907), vol. 24. The milieu of his later life is best evoked by Eckermann's *Gespräche mit Goethe in den letzten Jahren seines Lebens*, ed. H. H. Houben (Wiesbaden: F. A. Brockhaus, 1959).

In answering the question thus raised of why the French Revolution failed to produce "a crop of works of genius" equal to those of other great epochs of national life, Arnold reinforces his prescription for a critical detachment from immediate practical applications. By "quitting the intellectual sphere and rushing furiously into the political sphere," the Revolution aborted its creative, literary potential (III, 266). It did not, however, remain "barren of good." Because of the Revolution, France remains "the country in Europe where *the people* is most alive" (III, 265). Arnold was deeply impressed by the superior dignity and intelligence of the French common people. They are, he says, remarkably ignorant of facts, but at the same time they are responsive to political and social ideas of an elevated order, and they are attuned to the voice of reason. "It is the bright feature in her civilization that her common people can understand and appreciate language which elsewhere meets with a response only from the educated and refined classes" ("England and the Italian Question," I, 78–79; see also II, 153 and II, 9–10).

In different ways, then, both Germany and France offer stimulus and support to the modern spirit. England, in contrast, possesses neither the superior culture of the German elite nor the broad basis of rational enthusiasm that has animated France. The English common people "is at present more raw, to say the very least, less enviable-looking, further removed from civilised and humane life, than the common people almost anywhere" (*Friendship's Garland*, V, 18). The middle class is "acute and energetic, but tasteless, narrow-minded, and ignoble" ("Democracy," II, 25). The members of the professional class, to which Arnold himself belonged, are "by income and social position" aligned with the middle class; however, because they are educated at the aristocratic schools, they are "mainly identified in thought, feeling, and manners with the aristocratic class" (II, 88 and cf. V, 23). The modern spirit consists of an incessant movement of ideas, a heightened critical consciousness. An aristocracy is, Arnold says, by its very nature impervious to ideas. "Themselves a power reposing on all which is most solid, material, and visible, they are slow to attach any great importance to influences impalpable, spiritual, and viewless" (II, 11). If the best life of humanity resides in a heightened spiritual activity, the social predominance of an aristocracy limits not only its own members but, by the influence of its example, the rest of society as well. The aristocracy represents "the material ideal of splendour of wealth, and weight of property. And this ideal is the ideal truly operative upon our middle classes at this moment" (II, 321). The religious preoccupations of the middle classes do not adequately serve to counteract the materialist tendency, for popular religion has tended to place its emphasis on a materialized conception of beatitude and to rely on "motives of reward and punishment" (III, 148). The lower classes—for whom the aristocratic ideal is hopelessly out of reach, and "for whom in a middle class, narrow, ungenial, and unattractive, there is no adequate ideal"—are thrown back upon a brutal and dissolute sensuality (II, 324). Altogether, although exceptions may arise from any of the three major classes (V, 145), the social structure of England provides no suitable framework for the realization of a modern Hellenic ideal.

On the basis of this analysis Arnold counsels throughout his career the gradual, nonviolent disestablishment of the English aristocracy. At one time, he holds, the aristocracy was both socially necessary and culturally propitious. In the medieval period it provided points of social cohesion that replaced the shattered political system of imperial Rome (V, 203). As late even as the eighteenth century it possessed that superior personal dignity and elevation of character generated "by the possession of power, by the importance and responsibility of high station, by habitually dealing with great things, by being placed above the necessity of constantly struggling for little things" (II, 6). The example of nobility afforded by such an aristocracy had a refining and restraining effect on the population at large. It provided "a kind of outward shadow" of the Hellenic ideal (II, 318). In the contemporary world the aristocracy, ill-adapted to the social and intellectual needs of the modern spirit, has itself degenerated. It no longer presents an image of true nobility but rather of empty vanity and idle luxury. The point is put most succinctly by Arminius, who admonishes Arnold that the aristocracy "by all the power of example of a class high-placed, rich, idle, self-indulgent, without mental life . . . teaches your Philistines to live fast. But it no longer rules; at most it but administers; the Philistines rule" (V, 330). The middle and lower classes are thus coming into political power without any adequate standards of excellence to guide them. The consequence of such a situation Arnold finds best exemplified in the American culture that elevates the common man, systematically disparages all standards of personal and social superiority, and has, despite its material success, created a civilization marked by vulgarity and intellectual mediocrity (V, 241).

From the detached perspective of a spokesman for culture, Arnold proposes two practical solutions for the English sociocultural problem: an improved public education for the middle class and the adoption of a more positive attitude toward the state as the agent of national well-being. The two proposals are both causally interdependent and thematically concordant. A stronger power of state action appears as the precondition for establishing a national system of standardized public instruction, and this improved educational system would in turn give the middle classes a greater sense of belonging to the nation in its collective and corporate character, that is, the state. "By public establishment they [schools] may communicate to those reared in them the sense of being brought in contact with their country, with the national life, with the life of the world; and they will expand and dignify their spirits by communicating this sense to them" (II, 323). Thus, a stronger state would indirectly have an ennobling effect on the middle class. (Despite his impatience with and distaste for this class, Arnold believes that its energy and earnestness make it "the best stuff in this nation" [VIII, 347].) Moreover, the state could also have a more direct influence on the character of the middle class. A nation needs, Arnold says, "an ideal higher than that of an ordinary man, taken by himself" (II, 18), and he suggests that the state itself could become a medium for experience elevated above the "ordinary self," the self of individual and class interests. Assuming that there are sufficient means "for securing a correspondence between the acts of government and the will of the nation," Arnold supposes that through an expanded state power the nation might "acquire in the State an ideal of high reason and right feeling, representing its best self, commanding general respect, and forming a rallying-point for the intelligence and for the worthiest instincts of the community, which will herein find a true bond of union" (II, 19).

Arnold's primary concern in his political doctrine is still the perfection of the individual, but again he draws from the example of Athens, "where State-action was omnipresent," to demonstrate that a strong state "is not in itself unfavourable to the individual's perfection" (II, 314). He recognizes that state machinery can be and has been used to serve the interests of individuals or a class, and that such a use suppresses idealism rather than fosters it. He insists, however, that in an England so singularly devoted to individual initiative and so jealous of its personal liberties, the state would never be allowed to corrupt itself in this fashion. The Puritan middle class has the virtues of its defects. If it is narrow and stubborn, it is also fiercely moral and self-reliant. "Our middle class has secured for itself that centre of character and that moral force which are, I have said, the indispensable basis upon which perfection is to be founded. To securing them, its vigour in resisting the State, when the State tried to tyrannise over it, has contributed not a little" (II, 313). Social attitudes that at one historical moment serve the cause of human progress may become at another moment its most serious obstacle, and this may be so because of a change in circumstances that these very attitudes have helped to bring about. The only absolute standard, as Arnold says in *Culture and Anarchy,* is "the progress towards perfection" (V, 219), and the idea of progress necessarily entails a relativity of social values and social theories. If perfection is to be attained, or even approached, all the elements of culture must be regarded as building blocks at the free disposition of the critical intelligence. All social structures are erected in accordance with the needs of their times, and the only permanent authority is the mind that recognizes and submits itself to the stream of change.

The Cultural Dialectic

In his literary and social criticism Arnold adopts a historical vision in which the elements of culture combine differently for the good at different times, but he does not, as in the 1852 poem "Revolutions," regard history as a senseless jumble. In "The Modern Element" he commits himself both to an idea of cultural "development" and to the two basic terms of development, moral and intellectual (I, 19). Though described as complementary components of "freedom," these two terms are arranged in no specific and necessary historical order. Arnold merely says that at one time one principle is uppermost, then at another time the other. In "Democracy" Arnold defines the complementary relation of the two principles. "Culture without character is, no doubt, something frivolous, vain, and weak; but character without culture is, on the other hand, something raw, blind, and dangerous" (II, 24). At the same time he declares that the Puritan middle class, in maintaining its liberty of conscience and opinion, has rendered an "invaluable" service to the whole English community. From this position Arnold advances, in "A French Eton," to the idea that will form the nucleus of his historical dialectic. The Puritan resistance was not only valuable but necessary to progress, "the indispensable basis upon which perfection is to be founded."

In *Culture and Anarchy* Arnold expands the necessary function of the Puritan reaction from an English to a general European progress, and he also extends the principle of moral reaction to account for the dynamics of all of Western cultural history. The modern spirit, the cutting edge of human progress, is still Hellenism, but progress as a whole process consists not only of Hellenism but also of its dialectical counterforce, Hebraism. "For more than two hundred years the main stream of man's advance has moved towards knowing himself and the world, seeing things as they are, spontaneity of consciousness; the main impulse of a great part, and that the strongest part, of our nation has been towards strictness of conscience" (V, 175). Arnold calls this English tendency a "contravention of the natural order" and assigns it as the chief cause of the general decline in English affairs, political and literary. At the same time, however, he concedes to it a rationale of world-historical scope. Puritanism arose as a reaction "against the moral indifference and lax rule of conduct which in the sixteenth century came in with the Renascence" (V, 174). The effect of this reaction on the Puritans themselves, however necessary it may have been for their eventual perfection, has been to render their actual lives ugly, dismal, and incomplete. Nonetheless, "as we said of the former defeat of Hellenism, if Hellenism was defeated, this shows that Hellenism was imperfect, and that its ascendency at that moment would not have been for the world's good."

The "former defeat" of Hellenism is the collapse of the ancient world and its replacement by Christianity. In "Pagan and Mediaeval" Arnold had already held that the pagan ethos, ruled by the senses and understanding, was inadequate, and he offered as evidence the historical fact that humanity could not "live by it" (III, 227). This thesis left Arnold with a theoretical gap, the problem of explaining why there occurred any decline from the Hellenic to the Hellenistic and Roman civilizations. This gap reveals itself in Arnold's turnabout at the end of "Pagan and Mediaeval," where after demonstrating the superficiality of late pagan religious sentiment he reminds us "that before this state of things appeared, there was an epoch in Greek life,—in Pagan life,—of the highest possible beauty and value" (III, 230). By using the word *appeared* Arnold withdraws from any attempt at causal explanation. There was one phase, and then there was another. In "The Modern Element" Arnold had offered as an explanation for the decline of Athens its defeat in the Peloponnesian War—a defeat that left it, in diametrical contrast to Rome, a "head without a body," an ethos without an adequate "material basis" (I, 30). In "Pagan and Mediaeval" Arnold still takes the Peloponnesian War as marking the end of Athenian vigor, and in *Culture and Anarchy* he makes limited concessions to the usefulness modern industrialism may have in laying "broad foundations of material well-being for the society of the future" (V, 105). Nonetheless, material determinism is ultimately alien to the humanistic cast of his mind. In his analysis of contemporary political affairs he attributes the difficulties of the English to a lack of intelligence and the difficulties of the French to a lack of moral rigor. In the same fashion, on the largest scale, the dominant tendency of his thought is to place the driving forces of history inside human nature itself. He seeks the rationale for historical change in the adaptation of cultures—a sort of cultural tropism—to the ideals of moral salvation and intellectual deliverance. Accordingly, in *Culture and Anarchy* Arnold adjusts his historical analysis in such a way that both degenerate Hellenism and the Hellenic culture proper display a moral deficiency that generates its dialectical antithesis of Hebraism. "Apparently it was the Hellenic conception of human nature which was unsound, for the world could not live by it" (V, 169).

By allowing Hellenism to have been inadequate to the needs of humanity Arnold preserves both the progressive unity of history and its humanistic foundation, the instinct for a development towards perfection. At the same time, however, through the idea of a progressive development of human potential, he preserves Hellenism as the archetype for the teleological ideal of perfection. Hellenism was not, he says, "absolutely" unsound, "but it was unsound at that particular moment of man's development, it was premature. The indispensable basis of conduct and self-control, the platform upon which alone the perfection aimed at by Greece can come into bloom, was not to be reached by our race so easily; centuries of probation and discipline were needed to bring us to it" (V, 169). The essential character of Hebraism is the concern for "conduct," for acting in strict accordance with a prescribed moral code. It finds its motive power in the resistance to "sin"—the indulgence of selfish appetites, most especially "the flesh with its affections and lusts" (V, 167). Its positive force is the power of self-control; although Christianity has improved the method, it has done nothing to alter this fundamental character of Hebraism (V, 165). The main Hebraic phase of world history, the Christian interregnum, arose and flourished as a "self-conquest and rescue from the thrall of vile affections, not by obedience to the letter of a law, but by conformity to the image of a self-sacrificing example. To a world stricken with moral enervation Christianity offered its spectacle of an inspired self-sacrifice" (V, 169). The ancient world suffered from moral enervation because the Hellenic ideal made no sufficient provision against the weakness of human nature at that time. By concentrating on intellectual and aesthetic harmony the Greeks left mankind vulnerable to the miseries of disorder and cruelty arising from an unconquered "animality" (V, 101). Moreover, the Greek ethos could not provide consolation for sickness and sorrow ("Pagan and Mediaeval"). By making self-renouncement the law of life Christianity enabled the mass of mankind to endure the suffering that was inevitably to be their portion (V, 207).

In outline, then, Arnold's historical system has four main phases divided equally between Hebraism and Hellenism. "Between these two points of influence moves our world" (V, 163–64). The first two phases display a simple alternation of the two tendencies. The third and fourth phases comprise the Renaissance, gradually expanding into the neopaganism of the eighteenth and nineteenth centuries, and the Reformation. These last two phases take place contemporaneously and within a shorter chronological compass than the first two. Both Hebraism and Hellenism establish their own internal and inclusive standards of value, but they obtain their ultimate justification as components of a unified historical process that transcends the achievements of either of them. Hellenism is moved from its static condition as an ideal of individual perfection and rendered as a motive force of historical development. Christianity appears neither as it does to its adherents, as an end in itself, nor as it does to its enemies, as a wasteland of error and delusion. It serves a necessary historical function, to have made "the moral and religious fibre in humanity . . . more braced and developed than it had yet been" (V, 100). In similar fashion, when the intellectual and aesthetic impulses again came into force during the Renaissance, the crosscurrent of the Reformation and English Puritanism restrained the mainstream of Hellenism from losing itself in a hedonistic dissolution.

Because Hebraism and Hellenism have the same general purpose, "man's perfection or salvation" (V, 164), and because both tendencies are necessary components of this perfection, Arnold explicitly denies archetypal priority to either of them. "Hebraism and Hellenism are, neither of them, the *law* of human development, as their admirers are prone to make them; they are, each of them, *contributions*" (V, 170–71). Accordingly, in a preface composed after the rest of *Culture and Anarchy*, Arnold warns that, although he has himself elevated Hellenism over Hebraism, one must be prepared at any time to alter this evaluation and to reassign preeminence to the Hebraic character:

> Now, and for us, it is a time to Hellenise, and to praise knowing; for we have Hebraised too much, and have over-valued doing. But the habits and discipline received from Hebraism remain for our race an eternal possession; and, as humanity is constituted, one must never assign to them the second rank to-day, without being prepared to restore to them the first rank to-morrow.
>
> (V, 255)

This is the perspective adopted in "The Modern Element," a perspective from which Arnold regards the contemporary world as composed of various inherited cultural aptitudes that may be applied and adjusted in response to whatever needs are most pressing at any given time. Nonetheless, within the dialectical scheme of *Culture and Anarchy*, Arnold does commit himself to Hellenism as the originative and directive force of cultural history and so, in this sense, to Hellenism as "the law of human development." Hebraism appears as a supplementary, corrective agency that, because it regards intellectual deliverance as inessential to salvation, cannot of itself fashion an adequate ideal of perfection. Although pure Hellenism cannot of itself attain perfection, it does fashion an ideal that theoretically includes the Hebraic contribution. The Greeks arrived "at the idea of a comprehensive adjustment of the claims of both the sides in man, the moral as well as the intellectual, of a full estimate of both, and of a reconciliation of both" (V, 179).

Arnold's Hellenic ideal answers to his deepest intellectual instinct, the rationalist presupposition that "perfection" entails completeness and unity of consciousness. There is nothing more alien to him than the empiricists' presupposition that all we can or need to know are fragmentary perceptions given by the senses and mechanically arranged by "fictional" abstract generalizations. The classical statement of this mechanical sensationalism is presented by Locke in *An Essay Concerning Human Understanding*. Locke maintains that "all things that exist are only particulars," so that "*general* and *universal* belong not to the real existence of things; but are the inventions and creatures of the understanding, made by it for its own use, and concern only signs, whether words or ideas."[18] These presuppositions are the source for Empedocles' anguish, his morbid conviction that "the All" is never to be grasped and that reality can only be filtered and distorted through the "forms, and modes, and stifling veils" of thought. The historical process is for Empedocles merely a cyclical reenactment of a process of philosophical disillusionment and despair. One may best regard Arnold's Empedocles as representing the failure of English Romanticism to overcome the spiritual aridity of Locke's mechanical sensationalism through the force of emotional enthusiasm alone and without actually replacing Locke's philosophic presuppositions. By shifting to a relativistic historical vision Arnold provisionally frees himself from Empedocles' despair, but he does not thereby either satisfy or abandon the need for a rationalist fulfillment, a complete and unified consciousness.

All of Arnold's wide-ranging, seemingly diverse studies, from "The Modern Element" through *Culture and Anarchy*, are unified by his central motive: the search for a way to render historical change concordant with rationalist universalism. Arnold's first step—theoretically, not chronologically—toward a resolution of the cosmological and historical problem is simply to reject the Ro-

18. John Locke, *An Essay Concerning Human Understanding*, ed. Alexander Campbell Fraser, 2 vols. (New York: Dover, 1959), 2:16, 21. For Arnold's early interest in Locke and a comparison of Locke with Spinoza, see *LC*, pp. 116–17.

mantic assumption that "the All" is a formless infinity inaccessible to the divisive analytical categories of the mind. Arnold's advance beyond this position may be measured by comparing two statements on the nature of Hebraism and Hellenism. The first is from the essay on Heine, and its Romantic aesthetic already appears there as a somewhat embarrassed vestige of an obsolete cosmology. Hebraism and Hellenism both, Arnold says, "reach the infinite, which is the true goal of all poetry and all art,—the Greek spirit by beauty, the Hebrew spirit by sublimity" (III, 128). By the time of writing *Culture and Anarchy* Arnold has abandoned this position. The goal of both Hebraism and Hellenism is no longer "the infinite" but the universal order, an order accessible to rational intuition. "At the bottom of both the Greek and the Hebrew notion is the desire, native in man, for reason and the will of God, the feeling after the universal order,—in a word, the love of God" (V, 165).

In the essay on Heine, Arnold's attempt to reconcile the concepts of Hebraism and Hellenism with his residual Romanticism leads him into theoretical difficulties from which he will later extricate himself by substituting a classical cosmology and aesthetic for the Romantic. His description of the Greek aesthetic as represented in Heine's work clashes with his claim that Hellenism aims at the infinite. "By his perfection of literary form, by his love of clearness, by his love of beauty, Heine is Greek" (III, 128). Whenever Arnold himself has attempted to approach the infinite, for example, as in "The Future," he has done so through a dissolution of distinct form and a diminution of light. Arnold's description of the Greek aesthetic is persuasive, but it stands in conflict with his residual Romanticism. His description of Hebraism, again as exemplified by Heine, is more in accord with his Romanticism, but it is not a completely persuasive characterization of Hebraism. "By his intensity, by his untamableness, by his 'longing which cannot be uttered,' he is Hebrew" (III, 128). The attribution of "untamableness," however apt it may be for Heine, conflicts with Arnold's depictions of Hebraism in other works. In the essay on Marcus Aurelius Arnold describes the Jews as "that isolated, fierce, and stubborn race" (III, 144), but this description concerns itself with the political identity of the Jews in the Roman world. In "Spinoza and the Bible" Arnold remarks that the dominant character of the Hebrew religion is its devotion to "obedience" (III,

166), a point he frequently reiterates in *Culture and Anarchy.* In the passage where Arnold contrasts the different ways by which Hebraism and Hellenism strive after "the universal order," he significantly modifies his earlier, Romantic description of Hebraism. "Hebraism seizes upon certain plain, capital intimations of the universal order, and rivets itself, one may say, with unequalled grandeur of earnestness and intensity on the study and observance of them" (V, 165). The "intensity" remains, but it has been changed from a boundless yearning after the ineffable into a fervent adherence to a prescribed order.

Although Arnold is not, at this point, advocating Hebraism to his contemporaries, he is explaining its historical function and describing it as a valid intuition of an objective moral order. With a shift of emphasis from moral to intellectual order Arnold makes the same claim for Hellenism. "Greek intelligence has obviously for its essence the instinct for what Plato calls the true, firm, intelligible law of things" (V, 178). For Arnold this intelligible law is not only, as for Plato, moral and aesthetic but historical as well. The purpose of culture is "to draw towards a knowledge of the universal order which seems to be intended and aimed at in the world, and which it is a man's happiness to go along with or his misery to go counter to,—to learn, in short, the will of God" (V, 93). Right reason is the recognition of the will of God, a rational intuition of absolute truth and value, and the will of God manifests itself as a historical process tending toward the realization of the Hellenic ideal, "a harmonious expansion of *all* the powers which make the worth and beauty of human nature" (V, 94). Although Arnold speaks of the historical process as something "intended," his God is not a "person" external to the universal order but rather the summary term of that order. In his 1867 essay on the American theologist Theodore Parker, Arnold says that "science" can no longer accept a theistic concept of a God who has created the world and "set this movement a-going on a foreknown plan, and who sits *outside* of it watching its operation" (V, 83). What the scientific intellect can accept is "the idea that the world is in a course of development, of *becoming,* towards a perfection infinitely greater than we now can even conceive, the idea of a *tendance à l'ordre* present in the universe." God is himself the tendency to order, and he is identified in Arnold's thinking with the human instinct for development. That is to say, there is no God outside of the conditions established for the spiritual growth of humanity. Arnold thus freely combines the theological language of "providence" and "intention" with the "scientific" language of teleological evolution. The instinct for perfection is itself a "religious devotion to that providential order which forbids the final supremacy of imperfect things" ("A French Eton," II, 320). The providential order reveals itself in the historical dialectic of Hebraism and Hellenism, both of which are motivated internally by the instinct for perfection. The perfection of the individual thus depends on a concordance between the constitution of the individual mind and the shape of Western cultural history.

Infinity is not altogether banished from Arnold's cosmology, but it is removed from its theoretical position as a static absolute external to human experience and is integrated with the intellective dynamic of cultural history. "God" is himself both the abstract ideal of perfect being and knowing, an "unattainable but irresistible lode-star" (II, 325), and also the historical process through which humanity advances in pursuit of this ideal. This cosmological concept provides a resolution to the plight of Empedocles and serves as the unifying principle of Arnold's social and cultural theory. We may trace its development from "Democracy," through the critical essays, to its culmination in *Culture and Anarchy*.

In "Democracy" Arnold establishes his ideal of "perfection" as the union of a strong character and a high culture. This perfect adjustment, Arnold says, "will never be reached; but to recognise a period of transformation when it comes, and to adapt themselves honestly and rationally to its laws, is perhaps the nearest approach to perfection of which men and nations are capable" (II, 29). The "period of transformation" appears here, as in "The Modern Element," as an arbitrary "event," something that merely happens from some cause external to human motivation and which men cannot direct but to which they can "adapt." Arnold's concern here is for a peaceful transition to a new social order, but his mode of discussing social change naturally situates itself in a philosophical context. In order to free his countrymen from the anxiety of change, he points out that customs and habits are not necessary states of nature but only contrivances for satisfying given social needs; as the needs change, so must the contrivances. The refuge he offers from this flux is an abstract substance or nature entirely free from change. "Human thought, which made all institutions, inevitably saps them, resting only in that which is absolute and eternal" (II, 29). The language here harks back to that of the 1853 Preface. Arnold is not, to be sure, counseling resistance to and withdrawal from the flux of contemporary life. Quite the contrary. Nonetheless, he does imply an essential division between the ideal, unchanging absolute and the phenomenal world of arbitrary events and unstable adaptations.

In "A French Eton," written two years later, Arnold persists in requiring for perfection the union of moral and intellectual excellence, but he introduces an important new element to his idealism, the idea of an infinite expansion of human powers. "It is in making endless additions to itself, in the endless expansion of its powers, in endless growth in wisdom and beauty, that the spirit of the human race finds its ideal; to reach this ideal, culture is an indispensable aid, and that is the true value of culture" (II, 318). This statement advances on Arnold's previous views in two ways. First, the idea of an intellectual deliverance, which in "The Modern Element" consisted of a comprehension of past and present, is now given a forward impetus. It no longer simply assimilates a given world complex but itself possesses an originative power. The locus of historical change is shifted from external events to the activity of the mind itself. The mind is not only, as it were, driven into motion from behind and outside; it drives itself by means of its dynamic relation to a potential future state. Second, the ideal is no longer figured as a static and externalized absolute in which the mind may rest but as the principle of dynamic forward motion. By figuring expansion as "endless," Arnold gives to infinity itself a dynamic aspect and integrates it with the process of human intellectual growth. The idea of "expansion" has been extended from a social and cultural phase into an absolute ideal, that is, the ideal has become identified with the modern spirit.

By integrating the ideal with the processes of mind and of history, Arnold has marked out a positive advance on the cosmology of Empedocles. However, as it is presented in "A French Eton," his bold assertion of endless expansion could not stand without support and qualification. As a cosmological hypothesis it is defective in two respects. The first defect is that it is too exclusively subjective, and the second is that it is too simply positive. To begin with the first defect, Arnold's hypothesis provides for no adequate ground of value outside the individual self. In "A French Eton" Arnold has recourse to the idea of the state as a medium for the "best self," a means for transcending the "ordinary self." In *Culture and Anarchy,* however, he recognizes that the state, as a collection of individuals, must itself be grounded on some principle of authority besides the abstracted, collective will of those individuals. He finds his principle of authority in "right reason"—the intelligible, objective law of the good and the beautiful—and he makes of the state not the basis but the vessel for this right reason.[19] In reaction against the recent working-class disturbances, the Hyde Park riots, Arnold says that the state, already "precious," must become yet more so "as, believing in right reason, and having faith in the progress of humanity towards perfection, and ever labouring for this end, we grow to have clearer sight of the ideas of right reason, and of the elements and helps of perfection, and come gradually to fill the framework of the State with them" (V, 223). The best self is not created, as in "A French Eton," by conformity to the idea of the state; the state is constructed in conformity with the best self, a self that includes the existence of a state among its rational intuitions of moral good.

In order to get to this idea of a right reason, Arnold must make an allowance for an objective system of laws to which the expanding human faculties may accord themselves, and this he does in the essay "Spinoza and the Bible" (1863). Spinoza's works, Arnold says, deserve to and probably will become "in the history of modern philosophy the central point of interest" (III, 159).[20] What is of most interest to Arnold in Spinoza's philosophy is its union of a "modern" scientific spirit and a quasi-religious conception of nature. In his religious thinking Spinoza is "a child of modern Europe" (III, 158). Following Heine, Arnold locates Spinoza's modernity in his rejection of an externalized, personal God who

19. Douglas Bush provides a brief but helpful historical account of the concept of right reason in *Matthew Arnold,* pp. 153–54. Bush seems wrong in maintaining that Arnold does not himself claim some form of divine authority for right reason. More extensive historical accounts of right reason are given by Robert Hoopes in *Right Reason in the English Renaissance* (Cambridge, Mass.: Harvard University Press, 1962), and by C. A. Patrides in *The Cambridge Platonists* (London: E. Arnold, 1969).

20. William Robbins gives an excellent summary of the points of congruence between the religious ideas of Spinoza and Arnold. *The Ethical Idealism of Matthew Arnold* (London: William Heinemann, 1959), pp. 68–69.

has arranged the world according to a humanly oriented plan.[21] "His denial of final causes is essentially alien to the spirit of the Old Testament, and his cheerful and self-sufficing stoicism is essentially alien to the spirit of the New" (III, 177). Spinoza was, nonetheless, profoundly religious. "His whole soul was filled with desire of the love and knowledge of God, and of that only" (III, 179). Spinoza transcends conventional religion through the quality of his love. It is not personal and dramatic but detached and intellectual. "He makes the love of God to consist in the knowledge of God; and, as we know God only through his manifestation of himself in the laws of all nature, it is by knowing these laws that we love God, and the more we know them the more we love him" (III, 178). It is by retaining God as the *summum bonum,* the unity of natural law accessible to right reason, that Spinoza "maintains a profound affinity with that which is truest in religion, and inspires an indestructible interest" (III, 178). Spinoza's philosophical importance for Arnold consists in his establishment of a rational ideal that he is still able to treat with "the power of edification." His usefulness is limited, however, by the ahistoricity of his universal order and by the exclusively rational character of his religious devotion. Arnold's Hellenic ideal requires not only a rational unity of consciousness but a complete human development.

In order to understand what Arnold means by "right reason," we should consider the implications of a phrase Arnold sometimes substitutes for it—"reason and the will of God." As a standard in the sphere of value, right reason, contrary to the revelations of mathematics and logic, has both a pathetic, affective component and a component of conscious determination or choice. It is thus far subjective or personal—qualities that are denoted in the idea of God as a person with a "will." However, insofar as ethical and aesthetic choices are "right," they derive their validity from universal principles and are not dependent on the eccentricities of individual preference. God, as the summary term of the universal order, serves to represent the objective quality of the principles

21. "The God of the pantheists is distinguished from the God of the theists in this respect, that he is in the world itself, whereas the latter is entirely outside of, or what is the same thing, above the world." Heine says that Spinoza, for so long a time mocked and abused, "rises up in our present day to sole spiritual mastery" [my translation]. Heine, *History of Religion and Philosophy, Sämtliche Schriften,* 3:566 and 561. Also see Goethe, *Dichtung und Warheit,* beginning of book 16.

of right reason. Arnold, as we have seen, finds a modern philosophical grounding for these views in Spinoza, and he finds aesthetic and political formulations of them in the English neoclassical writers, to whom he frequently alludes in *Culture and Anarchy*.

Since Arnold's own universal order, unlike that of Spinoza and the English neoclassicists, is of a progressive historical character, he can allow for only one absolute principle of value: the idea of human perfection as a harmonious expansion of all the faculties. From this one principle, he is able to deduce very specific subordinate principles that he can apply to such contemporary political issues as the Irish church, state control of education, free trade, and marriage to a deceased wife's sister. The weak link in Arnold's rational politics—if we grant him his a priori standard of perfection—is the assumption of logical inevitability in the results that are to flow from the alternative policies he considers. The great merit of his scheme is that it enables him to judge of political issues within a broad but clearly defined framework of humane values that are both grounded in tradition and susceptible to modification in accord with a stable principle of progressive development.

In the aesthetic realm Arnold's ideal of a right reason translates into a standard of profound moral vision within a unified structure of representation. In Arnold's own critical practice the standard also requires the more elusive accessory qualities of felicity in style (diction and rhythm), naturalistic evocation, and the revelation through style of artistic character. For the "rational" validation of this aesthetic standard, Arnold appeals implicitly to the "justness of spirit" among cultivated readers (III, 107). Arnold's assumption that there exist objective, universally accessible values in art depends ultimately on the authority of his historical scheme. The possible attainment of evaluative consensus among qualified judges presupposes a homogeneity of sensibility founded on a common cultural heritage, and this heritage is itself regarded as the product of a necessary historical progression in accordance with quasi-organic laws of human development.

The second defect of Arnold's cosmological hypothesis of universal expansion is that—like the idyll of Theocritus Arnold chooses in "Pagan and Mediaeval" to represent the pagan "religion of pleasure"—it is too simply positive. If it is too much an abstract theoretical construct to be stamped by "the clear, positive, happy pagan character" of Theocritus, it still shares the cardinal defect of Theocritus' hymn—the incapacity to comprehend, withstand, or absorb adversity (III, 229). Arnold indirectly addresses himself to this defect in his discussion of the stoic optimism of Marcus Aurelius. On behalf of "science" Arnold rejects two of Marcus Aurelius' propositions: first, that "whatever happens to every man *is for the interest of the universal*"; and second, that "the whole course of the universe . . . has a providential reference to man's welfare: '*all other things have been made for the sake of rational beings*' " (III, 155). Although he rejects such statements "thus absolutely used," Arnold accepts as "true and useful" the psychologistic "turn" Marcus Aurelius gives to them. " 'The ruling part of man can make a material for itself out of that which opposes it, as fire lays hold of what falls into it, and rises higher by means of this very material' " (III, 156). In its simplest application this idea of constructive adversity serves as a guiding principle for Arnold's practical social criticism. He frequently declares that it is more useful for a nation to hear a recitation of its faults than of its virtues. It is thereby startled out of complacency and required to enlarge itself by the absorption of alien material. The French need to be told that they are wanting in character, the Germans in taste and delicacy, the Italians in energy and honesty, the Americans in refinement, and the English in intelligence, for "a nation is really civilised by acquiring the qualities it by nature is wanting in."[22]

To extend this principle of constructive adversity from a law of individual and national growth into a general law of historical development requires only a short and easy theoretical step. In the essay on Theodore Parker, Arnold again, as in "Marcus Aurelius," rejects the rationalist theodicy, but he adopts in its place a concept of a historical "tendency to order." His theoretical task thus becomes a demonstration of the ways in which the oppositional forces of Hebraism and Hellenism may be beneficial each to the other and both together to humanity. Arnold finds that if Hebraism braces the Hellenic character and yields it greater strength for sustaining its ideal, Hellenism provides light and guidance to the Hebraic powers of determination. Hellenism, the free play of the mind, may "bring new life and movement into that side of us with which alone Hebraism concerns itself, and awaken a healthier and less mechanical movement there" (V, 187). This is in fact, Arnold

22. *Letters* 1:326 (June 21, 1865).

says, what happened in the transition from the Hebrew religion to Christianity. The old rule of law had become external and mechanical. By "criticising a fixed rule" and requiring a more vital and spontaneous recognition of moral law as an inward experience —that is, through a suffusion of Hellenism—Paul renewed Hebraism (V, 188). A converse process appears at work in the Reformation and Renaissance. The Reformation was basically "a reaction of the moral and spiritual sense against the carnal and pagan sense" (III, 226); but nonetheless, because of its insistence on the primacy of individual religious experience and opinion, "Protestantism, though in a blind and stumbling manner, carried forward the Renascence" (III, 281).

Arnold maintains that though they are divergent in method, Hebraism and Hellenism possess no intrinsically exclusive quality. In history and in contemporary civilization, however, they appear as rival and opposed. When one tendency has been uppermost, the needs that were satisfied by the other have been neglected. This sort of cultural leapfrog is unsatisfactory. It produces "a certain confusion" (V, 175). Not only does it create an immediate sense of deprivation for either the intellectual or the ethical side of man, but it also engenders a cosmological sense of frustration and futility, a sense of an arbitrary alternation tending to no definite end. Arnold has developed his cultural dialectic as an alternative to the futile historical cyclism of Empedocles. If the complementary progression is not itself to degenerate into an inhuman and mechanical process, it must achieve a unity of purpose. It must be tending toward the realization of some human ideal of good, and this ideal must involve in itself the idea of completion. Hebraism, as we have seen, by concentrating its energy in the moral effort of a resistance to passion rather than in comprehension and synthesis, incapacitates itself for the formation of an adequate ideal of perfection. If there is to be any consummation of the historical process, it must be through the subordination of the Hebraic temper to the Hellenic ideal of perfection.

> For is not this the right crown of the long discipline of Hebraism . . . that when in the fulness of time it has reason and beauty offered to it, and the law of things as they really are, it should at last walk by this true light with the same staunchness and zeal with which it formerly walked by its imperfect light? And thus man's two great natural forces, Hebraism and Hellenism, will no longer be dissociated

> and rival, but will be a joint force of right thinking and strong doing to carry him on towards perfection. This is what the lovers of culture may perhaps dare to augur for such a nation as ours. (v, 225–26)

The ideal of perfection presents itself in two aspects. In his more optimistic moments Arnold thinks that a full development and harmonious relation of all the moral and intellectual faculties is attainable. It is this sort of relative human perfection that would best enable humanity to bring itself into accord with the endless expansion toward an ever-receding ideal of perfect being and knowing, that is, toward God.[23] Arnold approvingly quotes Martin Luther's definition of God: "A God is simply *that* whereon the human heart rests with trust, faith, hope, and love" (V, 252). Arnold's own hope and faith "rest" on the ideal of a spiritual progress in accordance with right reason. In "Democracy" Arnold had said that the human mind rests only in what is "absolute and eternal." By the time of writing *Culture and Anarchy* he has come to regard the "absolute" not as state or substance but as the historical process of growth. Hebraism reifies the absolute as a fixed order, and insofar as certain moral laws are necessary and permanent acquisitions of the race, Hebraism is right to have fixed on them. Hellenism, however, gives the more fundamental principle of the cosmological order and so the more complete knowledge of God. "Hellenism, surely, or the habit of fixing our mind upon the intelligible law of things, is most salutary if it makes us see that the only absolute good, the only absolute and eternal object prescribed to us by God's law, or the divine order of things, is the progress towards perfection,—our own progress towards it and the progress of humanity" (V, 219).

23. Edward Alexander rightly argues that "Arnold conceived of the dialectic of history as equivalent to the growth and development of the human spirit." However, he also maintains that in advocating Hellenism at the expense of Hebraism, Arnold succumbs to the one-sidedness he condemned, and he declares that Arnold wanted "historical oscillation to cease and give way to fixity." *Matthew Arnold and John Stuart Mill* (London: Routledge and Kegan Paul, 1965), pp. 51, 53, 54 (and see pp. 258–59). Both of these objections seem to miss the mark. In his comparisons of Mill and Arnold, Alexander tends to take Mill as the pattern to which Arnold is made to fit or against which he is measured and found wanting. His comparisons are, nonetheless, frequently instructive.

3 *Poetry and Preservation*

The Resurgence of Israel

Culture and Anarchy marks the apogee of Arnold's theoretical development. In the works of his next two decades he will make evaluative rearrangements in the components of his system, but these variations can all be interpreted within the theoretical framework developed in the early essays and fixed in *Culture and Anarchy*. The second phase of his critical career, the decade of religious writing, can best be interpreted as a microcosmic epoch of Hebraistic "concentration" within Arnold's own history. The constructive aspects of Arnold's religious thought may be seen as falling into accord not only with his general scheme of cultural categories but also with his advocacy of the Hellenic ideal and the modern spirit. The exclusive intensity of his Hebraism derives from events, personal grief and social upheaval, which are external to his theoretical construct. Moreover, in his earlier work Arnold has already described and criticized the exclusiveness of the Hebraic temper. The third phase, his final decade of literary and social criticism, appears as an effort of synthesis between his two earlier phases. The critical modern spirit is reinstated as the driving force of civilization, but this spirit now divides its empire more evenly with "conduct" and with the heart and imagination. In this third phase the fervor of moral concentration that had sustained Arnold in his religious writing transforms itself into a revitalized devotion to poetry as the most profound voice of moral life. Accordingly, there is a positive revaluation of the English Romantic poets—at least of Wordsworth, Byron, and Keats. Arnold does not, however, readopt a Romantic cosmology. He carefully segregates Wordsworth's "theory of Nature" from what is of use to him in the poetry, the emotionally charged utterance of moral truth (VIII, 250).

Arnold's claim, in *Culture and Anarchy,* that the historical contributions of Hebraism and Hellenism are somehow preserved within the cultural stream provides a solution for the Empedoclean plight of a cyclical history, but it imposes on Arnold the task of demonstrating in precisely what way this preservation takes place. If at times Arnold almost seems to be relying uncritically on the Lamarckian theory of the physical inheritance of acquired characteristics, the main tendency of his cultural theory is set firmly against any mechanical reliance on automatic processes. He rejects out of hand "the specially British form of Quietism, or a devout, but excessive, reliance on an over-ruling Providence. Providence, as the moralists are careful to tell us, generally works in human affairs by human means" (V, 159). The human means that Arnold designates as the caretaker of the providential order is culture, and he defines culture as a conscious, strenuous effort "to come at reason and the will of God by means of reading, observing, and thinking" (V, 129). The lessons of the past can be retained only through the constantly renewed effort of study and intellectual assimilation. The natural state of man is one of aesthetic vulgarity, moral savagery, and social recalcitrance. The course of history consists of a struggle to overcome the animalistic limitations of the natural state, and it is a course that must be spiritually recreated at each new stage of growth (VII, 229 and VIII, 38). If man has an instinct for perfection, he also has a contrary and more easily satisfied instinct to comply with the demands of his ordinary self; this second instinct is served by the "philosophical theory rife among us, to the effect that without the labour of perverting ourselves by custom or example to relish right reason, but by continuing all of us to follow freely our natural taste for the bathos, we shall, by the mercy of Providence, and by a kind of natural tendency of things, come in due time to relish and follow right reason" (V, 156). Right reason is a spontaneous recognition of the aesthetic, moral, intellectual, and social laws that serve as the standards of human perfection. Though they bear an axiomatic conviction, these laws are revealed only to "the best self," the self that has attained to a disinterested love for the best that is known and thought in the world. Once this state of mind has been achieved, it becomes self-validating. What is revealed through culture is the axiomatic value of culture itself; that is, a perfected development of human potential finds its rationale within its own state of being.

Thus, for the Hellenic pole of Arnold's cultural dialectic, there is no apparent difficulty in the assumption of historical preservation. Modern Hellenism requires an intellectual assimilation of an intellectual ideal. The materials given for comprehension change over time; as new knowledge is introduced and the present becomes the past, both history and the contemporary world become more complex. However, the two essential purposes of culture—the achievement of "the true point of view" from which to observe the world and the harmonious development of all the faculties—remain the same. The preservation of the Hebraic pole appears in a more problematic guise; conventional religion presents itself not as a flexible and synthetic standard of cultural development but as a system of salvation that requires adherence to a fixed, "factual" account of the historical acts of God and his relations to men. Its moral code and its ideal temper of "sweet reasonableness" are bound up both with an initial body of supernatural beliefs and with a gradually acquired body of speculative propositions explicating those beliefs. In *Culture and Anarchy* Arnold circumvents the issue of supernatural belief and theological dogma. He presupposes without argument a position that he will spend the next ten years trying, with only ambiguous results, to substantiate; he supposes that Hebraism and Christianity are not essentially supernatural interpretations of history and nature but rather a set of moral intuitions and an attitude toward them—"a *temper*, a *behaviour*" ("A Psychological Parallel," VIII, 122). Granting this assumption, it still remains to be seen in what way a temper and a mode of behavior can be preserved throughout historical upheavals of knowledge and social organization. Arnold's answer, again, is culture. The Christian moral contribution is to be preserved only by retaining an intimate familiarity with the Christian organs of expression, with the Bible and the traditions and ceremonies of the church. The Apostles' Creed and the Nicene Creed are, Arnold says, "poetry for us; and poetry consecrated, moreover, by having been on the tongue of all our forefathers for two thousand years, and on our own tongue ever since we were born. As such, then, we can *feel* them, even when we no longer take them literally; while, as approximations to a profound truth, we can *use* them" (VIII, 136).

Arnold's campaign of poetic preservation requires him to attack on two fronts. His declaration that we can still use the utterances of conventional religion is directed against those militant modernists who regard all of Christianity as an exploded mythology, the remnants of which must be obliterated by mocking incredulity. The second front on which Arnold must operate directs itself against those conventional Christians for whom the value of Christian doctrine rests on the literal truth of the scriptural account of a miraculous providence. Here culture must not only preserve but select and adapt the materials given by the Christian tradition. The perspective we gain by "knowing the best that has been thought and known in the world" enables us "in particular relation to the Bible" to get *"the power, through reading, to estimate the proportion and relation in what we read"* (VI, 153). In practical terms what this means for Arnold is to adopt the two cardinal points of Spinoza's constructive Biblical criticism: first, to regard the declarations of the prophets as figurative approximations of moral insights; and second, to recognize that the sum of revelation is simply the command to believe in God as the objective principle or force of moral order, and so to lead a good life (III, 162–63). To use the Bible in this way requires a Hellenic flexibility of mind. As Arnold remarks in *Culture and Anarchy*, a man who knows only his Bible has no means for properly understanding even that (V, 184). Arnold maintains that for us still to be able to use the Bible it is essential that we regard it not as an infallible revelation but as a human artifact. "To understand that the language of the Bible is fluid, passing, and literary, not rigid, fixed, and scientific, is the first step towards a right understanding of the Bible. But to take this very step, some experience of how men have thought and expressed themselves, and some flexibility of spirit, are necessary; and this is culture" (*Literature and Dogma*, VI, 152).

To take the language of religion as literary, not "scientific," does not mean for Arnold that the Bible is without referential validity. He does not regard poetry as merely highly wrought, aesthetically pleasing emotionalism but as an impassioned revelation of moral truth. The central purpose of his religious work is to preserve the substance of this revelation by "insisting on the natural truth of Christianity" (VI, 143).[1] His method is to reinterpret the writings of Paul and the records of Jesus' speech so as to show that the foundations of their thought are morally naturalistic, that they possess a "plain, solid, and experimental sense" (VI, 202), and that their supernatural elements are adventitious and dispensable. His exegesis thus works out a set of interpretative translations from the "poetic" language of Christ and Paul into the prosaic language of empirical moralism. God is represented as simply the beneficent structure of the natural order, "the eternal and divine power from which all life and wholesome energy proceed" (VI, 37). Righteousness is whatever attitude and behavior tend to the higher and fuller life of humanity, and the example of Jesus is taken as the greatest "clue to righteousness" (VIII, 62 and VI, 41). The death and the resurrection of Christ are intended, Arnold maintains, as symbolic representations of dying to the "ordinary or passing self, of sense, appetite, desire" and rising to the "higher or enduring self, of reason, spirit, will" (VIII, 154). Reason and the spirit, in this usage, designate a recognition of solidarity with the common life of humanity. It is opposed to the impulses of the flesh, which are selfish and exclusive. "Now, the law of the spirit makes men one; it is only by the law in our members that we are many" (VI, 43). Identification with Christ does not operate, for Arnold, as a mystical absolution from sin and physical mortality but as a psychological absolution from egoism and an elevation into a disinterested love of humanity. "Whoever identifies himself with Christ, identifies himself with Christ's idea of the solidarity of men. The whole race is conceived as one body, having to die and rise with Christ, and forming by the joint action of its regenerate members the mystical body of Christ" (VI, 49). The "immortality" that derives from this identification is not an individual survival but a temporal participation in "the *eternal order*" (VII, 372); in accordance with the cosmological theory of Arnold's first phase, the eternal order itself consists of a principle of historical development

1. In "A Comment on Christmas" Arnold gives credit to Coleridge for being the initiator in England of the idea that "the essential matters of Christianity are necessary and eternal facts of nature or truths of reason" (X, 227). He remarks, however, that neither Coleridge nor his followers were able to substantiate this insight.

toward an ideal state of individual fulfillment and social concord.

Arnold applies this set of doctrinal translations throughout four books of Biblical and theological commentary and polemics, but the main outline of his system is quite simple. He sums it up, concisely but completely, in a single paragraph of a late essay, "A Comment on Christmas" (1885):

> Therefore, when we are asked: What really is Christmas, and what does it celebrate? we answer: The birthday of Jesus. But what, then, is the miracle of the Incarnation? A homage to the virtue of pureness, and to the manifestation of this virtue in Jesus. What is Lent, and the miracle of the temptation? A homage to the virtue of self-control and to the manifestation of this virtue in Jesus. What does Easter celebrate? Jesus victorious over death by dying. By dying how? Dying to re-live. To re-live in Paradise, in another world? No, in this. But if in this, what is the kingdom of God? The ideal society of the future. Then what is immortality? To live in the eternal order, which never dies. What is salvation by Jesus Christ? The attainment of this immortality. Through what means? Through faith in Jesus, and appropriation of his method, secret, and temper.
>
> (x, 234)

In *Literature and Dogma* Arnold describes the method of Jesus as "the setting up a great unceasing inward movement of attention and verification" in the matter of conduct (VI, 288). His "secret" is "necrosis," dying to the flesh and egoistic self (VI, 291). His temper is one of "sweet reasonableness" (VI, 115).

It should be evident that up to this point Arnold's reinterpretation of religion, although it concentrates on moral rather than intellectual salvation, entails no basic conflict with the claims of Hellenism. The God of Arnold's first book on religion, *Saint Paul and Protestantism,* is the same as that of *Culture and Anarchy,* "the least inadequate name for that universal order which the intellect feels after as a law and the heart feels after as a benefit" (VI, 9). The best self of Hellenism, associated with "sweetness and light," is closely akin to the higher self of Hebraism, associated with the sweet reasonableness of Christ. If the main impulse of Hellenism is toward discovering the law of a rational order, it finds a "benefit" in the axiomatic cultural ideal of a complete humanity; conversely, the benefit received by Hebraism in its devotion to God entails an intellectual recognition of a cosmological order. Thus, in the conclusion to *Saint Paul* Arnold reaffirms the Hellenic ideal of totality as a union of the two tendencies. "Hebraism strikes too exclusively upon one string in us; Hellenism does not address itself with serious energy enough to morals and righteousness. For our totality, for our general perfection, we need to unite the two" (VI, 125). His declared purpose is not to emphasize Hebraism at the expense of Hellenism but to elevate conventional religion so that it may "help, not hinder, man's totality" (VI, 127). He recognizes the difficulty in achieving this goal: "It may well be that for harmonising Hebraism with Hellenism more preparation is needed than man has yet had." Nonetheless, his goal remains fixed, and he can encourage himself with the thought that even an unsuccessful effort will contribute to "the final achievement."

It is important to note this point clearly in Arnold's career; it is the last time, until the publication seven years later of the first of the *Mixed Essays*, that Arnold will present himself as an advocate for the Hellenic ideal of perfection. In the three intervening books (*Literature and Dogma, God and the Bible, Last Essays on Church and Religion*) he succumbs entirely to the spirit of Hebraistic exclusiveness. In *Culture and Anarchy* Arnold had stated that "the greatest and most important of the efforts by which the human race has manifested its impulse to perfect itself" has been religion (V, 93), but he had immediately added that "culture goes beyond religion" in establishing a true idea of perfection, for it requires "a harmonious expansion of *all* the powers which make the beauty and worth of human nature, and is not consistent with the over-development of any one power at the expense of the rest" (V, 94). While granting the unique efficacy of the moral instruction contained in the Bible, he denied that it has "a reach and sufficiency co-extensive with all the wants of human nature" (V, 177). Beginning with *Literature and Dogma* (1873), Arnold reverses this judgment:

> Now, this religion of the Bible we say [the churches] cannot value more than we do. If we hesitate to adopt strictly their language about its *all*-importance, that is only because we take an uncommonly large view of human perfection, and say, speaking strictly, that there go to this certain things,—art, for instance, and science,—which the Bible hardly meddles with. The difference between us and them, however, is more a difference of theoretical statement than of practical

conclusion. Speaking practically, and looking at the very large part of human life engaged by the Bible, at the comparatively small part unengaged by it, we are quite willing, like the churches, to call the Bible and its religion *all*-important.

(VI, 149)

In his conclusion to *Literature and Dogma* Arnold, taking cognizance of the apparent contradiction between the positions taken in this work and his earlier works, expresses concern about "whether we shall not be reproached with inconsistency" (VI, 407). He concludes that he should not be so reproached, for "in praising culture, we have never denied that conduct, not culture, is three-fourths of human life." This is his only effort toward a theoretical reconciliation, and it is not a solution but an evasion.

The fractionalizing of human concerns is beside the point. The real issue is in what serves as the driving and guiding force of historical progress, and here Arnold has fashioned an inescapable contradiction. In *Culture and Anarchy* it is Hellenism that provides the dynamic structure, the archetype and goal of progress; in *Literature and Dogma* this is no longer the case. While he still maintains that it is conceivable that "the Aryan genius" may someday be able "to treat science and art with the same kind of seriousness as conduct," he conclusively states that for this "man is hardly yet ripe" (VI, 410). It is, moreover, not only for the present state of humanity that "the true God" is "the God of the Bible, *the Eternal who makes for righteousness*, from whom Jesus came forth," but it is also this God "whose spirit governs the course of humanity." The God of the Bible is a Hebrew God, and for Arnold, Hebraism now governs the progress of humanity. Culture no longer presents itself as a self-validating ideal but as a subordinate, corrective agency to the Hebraic spirit; it becomes the handmaid of moral theology. Aesthetic and intelligential laws are still "real," but the summary term of the cosmological order is righteousness. "Now, the indications on this *moral* side of that tendency, not of our making, by which things fulfil the law of their being, we do very much mean to denote and sum up when we speak of *the will of God*" (VI, 191). Arnold finds himself not quite prepared to concur with Bishop Butler, the eighteenth-century theologian, in branding the disinterested pursuit of knowledge as of no use except "as an entertainment or diversion," but his objection takes the form not of a doctrinal counter-assertion but of a mild plea for moderation. " 'Bringing things to light' is not properly to be spoken of, I think, quite in this fashion. Still, with the low *comparative* rank which Butler assigns to it we will not quarrel" ("The Church of England," VIII, 65–66). Arnold is himself willing to specify this rank. Since "conduct" occupies three-fourths of life, "there is but one-fourth of life left; and if we let art and science divide this one-fourth fairly between them, they will have just one-eighth of life each" (VI, 297). If it is difficult to take seriously this pretense of precise quantification, Arnold appears fully earnest when he says that "the subject of the Old Testament, *Salvation by righteousness*, the subject of the New, *Righteousness by Jesus Christ*, are in positive strict truth, man's most momentous matters of concern" (VI, 144), and that Jesus himself was concerned exclusively with intuitions of practical morality (VI, 297–98).

Given the correspondence, in Arnold's cultural dialectic, between the shape of history and the ideal structure of the individual mind, it seems almost inevitable that there should occur in his own career a period of Hebraistic reaffirmation. There were, moreover, personal reasons—the death of his sons—for Arnold's religious preoccupations during this period. It is not, however, dialectically inevitable that Arnold's religious devotion should render itself subject to censure from the perspective of his own Hellenic ideal, nor that he should, without adequately confronting the theoretical conflict, so thoroughly subvert the doctrine of a complete human development. Nor is this disjunction between the first two phases of Arnold's career to be accounted for by the influence of personal factors alone. The cause for Arnold's transformation from comprehensive Hellene to exclusive Hebrew may be found, rather, in his response to the problem of social stability within an era of intellectual expansion. Before attempting to uncover the source of Arnold's conversion, we shall examine the contributory personal reasons for the resurgence of a religious temper in his work.

In January 1868 Arnold lost an infant son. In November of the same year, while he was composing the preface to *Culture and Anarchy*, he also lost his oldest son, a sixteen-year-old invalid. Arnold's response to the first of these deaths was to turn his mind to religious renunciation. "And so this loss comes to me just after my forty-fifth birthday, with so much other 'suffering in the flesh,' —the departure of youth, cares of many kinds, an almost painful anxiety about public matters,—to remind me that *the time past of our life may suffice us*!—words which have haunted me for the last year or two, and that we 'should no longer live the rest of our time in the flesh to the lusts of men, but to the will of God.' "[2] Arnold's sorrow for his second loss converted itself into a religious "awakening," and this renewed sense of religious consolation already finds voice in the preface to *Culture and Anarchy*.[3] Arnold finds in Hebraism "the discipline by which alone man is enabled to rescue his life from thraldom to the passing moment and to his bodily senses, to ennoble it, and to make it eternal" (V, 255). Nonetheless, Arnold continues in this preface to criticize the Hebraic tendency "to sacrifice all other sides of our being to the religious side. . . . we have seen that it leads to a narrow and twisted growth of our religious side itself, and to a failure in perfection" (V, 238). Thus, when Arnold says that we must always be prepared to restore Hebraism to the first rank, he is speaking of a practical shift of cultural emphasis, not of a revolution in his own theoretical framework. When Arnold loses a third son in 1872, we may suppose this loss to have reinforced his absorption in "the fundamental idea" of Israel, the idea that "*Righteousness tendeth to life*" (VI, 206); we may not without further evidence suppose it sufficient to have subverted his Hellenic ideal.

In 1870–71, not long before he began work on *Literature and Dogma*, Arnold's concern for the preservation of Hebraic righteousness within his own culture was given new urgency by the calamity of France in the Franco-Prussian War. France had figured for Arnold as the chief social representative of the modern spirit. The simultaneous French afflictions of military defeat and internal anarchy appeared to Arnold as signal evidence for the insufficiency of an exclusive Hellenic modernism. Arnold draws from the French disaster a lesson of world-historical import:

> Immense as are her advantages and resources, it does not seem as if France *could* recover herself now as she did in 1815, or indeed could recover herself within our time at all. Whatever may be said of the harshness of such a sentence, it is yet true that her fall is mainly due to that want of a serious conception of righteousness and the need of it, the consequences of which so often show themselves in the world's history, and in regard to the Graeco-Latin nations more particularly. The fall of Greece, the fall of Rome, the fall of the

2. *Letters* 1:443–44 (January 4, 1868).
3. *Letters* 1:466 (December 24, 1868).

> brilliant Italy of the fifteenth century, and now the fall of France, are all examples. Nothing gives more freshness and depth to one's reading of the Bible than the sense that this is so, and that this testimony is perpetually being borne to the book of righteousness, though the nation out of which it came was itself a political failure so utter and miserable.[4]

These moralistic political judgments, though made in the excitement generated by contemporary events, will be elaborated and corroborated in Arnold's 1872 reviews of the second and third volumes of Curtius's *History of Greece*.[5] Arnold describes the Athenians as having by racial nature a character of "vivacity and mobility," and he considers this mobility, like that of the Celts (among whom he includes the French), an essential component of genius (III, 346). By itself, however, this mobility is incapable of producing anything of solid worth. The brilliance of the Athenian world Arnold attributes to the blending of the native temper with the moral influence of the Delphic religion, "the graver view of life and the thoughts which deepen man's consciousness" (V, 271). The Delphic discipline bears a direct analogy with the Hebraic component of modern culture. "Apollo was not only the nourisher of genius, he was also the author of every higher moral effort; he was the prophet of his father Zeus, in the highest view of Zeus, as the source of the ideas of moral order and of right" (V, 271). Arnold draws out this analogy between Hebraism and early Delphism at some length in *God and the Bible*, where he maintains that at its most fervent the religious impulse of the Athenians matches that of the Hebrews. "From Pindar, Aeschylus, and Sophocles, may be quoted sentences as religious as those which we find in Job or Isaiah" (VII, 209). The crucial difference in the two cultures is that in Athens this religious influence gradually declined, whereas in Israel it grew "into an enthusiasm, turbid, passionate, absorbing and all-pervasive, to *bring in everlasting righteousness*" (VII, 212).

4. *Letters* 2:55–56 (January 31, 1871). Peter Dale correctly notes that "after 1870 Arnold became increasingly concerned with the moral rather than intellectual needs of society, partly as a result of the collapse of his intellectual models, the French, before the German army in that year, for 'want of a serious conception of righteousness.'" *The Victorian Critic and the Idea of History: Carlyle, Arnold, Pater* (Cambridge, Mass.: Harvard University Press, 1977), p. 133.

5. In exception to the rule of chronological order in Super's edition of Arnold's prose works, the five Curtius reviews, extending from 1868 to 1876, are all placed together in volume 5.

In the Curtius reviews (five in all), and again in *God and the Bible,* Arnold attributes the Hellenic decline in part to an organic fatality. "The main element in our nature conquers at last; the steady, according to Aristotle's profound remark, becomes stupid, and the brilliant becomes non-sane. Dorian Sparta died in the end of dulness; Ionian Athens perished in the end for want of Ballast" (V, 271). This sort of racial determinism comes up throughout Arnold's writing, but it never gains a definite ascendency. Racial propensity is only one factor in culture. It can be modified both by social circumstances and by conscious efforts of control. If at times Arnold speaks of the indomitable influences of race, at other times he declares that "community of practice is more telling than community of origin" ("A French Critic on Goethe," VIII, 256). Insofar as Arnold does adopt a rule of racial determinism, the mixed origins of the English allow him a great latitude in application and control.

> Now we have Germanism enough to make us Philistines, and Normanism enough to make us imperious, and Celtism enough to make us self-conscious and awkward; but German fidelity to Nature, and Latin precision and clear reason, and Celtic quick-wittedness and spirituality, we fall short of. . . . So long as we are blindly and ignorantly rolled about by the forces of our nature, their contradiction baffles us and lames us; so soon as we have clearly discerned what they are, and begun to apply to them a law of measure, control, and guidance, they may be made to work for our good and to carry us forward.
>
> (III, 382–83)

Arnold employs the supposed racial tendencies of the English for whatever polemical program he has in hand. In *Celtic Literature* he emphasizes the un-Semitic, Indo-European (Hellenic) element. In *Culture and Anarchy,* however, while still marking this difference, he takes the English habit of Hebraizing as indicative of "the essential unity of man" (V, 173); in the final Curtius review he emphasizes the affinity, in moral seriousness, between the English and the Germans (V, 294).

Arnold's reversion to the innate moral firmness of the Germanic peoples, including the English, provides him with a certain desperate reassurance against the conclusions he reaches in his review of Greek history. In *Culture and Anarchy* he had represented the decline of Athens as an unavoidable phase of a world-historical process. In the second and third Curtius reviews, when he comes to make a more specifically social and political analysis of Athenian history, he finds a disturbingly close parallel between this situation and that of the contemporary world. The basis of the Athenian grandeur was the store of stability and character provided by both the old religion and the conservative political ethos of the era prior to the Persian War. The quick, new flame of democracy and intellectual expansion fed itself on the fuel of tradition. It cast a brilliant light but then quickly burnt itself out. "What Athens lived upon, in her brilliant Periclean period, was the stores of *Halt* and character accumulated through less seen and heard generations. . . . They were used, and used up, and then came the end; here is our moral" (V, 281). The review of Athenian history, in conjunction with the collapse of France, presents Arnold with the specter of a like decline in English and European culture. In his earlier work Arnold had spoken with partisan enthusiasm for the agency of the modern spirit in its dissolution of antiquated beliefs and institutions. "Culture" had both undone the old order and fashioned from its own nature a modern ideal of a perfected humanity. In his more enthusiastic moments he had spoken as if the conditions necessary for achieving this ideal had never been more propitious than at the present time.

> [Culture] needs times of faith and ardour, times when the intellectual horizon is opening and widening all round us, to flourish in. And is not the close and bounded intellectual horizon within which we have long lived and moved now lifting up, and are not new lights finding free passage to shine in upon us? For a long time there was no passage for them to make their way in upon us. . . . But now the iron force of adhesion to the old routine,—social, political, religious,—has wonderfully yielded; the iron force of exclusion of all which is new has wonderfully yielded.
>
> (V, 92)

By 1875 Arnold's attitude toward the modern spirit of dissolution and transformation has itself undergone a signal transformation. He now regards it not as a wonderful opportunity but as a threat, and he counts himself among "those who search earnestly,—amid that break-up of traditional and conventional notions respecting our life, its conduct, and its sanctions, which is undeniably befalling our age,—for some clear light and some sure stay" ("Bishop Butler and the Zeit-Geist," VIII, 48). The shift in attitude is summed up in the word *befalling*, a word that gives the operations of the modern spirit the air of calamity. In "The Function of Criticism" Arnold had called the French Revolution "the greatest, the most animating event in history." In an 1872 review of Renan's *La Réforme intellectuelle et morale* he likens it to a drunken frenzy of useless destruction. "Whoever gives us a just and rational constitution of human society will also confer a great boon on us and effect a great work; but what has the French Revolution accomplished towards this? Nothing" (VII, 47). Arnold does not, however, simply abandon his liberalism. He seeks some means by which the force of change and freedom may be grounded in a firm concentration on righteousness. "The moral we draw [from the history of Athenian democracy] is not that the aim of the party of progress was bad, but that it was inadequate" (V, 281). In Athens the moral influence of Delphism gradually failed. Consequently, when "the anchor-chains by which the ship of State held—the anchor-chains of the influence of family and property, and of the old institutions which made government 'an aristocratic work'—were cut," there was no adequate stay for the natural "mobility" of the people (V, 277). In Israel, however, the ideas of righteousness so laid hold upon the nation "as to be the master-element in his thoughts, the sheet-anchor of his life" (VII, 214).

Arnold's solution, then, for the threat of social disintegration is to advocate a reproduction of the Hebraic love of righteousness within his own culture. At the same time, however, he recognizes that if religion is to be preserved at all it cannot be allowed to conflict with the discoveries of modern criticism. In his attempt to resolve this dilemma he reduces Hebraism to moral fervor alone, but in doing so he will ultimately involve himself in an insoluble tangle of sophistry and question begging. He declares that the secret of Israel's religion is the power of emotion that attached them to their God: " '*the joy of the Eternal is your strength*' " (VII, 248). The Jewish God, Arnold holds, is himself nothing more than a poetic personification of the idea of righteousness. He is distinguished from Zeus, as the source of moral order, only by an intensity of concentration on this idea. "The monotheistic idea of Israel is simply *seriousness*" (VI, 185). Arnold contends that it is only the late Hebrew religion that, under the stress of political disaster, degenerates into "materialistic" supernaturalism. He locates this shift in the book of Daniel (VI, 211), and he maintains that it is the prevalence of this late supernaturalism that is responsible for the illusory appearance of mysticism in the discourse of Jesus. He argues that Christ was compelled by the limitations of his followers to employ messianic language but that his real beliefs were entirely naturalistic. His real purpose was not to found a supernatural religion but "to transform for every religious soul the popular Messias-ideal of his time" (VII, 371). In this purpose he failed, but he nonetheless worked a moral revolution in his hearers, and he left the moral nucleus of his message to be rediscovered in later, more critically sophisticated times (VII, 371 and VIII, 142).

Arnold's historical interpretation of Christianity is not, finally, convincing. As an early critic noted, his method is to take from the records of Jesus' speech whatever seems to suit his argument and to reject as spurious interpolation whatever is too strongly marked by supernaturalism. Arnold's defense against this criticism is circular. He appeals to "certain of the data" about Christ as support for his contention that Jesus was "misunderstood and misrepresented by his followers," but this supposedly sound core of information is precisely what is left after Arnold has rejected everything that does not suit his case (VIII, 161). Even after this process of selection is complete, the supernatural element in the materials that are left can be explained away only by a willful effort of rationalization (see VII, 335–36 and VIII, 145). Moreover, even if Jesus was misunderstood, his actual intentions are irrelevant to the question of his historical influence. Arnold tries to circumvent this problem by arguing that "the vital force" of the Christian doctrine derives not from its *Aberglaube*, or "extra belief" in miracles and immortality, but from the inspiring moral example of Jesus himself, "the boundless confidence, consolation, and attachment, which the whole being and discourse of Jesus inspire" (VII, 370). What this comes to is an argument that for two millennia Christians have themselves mistaken the source and character of their own religious ardor. This is a bold claim, but Arnold does not hesitate to make it. He maintains that Paul, because of the limitations of his time and race, was incapable of imagining a purely moral and natural religion; however, his subliminal or subconscious belief about the resurrection was, like Arnold's, a belief in a psychological transformation (VI, 51). Paul's conscious supernaturalism is, he holds, superficial and adventitious. "What is original and essential in him" is the effort "to find a moral side and significance for all the processes, however mystical, of the religious life, with a view of strengthening, in this way, their hold upon us and their command of all our nature" (VI, 51).

Arnold's own effort is not only to find a moral side and significance to religious processes, but to exclude mysticism altogether, and at the same time to preserve the full force of religious fervor within the cultural stream. The only difference he will allow to exist between ethics and religion is "a difference of degree" (VI, 176). In the same passage he adds, "Religion, if we follow the intention of human thought and human language in the use of the word, is ethics heightened, enkindled, lit up by feeling; the passage from morality to religion is made when to morality is applied emotion. And the true meaning of religion is thus, not simply *morality*, but *morality touched by emotion*." If we then ask what is the source of this emotion, Arnold can only reply that the source is morality itself. He cannot deny that emotion is in some way associated with the supernatural beliefs of conventional religion, but he tries to avoid the conclusion that the emotion actually derives from the beliefs. He calls the supernatural elements "accretions" to the "ground idea" that righteousness tends to life, and he uses them as evidence for the "strength" of this idea. He argues that morality, rather than being crushed by the appearance of prosperity among the evil, took a "magnificent flight" into illusory fancies of a personal divinity, immortality, and final judgment (VI, 211–12). Arnold remarks parenthetically that these fancies "also in a wonderful manner attract emotion to the ideas of conduct and morality, attract it to them and combine it with them." If, on the one hand, we take this proposition to imply that the source of the emotion is the *Aberglaube* itself, we must modify Arnold's definition of religion to read: religion equals conduct plus mystical illusion; it is this definition that Arnold has sought to repudiate. If, on the other hand, we say that the emotion of *Aberglaube* derives from its moral ground, Arnold's argument implies that the emotion that *Aberglaube* adds to morality it gets from morality to begin with.

There is a similar problem in Arnold's attempt to derive from the past effectiveness of Christianity a guarantee for its future survival. He again assumes that the moral principles constituting his new, secularized version of Christianity are in fact the constitutive principles of conventional Christianity.

> Men conscious of a bent for being modest, temperate, kindly, affectionate, find themselves shameless, dissolute, living in malice and envy, hateful and hating one another. The experience is as old as the world, and the misery of it. And it is no cure whatever to be told that the Pope is not infallible, or that miracles do not happen; but a cure, a divine cure, for the bondage and the misery, has been found for nearly two thousand years to lie in the word, the character, the influence of Jesus. In this cure resides the power and the permanence of the Christian religion.
>
> (VIII, 330)

Arnold's use of the word *divine* is a bit of poetic license that only minimally conceals the question-begging flaw in his argument. When applied to Christ, the word *divine* means, for Arnold, nothing more than an exceptionally efficacious but strictly human example of devotion to a principle of moral order, "*the not ourselves which makes for righteousness*" (VI, 196). This is not what the divinity of Christ has meant for most men throughout history.

Arnold was too acute not to have sensed the weakness in the line, or circles, of his reasoning, and it is perhaps in part because of this weakness that he is driven in his religious writing to sacrifice his Hellenic ideal to Hebraism. If Christianity has exercised a unique and lasting power over men's minds and lives but has nonetheless been misconceived from the very beginning, it is imperative for Arnold that he demonstrate in some fashion that the power does not derive from the misconception. He cannot logically prove that the emotion of religion depends more on morality than on mysticism, but he can and does demonstrate in his own person a Hebraism that, though stripped of all supernatural belief, still matches in exclusiveness and intensity the moral fervor of conventional Christianity. Arnold's personal demonstration of a purified but unenfeebled religious fervor can, however, do very little toward verifying the possibility of a general preservation of religion within modern culture, for his own religious method is both abstruse and self-contradictory. He uses the "added" emotion of traditional mystical language as a support for moral concentration, but at the same time he constantly subtracts the mystical element from this language and translates it into a system of empirical morality. The sheer mental agility that this method requires would render it inaccessible to those for whom Arnold most wishes religion to be preserved—the masses of men whom it enables to overcome "the plain faults of our animality" (V, 101). There can be no doubt that Arnold himself found spiritual sustenance in the "poetry" of devotion, but the strain of his paradoxical method must eventually have told even on him. He remarks in an early essay that "it is one of the hardest tasks in the world to make new intellectual ideas harmonise truly with the religious life," but he had also remarked in the same essay that the "religious life resides not in an incessant movement of ideas, but in a feeling which attaches itself to certain fixed objects" (III, 69 and 67). Arnold's own religious life is a house divided against itself, for in order to allow himself to keep his emotional attachment to the Bible and the church, he must create an incessant movement of ideas within himself. The conflict here is not only theoretical but practical and emotional. Arnold feels that the value of religion resides in "the sense of the beauty and rest of religion, the sense that its charm lies in its grace and peace" (VIII, 84). Arnold's juggling of antinomies produces finally a sense not of grace and peace but of fretful futility.

Arnold himself never openly admits defeat in his religious work. In an 1883 preface to a popular, shortened edition of *Literature and Dogma,* he declares that it is "of all my books in prose, the one most important (if I may say so) and most capable of being useful" (VI, 141). His usefulness, as he describes it in a letter to his sister Frances, consists in demonstrating that, although a great change in religion must come and supernaturalism must "pass away," the transition can be made without "terror and despair," for everything essential to human progress "stands firm and unchanged."[6] Despite his deviations into exclusive Hebraism, the main purpose of Arnold's religious studies is to demonstrate that Christianity contains a rich and empirically valid moral contribution to cultural progress and to substitute this ideal of a secular progress for the "materialist" teleology of conventional religion. By redefining religion as an emotionally intensified morality, Arnold is enabled to predict, for the consolation of Christians and in support of the doctrine of cultural preservation, that Christianity has "an immense development still before it" (VI, 396). This statement appears toward the end of *Literature and Dogma* in the most emphatically Hebraistic period of Arnold's career, but a similar statement appears in the late essay "A Comment on Christmas."

6. *Letters* 2:139 (November 1874).

"The way, truth, and life have been found in Christianity, and will not now be found outside of it" (X, 232). What Arnold means by this is that "salvation does really depend on conformity to the line of Jesus" (X, 235), but only to this line as Arnold interprets it, which is as a line of moral rectitude. The future he predicts for Christianity is actually a future for a world of secular moral enlightenment. In a letter of 1881 Arnold declares that "the force which is shaping the future" is not to be found "with any of the orthodox religions, or with any of the neo-religious developments which propose to themselves to supersede them."[7] Reverting to the Hellenism of *Culture and Anarchy*, he complains that an exclusive preoccupation with religious issues places an unnatural constraint on human potential. "Man feels himself to be a more various and richly-endowed animal than the old religious theory of human life allowed, and he is endeavouring to give satisfaction to the long suppressed and still imperfectly-understood instincts of this varied nature." Once Arnold has regained this Hellenic perspective, he disparages those who treat religious questions as "all-absorbing," and in doing so he implicitly censures the provinciality of his own period of religious absorption. "The great centre-current of our time is a *lay* current."

Arnold's initial purpose in his religious writing is to preserve for Christianity a constructive power in the future of humanity. It is, however, through these very efforts of preservation that he is led gradually to abandon the intellectual pretensions of religion and so to consign it to a role as a guardian of the "poetry" of the past, but without influence on the course of the future. We may trace this decline in his hopes for a genuine growth of religious thought through the gradual reversal in the positions he assigns to Catholicism and Protestantism. In his early essay on Eugénie de Guérin, Arnold had contrasted Catholicism, as the church of the past, with Protestantism, as the church of the future. The historical claims of Catholicism and the sensuous, imaginative appeal of its ceremonies lend it "a noblesse and amplitude" that is lacking in Protestantism; but, "in revenge, Protestantism has a future before it, a prospect of growth in alliance with the vital movement of modern society; while Catholicism appears to be bent on widening the breach between itself and the modern spirit" (III, 96–97). By the time of writing the *Mixed Essays* (published in 1879), Arnold

7. *Letters* 2:220 (March 25, 1881).

has given up all hope of uniting conventional religion with the modern spirit, and he accordingly revises his prophecy on the prospects of Catholicism and Protestantism. The Protestant sects, depending for their influence on their doctrines, will "dissolve and perish" (VIII, 334). Catholicism, on the other hand, has "a great future before it," but this future depends on its being freed from sacerdotalism and dogma. "Its real superiority is in its charm for the imagination,—its poetry." The poetry consists of its history and its ceremonies, and Arnold hopes to retain these ceremonies as a way of publicly celebrating Christian morality. "Its forms will be retained, as symbolising with the force and charm of poetry a few cardinal facts and ideas, simple indeed, but indispensable and inexhaustible, and on which our race could lay hold only by materialising them." Arnold exempts the Anglican church from his prophecy of doom for Protestantism because it has retained the "forms" of Catholicism and because it has a historical life.

In *Saint Paul and Protestantism* Arnold had rebuked Puritanism—taken as quintessentially Protestant—with "sophisticating religion of the heart into theories of the head about election and justification" (VI, 69). He had, nonetheless, left open the possibility of an intellectual growth of religion. The mistake of Puritanism was to fix itself on specific doctrines. The historic churches, however, have been "charged ever since the rise of Christianity with the task of developing the immense and complex store of ideas contained in Christianity" (VI, 73). Because they are not founded on precise and limited theological propositions, these historic churches have the flexibility necessary for gradually assimilating modern ideas. They thus possess a "power of growth" (VI, 92 and 75). The primary function of the church is to serve as the keeper of the Biblical revelation, and Arnold concurred, at this time, with Butler's opinion that " '*the Bible contains many truths as yet undiscovered*' " (VI, 89). He maintains that the faulty doctrines of the early church resulted from no intrinsic deficiency in the intellectual potential of theology but rather "simply from the natural operation of the law of development, which for success in philosophy and criticism requires certain conditions that in the early and mediaeval church were not to be found" (VI, 91).

One might reasonably object that there is something specious in this rhetorical dissociation of historical "conditions" from the actual intellectual tendencies of the church—as if these conditions could be arbitrarily superadded or deducted from the cultural complex, and as if the church had itself had no influence on the intellectual conditions in which it operated. A more serious problem for Arnold, however, is that this line of argument runs counter to the tactic by which he hopes to save Christian morality from the collapse of supernaturalism. The main thrust of his defense of Christianity is that in its origin and essential character it is not theoretical at all, that it offers no interpretation of history or of nature—these are the realms of "science"—and that it restricts itself to giving practical advice on conduct. If Christianity makes no pretense of offering objective knowledge, it can hardly be called false, and its moral core is safe. At the same time, however, it must renounce all expectation of intellectual growth.

It is in accordance with this line of argument that Arnold is led, in 1878, to modify his earlier views and to declare that the inadequacy of early church doctrine derives not from the historical accident of being developed in unpropitious conditions but from the very nature of the Biblical revelation:

> The need for beauty is a real and now rapidly growing need in man; Puritanism cannot satisfy it, Catholicism and the English Church can. The need for intellect and knowledge in him, indeed, neither Puritanism, nor Catholicism, nor the English Church can at present satisfy. That need has to seek satisfaction nowadays elsewhere,—through the modern spirit, science, literature. But, as one drops the false science of the Churches, one perceives that what they had to deal with was so simple that it did not require science. Their beauty remains, investing certain elementary truths of inestimable depth and value, yet of extreme simplicity.
>
> (VIII, 343)

The modern spirit must still take account of the permanent contributions of Christian morality, but it can receive from Christianity no assistance in its formulation of a critical synthesis, an intellectual deliverance, for the present and the future.

A Full Humanity

Once religion has been reduced to poetic moralism, there is only a short and inevitable step to the replacement of religion with poetry proper. When Arnold takes this step, his religious thought comes full circle and rejoins the Hellenism of his first phase. In a letter to Clough in 1852 Arnold had declared that poetry must become "a complete magister vitae as the poetry of the ancients did: by including, as theirs did, religion with poetry, instead of existing as poetry only, and leaving religious wants to be supplied by the Christian religion, as a power existing independent of the poetical power."[8] In *Culture and Anarchy* he declares not only that poetry must include religion but that, by assimilating "the religious idea of a devout energy," it is destined "to transform and govern" religion (V, 100). The final step, ironically enough the result of Arnold's labors on behalf of religion, is to render religion a museum of ritual and to give to poetry alone an active participation in the modern spirit. In his 1878 essay "On Poetry" Arnold says that "the reign of religion as morality touched with emotion is indeed indestructible," but he has already defined poetry as precisely this—moral ideas "touched with beauty, heightened by emotion" (IX, 63 and 62; cf. IX, 46). If poetry and religion are defined thus alike, poetry has an insuperable advantage in pursuing its purpose directly and being unencumbered by the vestiges of a supernatural "science":

> Our religion has materialised itself in the fact—the supposed fact; it has attached its emotion to the fact. For poetry the idea is everything; the rest is its world of illusion, of divine illusion; it attaches its emotion to the idea, the idea *is* the fact. The strongest part of our religion to-day is its unconscious poetry. The future of poetry is immense, because in conscious poetry, where it is worthy of its high destinies, our race, as time goes on, will find an ever surer and surer stay.
>
> (IX, 63)

Poetry proper, Arnold says, "thinks emotionally," and in order to preserve conventional religion as poetry, he has been forced to deny to it the power of thought altogether. Its conscious, intellective content is of no validity; but it is on this content that, for its practitioners, the subconscious poetic content depends for its effect. In secular poetry thought operates within a legitimate sphere as a merely human commentary on human life, and it is integrated with feeling so as to produce a complete and valid form of recognition and utterance (IX, 44 and 39).

This conclusion to the sequence of Arnold's religious commen-

8. *LC*, p. 124.

taries leaves him with very much the same situation he had discovered in the high period of Athenian culture, the period when "Greek poetry was now more religious than Greek religion, and partly supplied its place" (VII, 209). However, by the time that Arnold comes to advocate poetry as a religious "stay," he has recovered from his fear of repeating the Athenian decline and regained confidence in the general progress of humanity. He readopts the liberal ideal, "to rely for success on the better feelings and higher intelligence of mankind" (VIII, 325), and he identifies this higher intelligence once more with the Hellenic archetype. It is possible to mark with some precision the point at which Arnold emerges from his phase of Hebraic concentration. "A French Critic on Milton," written in 1876, is the first of his essays written after the *Last Essays on Church and Religion* and collected in *Mixed Essays*. In this essay Arnold declares that "human progress consists in a continual increase in the number of those who, ceasing to live by the animal life alone and to feel the pleasures of sense only, come to participate in the intellectual life also, and to find enjoyment in the things of the mind" (VIII, 169). In the preface to *Last Essays*, written at about the same time, Arnold had made the same distinction between the lower self of sensual appetite and the "higher self" of the mind, but the method he recommended for cultivating the higher self was to fasten on "certain examples, precepts and sayings" that reinforce the higher self, and not to go "skipping about all over the the world for various renderings of it" (VIII, 154–55). In the Milton essay the other Arnold, the Hellenic, advises just the opposite. Those who have awakened to the life of the mind find that "it is their business to learn the real truth about the important men, and things, and books, which interest the human mind. For thus is gradually to be acquired a stock of sound ideas, in which the mind will habitually move, and which alone can give to our judgments security and solidity" (VIII, 170). The activity of the critical intelligence has become once again the only sure way to salvation.

There are, finally, two Arnolds—the Hebraic and the Hellenic. They may be seen standing side by side in his *Note-Books*, which are at once a remarkably diverse collect of quotations from world literature and also, as its editors say, a book of devotion in which Arnold meditatively reiterates pious quotations from the Bible, the *Imitatio Christi*, and Bishop Wilson. In the preface to *Culture and Anarchy* Arnold remarks that "the religious side" is "always tending in every serious man to predominance over our other spiritual sides" (V, 239). The Hebraic Arnold, in correspondence with his Hellenic definition of Hebraism, is always tending to an exclusive concentration on righteousness. The Hellenic Arnold does, however, make a provision for the Hebraic, and it is the Hellenic ideal of expansion toward a full humanity that dominates the last phase of Arnold's career.

Arnold's renewed advocacy of the modern spirit appears most strikingly in the 1878 essay "Equality." Arnold himself tacitly indicates the significance of this essay by placing it second in the *Mixed Essays,* just after "Democracy," the 1861 introduction to his official report on the French educational system. The purpose of both essays is to establish an ideal of civilization by defining a standard of human perfection and describing the social conditions that serve to further its attainment. As in *Culture and Anarchy,* the standard of excellence is a union of conduct and culture. "In modern epochs the part of a high reason, of ideas, acquires constantly increasing importance in the conduct of the world's affairs. A fine culture is the complement of a high reason, and it is in the conjunction of both with character, with energy, that the ideal for men and nations is to be placed" (II, 24). In "Equality" Arnold explicitly identifies this "conjunction" as a merging of the qualities of Hebraism and Hellenism; he calls it "civilisation" and defines it as "the humanisation of man in society." He attributes to it four distinct "powers," or human potentials (VIII, 286). Hebraism provides only the one power of conduct, but this is "the greatest of all" (VIII, 292). The other three powers are Hellenic. The "high reason" of "Democracy" becomes "the power of intellect and knowledge," and "a fine culture" is broken down into "the power of social life and manners" and "the power of beauty."

In both "Democracy" and "Equality" Arnold's social thesis is that for the modern world the necessary precondition for the harmonious development of all these powers is social equality. Although the aristocracy has served a useful political purpose in the past and has established a high standard of manners, it now stands in the way of further progress. "The great inequality of classes and property, which came to us from the Middle Age . . . has the natural and necessary effect, under present circumstances, of materialising our upper class, vulgarising our middle class, and brutalising our lower class. And this is to fail in civilisation" (VIII, 299). Arnold's tone is militant, and there is no hint in it of his earlier anxiety about "that break-up of traditional and conventional notions respecting our life, its conduct, and its sanctions, which is undeniably befalling our age" (VIII, 48).[9] His temporary conversion to a conservative political and social outlook had never reached the point of an explicit intellectual repudiation of his cultural theory. Unlike his Hellenism, his Hebraic doctrines were not the result of a gradual intellectual development but of an emotional overreaction, in a man already weakened by personal grief, to the stress of local and temporary political events, the Franco-Prussian War.

In "Equality," when he reasserts his confidence in the modern spirit, he does so on the basis of a principle he had enunciated for a different purpose in "Democracy." In attempting to reassure the English that by yielding more power to the state they need not fear a weakening in the character of the individual, Arnold had declared that "it seems to me, then, that one may save one's self from much idle terror at names and shadows if one will be at the pains to remember what different conditions the different character of two nations must necessarily impose on the operation of any principle" (II, 16). The character of the French, like that of the Athenians, is enfeebled by a native "mobility" or frivolity. The character of the English, however, is marked by "energy and honesty," and these qualities secure them against any severe or chronic social disruption (VIII, 293). "No one who knows this country would deny that it is characterised, in a remarkable degree, by a sense of the power of conduct. Our feeling for religion is one part of this; our industry is another. What foreigners so much remark in us,—our public spirit, our love, amidst all our liberty, for public order and for stability,—are parts of it too" (VIII, 287).

The four powers of civilization are complementary; they do not conflict with one another. A failure of civilization can thus result only from a defect of one of these qualities, and this defect cannot be attributed to the action of any of the other qualities. The chief

9. Although it is true that the Hellenism of Arnold's last decade is in general less single-minded than that of *Essays in Criticism* and *Culture and Anarchy*, David DeLaura seems to overstate the case when he declares that "after his return to politics and literature in 1877, Arnold never again adopts quite the supremely self-confident 'Greek' air of the sixties." *Hebrew and Hellene in Victorian England: Newman, Arnold, and Pater* (Austin: University of Texas Press, 1969), pp. 180–81.

distinction of the French is their "congenital sense for the power of social intercourse and manners" (VIII, 289), and this sense provided the moving force behind the French Revolution and the subsequent introduction of social equality in France. In his Hebraic phase Arnold had repudiated the French Revolution; he now reverts to his former position, that the Revolution not only wrecked the old order but also served a creative and constructive function. In his essay on Gray, Arnold calls it the "great historical manifestation" of "that European renewing of men's minds" (IX, 201). In "Equality" he already takes the position that the purpose of the Revolution, the institution of equality, was in itself good; not only is equality not the cause of the political troubles of the French, it acts as a healing influence for these troubles. "Well then, if a nation laying no sufficient hold upon the powers of beauty and knowledge, and a most failing and feeble hold upon the power of conduct, comes to demoralisation and intellectual stoppage and fearful troubles, we need not be inordinately surprised. What we should rather marvel at is the healing and bountiful operation of Nature, whereby the laying firm hold on one real element in our humanisation has had for France results so beneficent" (VIII, 292–93). Conversely, if the English have not suffered from a want of conduct, they have suffered from a want of the "spirit of society," which in the modern age entails social equality. It should also be noted, however, that, although Arnold still believes that a broad social basis is beneficial to the development of a high culture, he nonetheless reserves an elitist conviction that the majority of any nation is unsound and that the preservation of culture ultimately depends on a "remnant" of the better disposed (see V, 292 and the essay "Numbers" from *Discourses in America*).

The four powers of civilization provide Arnold with a static paradigm by means of which he may evaluate ancient and modern civilizations, but they do not, in themselves, contain any principle of development toward harmonious union. The power of intellect and knowledge, which distinguishes the Germans, may exist quite independently of manners, beauty, and even character. The sense of beauty, for which Arnold praises the Italians, may be maintained in a state of ignorance and moral dissolution. The French give Arnold ample occasion for remarking on the low standard of civilization that may develop among a people heedless of the value of conduct or morality. In the last few years of his life Arnold becomes ever more disillusioned with French society, and he comments with bitter irony on the tendency of the English middle class, as it "slowly awakens from its intellectual sleep of two centuries" (IX, 236), to overlook Racine and Voltaire but respond avidly to contemporary, popular French literature. Arnold feels that the modern spirit, working on the French character, has finally produced a culture that is dominated by the *homme sensuel moyen* and that takes as its highest ideal "the great goddess" Aselgeia, or Lubricity (IX, 77 and X, 155). The last power, conduct, by which Arnold exclusively characterizes the English Puritans, offers by itself a life that is ugly, narrow, and dull.

In order, then, to unify these four powers within an organic scheme of cultural progress, Arnold has recourse to a fifth power that comprehends the other four and that possesses an intrinsic principle of dynamism. In the preface to *Mixed Essays* he identifies this principle and assigns it to the primary rank among the vital forces directing both individuals and the cultural body as a whole. "First and foremost of the necessary means towards man's civilisation we must name *expansion.* The need of expansion is as genuine an instinct in man as the need in plants for the light, or the need in man himself for going upright" (VIII, 371). Arnold's evolutionism differs from Darwin's in that it does not explain development as an offshoot or by-product of the instincts of self-preservation and reproduction but rather designates development as itself a primary instinct. Regarding it from its teleological aspect, Arnold calls it "that instinct of perfection, which is the master-power in humanity" (VIII, 290). By presupposing this "instinct" as the necessary basis for "man's whole effort to civilise himself" (VIII, 371), Arnold is able to derive the four powers from a common source and to view them as directed toward a common end, despite the fact that they are frequently found operating in semi-isolation one from another.

This system of five powers, which Arnold reiterates and applies throughout the essays of his last years, does not essentially differ from the system of his first phase. The structure of history remains, at bottom, a dialectical alternation of the forces of expansion and concentration. The force of expansion is closely associated with Hellenic intellectual spontaneity and flexibility, and the conservative agency is associated with the Hebraic concentration on conduct. The concern for beauty and manners is a subsidiary element of Hellenism. There is, however, one theoretical advance over the earlier system. By explicitly denoting expansion as the primary force of development, Arnold is able to identify concentration as a subordinate and derivative force within the whole dynamic structure of cultural progress. By means of this theoretical modification Arnold can articulate more precisely than before the nature of a future reconciliation between the oppositional forces of Hebraism and Hellenism. That these two forces are still the basic terms of his system Arnold makes apparent in "A Speech at Eton," where he sketches an outline of cultural history by following the diverse fortunes of the Greek concept of *eutrapelia*, or "flexibility." "Lucidity of thought, clearness and propriety of language, freedom from prejudice and freedom from stiffness, openness of mind, amiability of manners,—all these seem to go along with a certain happy flexibility of nature, and to depend upon it" (IX, 24). These are the qualities of the Hellenic intelligence, and in devoting itself to them, Athens became distracted and diverted from the concern with conduct (IX, 32). The antithesis to the Greek nature appears in Christianity and reaches its extreme development in the medieval world, where flexibility was "quite banished, clear straightforward Attic thinking quite lost; restraint, stoppage, and prejudice, regnant" (IX, 34). The third main phase of culture, the modern age, is distinguished by a revival of "fearless thinking and flexibility." The triumphant tone echoes that of the early essays, but it is qualified now by a note of caution. Arnold regards the reemergence of Hellenic qualities as "again, perhaps, not without their accompaniment of danger" (IX, 34).

In his earlier work Arnold has found no means for resisting this danger except through emphasizing the oppositional force of Hebraism. By refusing to designate either Hebraism or Hellenism as "the *law* of human development," Arnold had left them both as semiautonomous agencies and had provided himself with no theoretical means for reconciling them. Having himself advocated a militant Hellenism, he found it necessary to turn about and press with equal vigor a single-minded Hebraism. In his last phase, however, Arnold frees himself from this polemical dualism. His response now to the danger in the modern "flexibility" of mind is to seek in the primary, originative force of expansion a tendency toward union between flexibility and conduct. On the one hand, insofar as expansion is to be identified with Hellenic flexibility, Arnold gives Hellenism the function of reconciliation. The moral to be drawn from cultural history "is, not that flexibility is a bad thing, but that the Greek flexibility was really not flexible enough, because it could not enough bend itself to the moral ideas which are so large a part of life" (IX, 34). It is, presumably, within the scope of modern criticism to achieve this last degree of flexibility and so to effect a comprehensive synthesis of all the human faculties. On the other hand, insofar as the power of conduct also originates in the primary drive for expansion or progress, Arnold also gives Hebraism a conciliatory function. In the preface to *Discourses in America* he declares that the law of conduct "gradually widens, indeed, so as to include light as well as honesty and energy; to make light, also, a moral cause. Unless we are transformed we cannot finally stand, and without more light we cannot be transformed" (X, 240). In these two dialectical formulations, where both poles of the cultural process comprehend or generate the other, Arnold comes the closest he will ever come to a theoretical resolution of the oppositional forces in his cultural system.

On a plane less abstract, considering the critical intelligence and the religious temper simply as two facts of his contemporary world, Arnold finds reason for hope in the circumstances wherein they will meet and mingle in England. "Negative lucidity," the recognition of incongruity and absurdity in the old order of beliefs and institutions, "is inevitable and indispensable" as the "condition of all serious construction for the future. . . . If we see it accompanied in France by much that we shrink from, we should reflect that in England it will have influences joined with it which it has not in France—the natural seriousness of our people, their sense of reverence and respect, their love for the past. Come it must; and here, where it has been so late in coming, it will probably be for the first time seen to come without danger" ("A Liverpool Address," X, 87–88). England, so long outside the mainstream of European culture, thus becomes the focal point of Arnold's hope for the civilization of the future. It is perhaps partly for this reason that in the last three years of his life Arnold devotes so much of his time to commenting on contemporary English political affairs. Much of this material, if not entirely ephemeral, is of small interest for Arnold's general cultural theory.[10]

The Romantic Revaluation

Arnold's *Essays in Criticism, Second Series,* written in 1879 and the early 1880s, contains several of the essays by which he is best known today. His introductions to the Romantic poets and "The Study of Poetry" should not, however, be considered absolutely as definitive statements of his attitudes and affiliations in respect to poetry. They may better be understood comparatively, in relation to the development of his thought throughout his career; they nonetheless serve (along with "Literature and Science" from *Discourses in America*) as part of Arnold's contribution in his third phase to the "serious construction of the future." As in the first phase of his career, this construction relies on both poetry and criticism, but their relative status undergoes something of a change. Arnold retains from his religious period a certain apprehension about the destructive character of the critical intelligence, and the earnestness with which he seeks in poetry a "sure stay" for the modern world leads him to a far more appreciative evaluation of the nineteenth-century English poets than he had given in the first series of *Essays in Criticism.* The creation of a comprehensive intellectual synthesis remains, nonetheless, the function of criticism.

In a letter to his brother, written in 1857, at about the same time as "The Modern Element," Arnold had prophesied an imminent devaluation of the English Romantic poets. "A great transformation in the intellectual nature of the English, and, consequently, in their estimate of their own writers, is, I have long felt, inevitable. When this transformation comes the popularity of Wordsworth, Shelley, Coleridge, and others, remarkable men as they were, will not be the better for it."[11] As it turned out, the chief agent of this devaluation was to be Arnold himself. Arnold's own

10. For a discussion of Arnold's political writings in this period, see chapter 6 of Patrick J. McCarthy's *Matthew Arnold and the Three Classes* (New York: Columbia University Press, 1964). Altogether, McCarthy's book provides a very readable account of the immediate social and political background to Arnold's work.

11. Lowe, "Two Arnold Letters," *Modern Philology* 52 (1955): 262–63.

needs at this time were for an adequate interpretation of cultural history, and for this the Romantics could offer him little. Wordsworth had retreated in confusion from the modern spirit. Byron, Arnold says in "Memorial Verses," "taught us little." Keats had reanimated the sensual luxuriousness of Elizabethan poetry, but he did not have an adequate "idea of the world" by means of which he could escape from a "confused multitudinousness." When Arnold returns to the Romantics in his later years, these judgments remain firm. What changes is not his estimate of the intellectual power of the Romantics, but his own needs and the needs of his culture as he sees them reflected in himself. The poet who will most profit from Arnold's revaluation is Wordsworth, and in a letter of 1880 Arnold describes Wordsworth as, like Burke, "a great force in that epoch of concentration, as I call it, which arose in England in opposition to the epoch of expansion declaring itself in the French Revolution."[12] In "Heinrich Heine" Arnold had complained that Wordsworth had retired "into a monastery." In his 1883 "Address to the Wordsworth Society" he repeats this charge, but this time he means it as praise. He announces his own gradual retirement from the world and explains that since in modern times one can no longer enter a monastery he has decided to join the Wordsworth Society instead. "The two things are not so very different. A monastery is under the rules of poverty, chastity, and obedience. Well, and he who comes under the discipline of Wordsworth comes under those same rules. Wordsworth constantly both preached and practised them" (X, 131).

Arnold's struggle to assimilate the critical materials of the European mainstream and to fashion from them an intellectual deliverance has been largely successful. Consequently, his attention in the 1880s is diverted from the pursuit of criticism, the relations of ideas, to the pursuit of those moral and emotional qualities that will help to preserve continuity within cultural change. Poetry must take the place of religion, and religion is characterized not by intellectual activity but by devotion. The poetry that will best serve the purpose of replacing religion is not intellectual and objective but intuitive and expressive. For this reason Arnold disparages eighteenth-century poetry, "whose task was such as to call forth in general men's powers of understanding, wit and cleverness," and he elevates Romantic poetry for its power to call forth

12. *Letters* 2:192 (January 21, 1880).

the "deepest powers of mind and soul" (IX, 200). Arnold had already, in his first phase, drawn an association between the faculties engaged by poetry and religion, and in *God and the Bible* he had reinforced this association. "For the power of Christianity has been in the immense emotion which it has excited; in its engaging, for the government of man's conduct, the mighty forces of love, reverence, gratitude, hope, pity, and awe,—all that host of allies which Wordsworth includes under the one name of *imagination*" (VII, 377).

Wordsworth himself, whom Arnold calls "one of the best and deepest spiritual influences of our century," becomes the main figure on whom Arnold relies for the task of "again cementing the alliance between the imagination and conduct" (VII, 378).[13] His crucial importance within Arnold's cultural scheme does not, however, prevent Arnold from pointing out the limitations of his range and significance. At its best, literature offers a "criticism of life by gifted men, alive and active with extraordinary power at an unusual number of points" ("Literature and Science," X, 68), and Wordsworth can satisfy only part of these criteria. His virtue is vital intensity, not variety and comprehensiveness. Arnold ranks Wordsworth below only Shakespeare and Milton among the English poets, but he notes that Wordsworth is remarkable neither for a wide "culture" nor for "mental lucidity" (IX, 230). Wordsworth's greatness derives rather from "the extraordinary power" with which he "feels the joy offered to us in nature, the joy offered to us in the simple primary affections and duties" (IX, 51). The joy that Wordsworth himself feels becomes for Arnold a primary religious source. Like righteousness itself, Wordsworth's simple and profound treatment of moral ideas tends to "life" (IX, 48). It does not, however, tend to give an intellectually satisfying account of itself. Arnold excludes Wordsworth's longer philosophical poems from his collection of Wordsworth's verse, he disparages the "Intimations" ode, and he roundly declares that "we cannot do him justice until we dismiss his formal philosophy" (IX, 48). The works he selects "most perfectly to show Wordsworth's unique power" are simple, unassuming poems: "Michael," "The Fountain," and "The Highland Reaper" (IX, 54). This selection seems almost eccentric, but Arnold bases his judgment on the unadulterated presence in these poems of what he holds to be Wordsworth's distinc-

13. *Letters* 2:191 (January 21, 1880).

tive merits: "the profound sincereness with which Wordsworth feels his subject, and also . . . the profoundly sincere and natural character of his subject itself" (IX, 53). It is this "sincereness," the instinct for what is sound and genuine, that enables Wordsworth, despite his limitations, to help fashion the new spiritual basis for the modern world.

Arnold's estimate of Wordsworth provides the pattern for his revaluation of Byron; he regards Byron as inferior in rank to Wordsworth but standing out with him above the other Romantics, "first and pre-eminent in actual performance, a glorious pair, among the English poets of this century" (IX, 236). Byron's virtue, like that of Wordsworth, is the "excellence of sincerity and strength," and as in Wordsworth it is an excellence that derives from sources inaccessible to the intellect and thus undamaged by defects of reflective power, cultivation, or even artistic tact. "Nature herself seems to take the pen from him as she took it from Wordsworth, and to write for him as she wrote for Wordsworth, though in a different fashion, with her own penetrating simplicity" (IX, 234). Wordsworth and Byron are paired as representing complementary forces of moral character, the power of sympathy and the power of passionate resistance. Wordsworth's bent is the more positive and constructive and, for this reason, greater. "Wordsworth has an insight into permanent sources of joy and consolation for mankind which Byron has not; his poetry gives us more which we may rest upon than Byron's" (IX, 236). If Wordsworth's vital sympathy with common humanity is akin to righteousness, Byron's power of resistance to cant and absurdity is a sort of negative righteousness. The tenderness and gentleness in Wordsworth's humane spirit required for its preservation a degree of compromise with the established order of society. As Arnold says in the first "Obermann," "Wordsworth's eyes avert their ken / From half of human fate." Byron, in contrast, found his greatest source of strength in his opposition to the "system of established facts and dominant ideas" in post-Napoleonic England. "The falsehood, cynicism, insolence, misgovernment, oppression, with their unfailing crop of human misery . . . roused Byron to irreconcilable revolt and battle" (IX, 232). Byron's merit is not, even so, of an exclusively oppositional character. If there had been no sense of positive value inspiring his revolt, it would have lacked nobility, and Byron would have seemed to Arnold like Charlotte Brontë, whose mind, he says, "contains nothing but hunger, rebellion, and rage."[14] Besides "his astounding power and passion," Byron had also "a strong and deep sense for what is beautiful in nature, and for what is beautiful in human action and suffering" (IX, 234). Nonetheless, while Wordsworth is particularly characterized by his ability to transcend the merely personal and to see into the common life of humanity, Byron is characterized by the energy of his own personality, and this for Arnold is the lesser part of virtue.

Character is the basis of conduct, and in his last phase Arnold's preoccupation with the moral influence of poetry brings him to place special emphasis on the character of the poet. Style, taken as the manipulation of the formal elements of verse, had always seemed to him of secondary importance to style taken as a reflection of character. In his earlier years, however, he was more ready to allow for a poetry of "natural magic" distinct from the poetry of moral interpretation. In his 1850 "Memorial Verses" for Wordsworth, Arnold had celebrated Wordsworth's poetry primarily for its natural magic and had almost seemed to regard this magic as effecting a release from moral care:

He laid us as we lay at birth
On the cool flowery lap of earth,
Smiles broke from us and we had ease;
The hills were round us, and the breeze
Went o'er the sun-lit fields again;
Our foreheads felt the wind and rain.
Our youth return'd; for there was shed
On spirits that had long been dead,
Spirits dried up and closely furl'd,
The freshness of the early world.

. . . .

Others will teach us how to dare,
And against fear our breast to steel;
Others will strengthen us to bear—
But who, ah! who, will make us feel?

By the time of writing his introductory essay on Wordsworth, Arnold still grants Wordsworth's power of natural evocation, but he has decidedly shifted his evaluative emphasis to Wordsworth's power of moral interpretation, his evocation of "the simple, pri-

14. *Letters* 1:34 (April 14, 1853).

mary affections and duties." In similar fashion, in his early evaluation of Byron, Arnold had celebrated the sensational impact of Byron's "fount of fiery life." "With shivering heart the strife we saw / Of passion with eternal law" ("Memorial Verses"). When he returns to Byron thirty years later, Arnold speaks of a revolt not against "eternal law" but against British conventionalism, everything that was false and unsound in English civilization.

Arnold's most complete single definition of poetry, enunciated in the essay on Byron, appears to give equal weight to form and content. "Truth and seriousness of substance and matter, felicity and perfection of diction and manner, as these are exhibited in the best poets, are what constitute a criticism of life made in conformity with the laws of poetic truth and poetic beauty" (IX, 228). In his actual application of this definition Arnold renders "manner" dependent on character, and character he regards as largely constitutive of "substance and matter." In his essay "A French Critic on Milton," Arnold is willing to grant Edmond Scherer's contention that Milton's beliefs and the application of those beliefs to the fable of *Paradise Lost* are obsolete, " 'that if the work subsists it is in spite of the subject treated by it' " (VIII, 186). Nonetheless, he maintains that Milton can still be a living influence because "he is our great artist in style, our one first-rate master in the grand style" (VIII, 183). Style is itself converted into substance, something that can continue to sustain us by reflecting a quality of character:

> Some moral qualities seem to be connected in a man with his power of style. Milton's power of style, for instance, has for its great character *elevation*; and Milton's elevation clearly comes, in the main, from a moral quality in him,—his pureness. . . . These two, pureness and kindness, are, in very truth, the two signal Christian virtues. . . . In kindness, and in all which that word conveys or suggests, Milton does not shine. He had the temper of his Puritan party. . . . But, on the other hand, how high, clear, and splendid is his pureness; and how intimately does its might enter into the voice of his poetry!
> (VIII, 184–85)

It is by the use of this principle of the interdependence of style and character that Arnold is able to rehabilitate one more of the Romantic poets, Keats. In the early essay on Maurice de Guérin, Arnold had argued that Keats was characterized exclusively by his gift of natural magic (III, 34). In his introduction to Keats's poems in 1880, Arnold stands by this judgment, and he adds that "Keats was not ripe" for a poetry of "moral interpretation" (IX, 215). He finds, however, that Keats's passion for natural beauty "is not a passion of the sensuous or sentimental poet. It is an intellectual and spiritual passion" (IX, 213). Keats's sensuousness is purified by his "lucidity," and "lucidity is in itself akin to character and to high and severe work" (IX, 211). Arnold draws on a comparison with Milton to render the "fascinating felicity" of Keats's style and manner a quality of character, and character itself an intellectual "matter." Keats was not mature enough for the larger tasks of poetic construction, but "even in his pursuit of 'the pleasures of song' . . . there is that stamp of high work which is akin to character, which is character passing into intellectual production" (IX, 212). Character without talent can of course produce nothing in literature, but intellectual production of the highest order necessarily grounds itself in some moral quality of the artist. Literature is not, as T. S. Eliot would have it, a medium detached from the personality of the poet. The subjective qualities of the poet are themselves a part of the medium.

This stylistic subjectivism serves as a complement to the doctrine of historical relativism that Arnold had set out in "The Function of Criticism." Literature uses, he said, the best ideas current at the time, whatever those ideas may be. The worth of literature thus does not depend on the absolute truth or falsity of its ideas but on their humane significance, and this significance will be reflected in the poet's manner of treating them. Stylistic subjectivism works, as does historical relativism, toward preserving literature for its aesthetic and moral rather than "scientific" qualities. In his second essay on Milton, Arnold will go as far in this direction as to declare that "the mighty power of poetry and art. . . . resides chiefly in the refining and elevation wrought in us by the high and rare excellence of the great style" (XI, 331). In the lectures *On Translating Homer*, when Arnold had attempted to define the great or grand style, he had included the substance or matter as part of the style. "I think it will be found that the grand style arises in poetry, *when a noble nature, poetically gifted, treats with simplicity or with severity a serious subject*" (I, 188). From this point of view the "subject" may be obsolete, as are Homer's pantheon and the Christian cosmologies of Dante and Milton, but its "seriousness" relative to its author continues to have a moral effect on the reader. From the poets of his own age, however, Arnold requires not only this influence wrought by style but a contribution to "the serious construction of the future," and in this respect Wordsworth and Byron, alone of the English poets of the nineteenth century, satisfy Arnold's requirements:

> Keats had probably, indeed, a more consummate poetic gift than either of them; but he died having produced too little and being as yet too immature to rival them. I for my part can never even think of equalling with them any other of their contemporaries;—either Coleridge, poet and philosopher wrecked in a mist of opium; or Shelley, beautiful and ineffectual angel, beating in the void his luminous wings in vain.
>
> (IX, 236–37)

In Wordsworth, Arnold finds a poetry that reawakens the religious sense of a beneficent moral order, and religion, Arnold says, is "the deepest thing in human life" (X, 252). It is not, however, the whole of life, and Arnold's highest standard for literature, reflecting his ideal of "civilisation," requires that it work to unify all the "powers" of man. In "Literature and Science" Arnold is "particularly concerned" with the function of literature in relating the "pieces" of knowledge given by science to two other powers, beauty and conduct (X, 62). In his second essay on Sainte-Beuve he takes due notice also of the fourth power, the sense for society. "Now it so happens that the great place of France in the world is very much due to her eminent gift for social life and development; and this gift French literature has accompanied, fashioned, perfected, and continues to reflect. This gives a special interest to French literature, and an interest independent even of the excellence of individual French writers, high as that often is" (XI, 118–19). The literature of society, though segregated from the discussion of "Literature and Science," is of great importance for Arnold. Singling out Molière as "by far the chief name in French poetry," Arnold adds that Molière is also "one of the very greatest names in all literature" (IX, 72), and he places him, along with Shakespeare, Milton, and Goethe, in a list of the four greatest poets of the last three centuries. Of these four poets who answer adequately to Arnold's standard of civilization, only Goethe is "modern" in the sense of having to create a new spiritual basis, and Goethe, though the greatest poet of Germany, and a greater poet than Wordsworth, is still more important for Arnold as a critic than as a poet (IX, 54 and 41; VIII, 275). The poetic qualities of the heart and imagination, in alliance with moral character, are essential for the creation of a new spiritual basis. When they are isolated from the power of knowledge and intelligence, as they are in Wordsworth and Byron, they are not alone sufficient to create this basis.

Arnold has never lost the need for a complete view of the world, and for this view the qualities of intelligence are indispensable. Arnold's early Empedoclean yearning after the infinite had attempted to bypass the intelligence and seize "the All" through direct intuition. In the period from "The Modern Element" through *Culture and Anarchy,* he replaced this Romantic framework with a theoretical synthesis of historical progressivism and rationalism, and he never returns to the Empedoclean mode. In "Equality," even while reestablishing expansion and diversity as necessary components of civilization, he affirms that to keep within the measure of human aptitudes is a necessary condition for a right relation to "nature." "Civilisation is the humanisation of man in society. To be humanised is to comply with the true law of our human nature: *servare modum, finemque tenere, Naturamque sequi,* says Lucan; 'to keep our measure, and to hold fast our end, and to follow Nature.' To be humanised is to make progress towards this, our true and full humanity" (VIII, 286). Defending his liberal faith of relying on the better feelings and higher intelligence of mankind, Arnold confirms that the historical process is a growth toward a more perfect understanding of the natural order. He quotes approvingly this sentence from Condorcet: "The natural order of things tends to bring general opinion more and more into conformity with truth" (VIII, 327). In a late review of the French writer Amiel, Arnold's rejection of mystical passion reaffirms his conversion to an intelligible universe and gives us the clue to his rejection of Wordsworth's "philosophy":[15]

15. In his discussion of the philosophical character of Arnold's poetry, William Robbins argues that "the thought of absorption into an all-embracing Nothingness" was "never very real to Arnold." *The Ethical Idealism of Matthew Arnold* (London: William Heinemann, 1959), p. 96. However, the evidence he brings forward is the comment on Amiel, and this comment works against his thesis that Arnold's attitudes are consistent throughout his career. Robbins's sympathy for Arnold's religious efforts renders his views on Arnold's whole body of thought less cogent than they might be; nonetheless, despite poor or-

> The desire for the all, the impatience with what is partial and limited, the fascination of the infinite. . . . lend themselves well to poetry, but what are we to say of their value as ideas to be lived with, dilated on, made the governing ideas of life? Except for use in passing, and with the power to dismiss them again, they are unprofitable. . . . Nay, the thoughts which have positive truth and value . . . are precisely thoughts which counteract the "vague aspiration and indeterminate desire" possessing Amiel and filling his Journal: they are thoughts insisting on the need of limit, the feasibility of performance.
>
> (XI, 271–72)

The "desire for the all" and the need for "thoughts to be lived with" form the boundaries of Arnold's own intellectual universe. He resolves the conflict between these two needs, first, by adopting a belief in a rational world order correspondent to "the general world of thought," that is, to criticism (III, 40) and, second, by rendering the world of thought as a progressive historical growth toward a full humanity and a whole view. The aesthetic equivalent of this whole view is not Romantic and Christian but classical and pagan. "*Fit details strictly combined, in view of a large general result nobly conceived*; that is just where we English fail, where all our art fails" ("Literature and Science," X, 71). The unity of vision in Greek art provides Arnold throughout his life with an archetype of perfection, and yet he himself recognizes that, although "in many respects the ancients are far above us," nonetheless "there is something that we demand which they can never give" ("Wordsworth," IX, 54). Arnold does not say what this "something" is, but one may conjecture from the context that it is in part Wordsworth's inwardness and gentleness, his "sweet calm" (first "Obermann"). More importantly, what the ancient archetype of aesthetic unity cannot give is, by definition, that sense of division between a present reality and an ideal future state, which for Arnold generates the historical process—a process in which culture develops through ever greater complexity toward an inaccessible perfection of totality. The pristine, simple unity of the ancient sensibility renders ancient literature an absolute good, but it is by this very perfection that the ancients are, finally, most limited.

---

ganization and repetitiousness, the quality of scholarship and reflection in his book is of a very high order.

2

4 *The Style of Reason*

The Middle Way

The modern world begins in the eighteenth century, and in three main areas of Arnold's cultural theory—his classicism, his aesthetic and moral rationalism, and his religious traditionalism—his solutions to the modern problem draw directly from, and align him with, the major writers of the Augustan period in England: Dryden, Pope, Swift, and Johnson. Arnold judges English neoclassicism by comparison both with the French Enlightenment and with English Romanticism. Throughout his critical career, however, he pursues a dialogue with the English neoclassicists themselves, and even while judging them, he borrows materials for his judgments from them. Dryden and Johnson are the first two great critics of English literature, and if we accept Arnold's own evaluation of Coleridge, Arnold is the third. His two greatest predecessors provide Arnold with both a high standard of critical performance and a large body of opinions and ideas that contribute to the formulation of his critical doctrines. Pope and Swift help to fashion for Arnold the standards of style appropriate to the aesthetic and moral assumptions of a rationalist cosmology. Arnold quotes and echoes basic doctrinal statements of all four of the greatest neoclassicists, he establishes Swift and Johnson as touchstones for a sound modern prose, and he absorbs from Pope a good measure of the spirit and manner of his own didactic poetry. In order, then, to situate Arnold within the tradition of modern English literature, I shall in this chapter examine his relation to the Augustan age, how he places it within his cultural system, and what he takes from it.

Many of the ideas that Arnold shares with the neoclassicists have, of course, an origin in classical literature, and many remain current in modified form among Arnold's contemporaries. One must, therefore, be very cautious about the attribution of exclusive influence. Even so, once all due qualifications have been made, the distinct doctrinal affinities between Arnold and the neoclassicists, his extensive commentary on them, and the frequent cases in which there is at least a probability of direct borrowing seem to indicate that the neoclassicists play a much larger role in the development of Arnold's critical thought than has been generally recognized. We have yet to receive a comprehensive and critically adequate account of Arnold's relations to ancient literature (Warren D. Anderson's study, *Matthew Arnold and the Classical Tradition,* is of value mainly in identifying possible sources and allusions), but from the evidence adduced in this chapter, I would venture to suggest that much of Arnold's supposed classicism is in fact neoclassicism, that is, a classicism reflected through the prism of eighteenth-century aesthetics. The eighteenth-century writers generously acknowledged their own debts to ancient literature, and Arnold clearly listens to what they have to say about this literature. They are, moreover, close to Arnold in ways the ancient writers could not be. They are modern not only in idea but in time; they are, like Arnold, heirs to both the classical and Christian traditions; and they are English. The neoclassicists wrote in Arnold's own language, they lived in a society much more like his own than those of Rome and Athens, and they dealt critically with his own national literature.

Until the advent of Lessing in the latter half of the eighteenth century, the modern spirit appears as a significant force in only two nations, England and France. Although Arnold criticizes the English neoclassicists with a severe thoroughness and acknowledges the French Enlightenment to be "one of the most powerful and pervasive intellectual agencies that have ever existed" (III, 240), his own affinities of thought and feeling are ultimately closer to the English eighteenth century than to the French. Arnold begins his writing career as an elegist for a lost faith, and he pursues his goal of an intellectual deliverance by seeking a reconciliation between the two main areas of cultural life: religious devotion and intellectual activity. In France the Enlightenment did not so much lose as actively repudiate its Christian heritage. The philosophes were animated by the sense of a revolutionary historical mission, but in fulfilling this mission, they closed themselves off from the spiritual resources of the Christian past. In England the modern spirit, proceeding more reluctantly, achieved less sensational victories for "negative lucidity," but it more successfully preserved the ideal of a full humanity within the historical life of culture.

Through the work of its natural scientists and empirical philosophers, England provided the intellectual foundations for the French Enlightenment, but in England itself critical empiricism was seldom carried to its radical conclusions, and it did not overtly publish a revolutionary revision of traditional religious and social thought. Energy and originality, the qualities of genius, were necessary to begin the Enlightenment, but rational consistency, a quality of intelligence, was necessary to make it prevail. In England the modern spirit was not willing to enforce its claims for an exclusive command over the minds of men.

> There was great and free intellectual movement in England at the beginning of the eighteenth century; indeed, it was from England that the movement passed into France. But our nation had not that strong natural bent for lucidity which the French have; its bent was towards other things in preference. Our leading thinkers had not the genius and passion for lucidity which distinguishes Voltaire. In their free enquiry they soon found themselves coming into collision with a number of established facts, beliefs, conventions. Thereupon all sorts of practical considerations began to sway them; the danger signal went up, they often stopped short, turned their eyes another way, or drew down a curtain between themselves and the light.
>
> ("A LIVERPOOL ADDRESS," X, 86)

Arnold holds that even in England the eighteenth century, up to the time of the French Revolution, was primarily a period of expansion, of critical inquiry and increased social mobility, but this tendency was severely inhibited by powerful countercurrents of intellectual concentration. Johnson, whom Arnold refers to as "the greatest power in English letters during the eighteenth century," was a Tory and a Christian, "a strong force of conservatism and concentration, in an epoch which by its natural tendencies seemed to be moving towards expansion and freedom" (VIII, 309 and 319). Addison, the most popular and influential critic of the earlier part of the century, succeeded in part because of the moderation and conventionality that characterized and limited his criticism. Johnson credits Addison with having set the tone of refinement and civility in social life, and Arnold credits him with bringing a more gentle and civil tone into the manner of literary criticism. Neither credits him with any great profundity of thought. Johnson defends him on the basis that he made no pretense toward greatness and that within the modest range he set for himself he was successful. From his own perspective of uneasy but stubborn orthodoxy, Johnson finds the confident moderation of Addison's religion a source of comfort and a matter of praise.[1] Arnold, for whom orthodoxy presents itself more as a threat than as a safeguard to religion, can receive little help from the religious ideas of either Addison or Johnson, and the moderation that once made Addison a cultural influence now consigns him to merely historical interest. "Whatever his services to his time, Addison is for us now a writer whose range and force of thought are not considerable enough to make him interesting" (VIII, 249).

As an advocate of the modern spirit Arnold deprecates the English eighteenth century as not sufficiently radical. From the other side of his literary horizon, as an advocate of poetry and religious feeling, he disparages the whole eighteenth century, French and English, for its spiritual aridity. He sympathizes with Bishop Butler's frustration in trying to uphold the religious life among the frivolous skeptics of the court, and he regards Thomas Gray as a tragic victim of the *Zeitgeist*, a naturally poetic soul cramped and stifled in a culture dominated by the spirit of prose. The most radically Gallic and pagan of all English eighteenth-century thinkers is David Hume, and Arnold takes it as evidence of Gray's "seriousness" and "character" that he recoiled from both Hume and Voltaire (IX, 196). At the same time, however, Arnold conjectures that if Gray had been born later in the eighteenth century, he might have profited from "that European renewing of men's minds of which the great historical manifestation is the French Revolution" (IX, 201).

The English eighteenth century is an age of compromise. Seen in the most derogatory light, this means that it is animated neither by modernist zeal nor by religious or poetic passion; that is, it

1. See the concluding remarks in Johnson's *Life of Addison*.

has enough timid conservatism to make it dull and enough worldly sophistication to make it shallow. This is the view taken by the advance guard of the Romantic reaction, and it is a view that Arnold partly shares. One of Arnold's greatest strengths as a critic, however, is his power of balanced evaluation, and the case he prosecutes against the eighteenth century gives only half the story. The other half appears in the genuine approbation Arnold accords to "our age of prose and reason . . . our excellent and indispensable eighteenth century" (IX, 180). The eighteenth century is the first truly modern age in England, and it not only fulfilled a necessary historical function but continued to work as a living influence on Arnold. If it offers pure archetypes of neither Hellenism nor Hebraism (intellectual nor religious ardor), it does offer the first modern example of a synthesis between the two. If it did not fling itself with revolutionary enthusiasm into the future, neither did it divorce itself from the culture of the past, and if it failed of an exclusive religious intensity, neither did it close itself off from the life of the mind and the needs of the critical spirit.

In 1878 Arnold published an edition of six selected lives from Johnson's *Lives of the Poets*. The six he chose—Milton, Dryden, Swift, Addison, Pope, and Gray—all represent "names of the first class in English literature" and should serve, Arnold says, as a central point of reference for the student of English literature (VIII, 309).

> The six lives cover a period of literary and intellectual movement in which we are all profoundly interested. It is the passage of our nation to prose and reason; the passage to a type of thought and expression modern, European, and which on the whole is ours at the present day, from a type antiquated, peculiar, and which is ours no longer.
>
> (VIII, 312)

Taken in its narrowest possible signification, this statement can and has been read to mean only that the historical interest of the eighteenth century consists in its development of a serviceable style of prose, an achievement that though merely technical was nonetheless paid for through a spiritual loss.[2] Arnold himself,

2. See E. K. Brown, "Matthew Arnold and the Eighteenth Century," *University of Toronto Quarterly* 9 (1940): 203 and 213. Geoffrey Tillotson, like Brown, assumes that when Arnold calls the eighteenth century an age of prose, this appellation is necessarily to be taken as an insult. *Criticism and the Nine-*

however, says that the transition is not only to a type of "expression" that is modern but also to a type of "thought," and he calls this century and a half "an important period of our literary and intellectual history." The transition from the world of Milton to that of Dryden, Pope, and Swift represents not only a purification of prose style but a profound shifting in the basis of intellectual life. The passage from a mode of discourse fanciful and eccentric to one reasonable and natural corresponds to a change of sensibility, a transition from the old world dominated by the religious imagination to a new world that seeks its authority in reason and nature.

Of the six figures in Arnold's selection, Milton is the most intrinsically important writer; however, because he does not belong to the modern world, he has the least direct influence on Arnold's own thought. Arnold describes Milton as "a survivor from the great age of poetry," and he contrasts him to the Augustans, who were "mighty workers for the age of prose" (VIII, 318). Equally, Milton was a survivor from the last great age of firmly orthodox Christian faith. The publication of Milton's epic of religious confirmation precedes by only fifteen years the first major poem of serious, sustained skepticism in English. Dryden's *Religio Laici* systematically questions every major tenet of Christian doctrine, including the divinity of Christ, and Dryden can discover no adequate grounds for doctrinal confirmation. Dryden is not himself ready to embrace the consequences of his skepticism, and he concludes his penetrating inquiry with a remarkably unconvincing palinode. "Faith is not built on disquisitions vain; / The things we *must* believe are *few* and *plain*." For Dryden, sadly beleaguered by his own reluctant skepticism, Christianity is still the way of truth and life, if only one can find an authority sufficient to sanction and direct one's belief. Dryden finally finds this authority for himself in the Catholic church, but not before he has unwillingly undermined for his successors the foundations of all religious authority.

Pope, who considers himself Dryden's lineal descendant in poetry, never explicitly repudiates Christianity, but like Arnold he reduces it from dogma, a factual account of history and

teenth Century (London: Athlone Press, 1951), pp. 69 and 72. The articles by Tillotson and Brown pretty much exhaust the critical commentary on Arnold and the eighteenth century. Comments by other critics are for the most part limited to passing and parenthetical remarks of a general character.

nature, to tradition and ritual. In his "Imitation" of Horace's sixth "Epistle" from Book One, Pope easily translates Horace's veneration for the sacred groves and altars of Rome into his own pious regard for the Roman church, but his piety does not entail doctrinal adherence. Instead he adheres to "*Unerring Nature,* still divinely bright," which yields "One *clear, unchang'd,* and *Universal* Light" ("An Essay on Criticism," lines 70–71). Pope does not associate this light with the illumination of the Gospel but with the radiance of Homer. He explains that Vergil copied Homer because "*Nature* and *Homer* were, he found, the *same*" (line 135). Arnold, too, turns back to Greek art for the validation of his belief that through rational intuition man has access to objective laws of truth and beauty.

> Hellenism, and human life in the hands of Hellenism, is invested with a kind of aerial ease, clearness, and radiancy; they are full of what we call sweetness and light. . . . Greek intelligence has obviously for its essence the instinct for what Plato calls the true, firm, intelligible law of things; the law of light, of seeing things as they are. . . . Greek art and beauty rest on fidelity to nature,—the *best* nature,—and on a delicate discrimination of what this best nature is.
>
> (v, 167 and 178)

The phrase "sweetness and light" and its attribution to antique literature are drawn from Swift's *Battle of the Books.* Swift, like Pope, maintains a nominal orthodoxy, but he creates in his Houyhnhnms an ideal of human nature that is entirely pagan and rational. The word *Houyhnhnm,* in its etymological derivation, means "the Perfection of Nature," and Swift's rational animals have attained their perfection in isolation from the corrupted traditions of Christian civilization.[3] Even Johnson, sincerely orthodox as he was, takes refuge from Christian doctrine by adopting for his most extensive essay in moral philosophy the mode of the Oriental *conte.* The wisdom of Imlac in *Rasselas* is not that of a Christian theologian but of a modern Socrates.

Arnold's Hellenism, his reliance on the authority of reason and his association of this authority with the works of classical antiquity, detach him from the Romantic tradition and link him with the neoclassicists. In the second phase of his career, when Arnold turns from Hellenism to Hebraism and attempts to reconstruct

3. Jonathan Swift, *Gulliver's Travels,* bk. 4, chap. 3.

Christianity as essentially a moral code, he again builds on foundations laid by the Augustans. Dryden begins clearing the ground for this development by subordinating theological disputation to civil concord.

'Tis some Relief, that points not clearly known,
Without much hazard may be let alone:
And, after hearing what our Church can say,
If still our Reason runs another way,
That private Reason 'tis more Just to curb,
Than by disputes the publick Peace disturb.
For points obscure are of small use to learn:
But *Common quiet* is *Mankind's concern.*

(RELIGIO LAICI, LINES 443–50)

For Dryden there seems to be an irreconcilable conflict between what is discovered by reason and what is enjoined by established authority. His conclusion, here, is simply to let religion rest. As Arnold says, after the Restoration the time had come "when our nation felt the imperious need of freeing itself from the absorbing preoccupation which religion in the Puritan age had exercised" (IX, 179).

Pope, like Dryden, counsels against any public disruption on the basis of doctrinal differences. He goes beyond Dryden, however, in implying that the end and substance of religion is nothing more than, as Arnold calls it, a temper and a behavior.

For Modes of Faith, let graceless zealots fight;
His can't be wrong whose life is in the right:
In Faith and Hope the world will disagree,
But all Mankind's concern is Charity.

(ESSAY ON MAN, BK. 3, LINES 305–308)

For Pope religion is pragmatic. The validity of religious faith is to be tested, not by the "scientific" correspondence of doctrine to reality, but by the practical consequences of belief. Disagreements in "Faith" may be interpreted as referring only to doctrinal dissensions among various Christian sects, but "Hope" refers to the different expectations that men may hold in regard to personal immortality. Christ and the Christian scheme of salvation are not mentioned in the *Essay on Man*, and religious piety does not depend on adherence to any specifically Christian doctrine. It does depend, however, as it does for Arnold, on adherence to Christian morality. Whereas Dryden had held that religion should not be allowed to disturb one's sense of common humanity, for Pope common humanity has itself become religion.

In Swift's thinking, as in Pope's, the substance of religion has been tacitly transformed from doctrine to conduct. In his "Argument Against Abolishing Christianity" Swift veils his incredulity in a transparent irony, but there is a ring of conviction in his profession that "real" (that is, dogmatic) Christianity is a lost cause. "The System of the Gospel, after the Fate of other Systems is generally antiquated and exploded."[4] Like Arnold, however, he considers religion to be necessary for the restraint of animal passions, and he opposes the public disestablishment of religion on the basis of its social utility.

> IT is likewise proposed, as a great Advantage to the Publick, that if we once discard the System of the Gospel, all Religion will, of Course, be banished for ever; and consequently along with it, those grievous Prejudices of Education; which, under the Names of Virtue, Conscience, Honour, Justice, and the like, are so apt to disturb the Peace of human Minds.[5]

Arnold also defends the Anglican church for its social value. "I regard the Church of England as, in fact, a great national society for the promotion of what is commonly called *goodness*" (VIII, 65). Arnold's defense of the church is not, however, animated merely by the detached calculations of the social engineer. His piety toward the historical life of his culture binds him, as Pope and Swift are bound, to the traditions of Christian worship. "Not to break one's connexion with the past in one's religion is one of the strongest instincts in human nature."[6]

Arnold's efforts to mediate between the claims of modernism and the claims of tradition link him to the critical framework of the Augustan sensibility. There is, however, an important part of Arnold's own religious tradition in which the neoclassicists cannot share. The poetry of English Romanticism, especially that of Wordsworth, serves Arnold as a primary religious source, and as a post-Romantic Arnold takes a critical perspective on the neoclassical sensibility. In a letter of 1880 he remarks that in the eigh-

4. Jonathan Swift, *Prose Works*, ed. Herbert Davis, 14 vols. (Oxford: Shakespeare Head Press, 1939), 2:27.
5. Ibid., p. 33.
6. *Letters* 2:151 (June 1876).

teenth century "the people were just like ourselves, whilst the Elizabethan are not," but he also says that, although the eighteenth century "is very interesting," he himself would "not like to have lived in it."[7] The chief reason for Arnold's aversion is that the period suffered from a "defective poetry and criticism of poetry" (VIII, 317). The two major poets of the period are Dryden and Pope, and Arnold regards them both as possessing a genius not essentially poetic. Though working in the medium of verse, they turned their energies to the refinement of the English language as a vehicle for intelligence, for wit and sense.

> We are to regard Dryden as the puissant and glorious founder, Pope as the splendid high priest, of our age of prose and reason. . . . though they may in a certain sense be masters of the art of versification, Dryden and Pope are not classics of our poetry, they are classics of our prose.
>
> (IX, 180 AND 181)

It is only late in his career that Arnold determines to define the verse of Dryden and Pope as "prose," not poetry, but in doing so he gives a generic resolution to a problem that has occupied him from the beginning of his career. In a letter to his brother, written at the time of "The Modern Element," Arnold sketches out an evaluative scheme of historical epochs and the degree of adequacy displayed by the literature of each epoch. The Augustan age holds a peculiar place in this scheme; of all the epochs Arnold mentions, it is the only one besides that of Periclean Athens that he regards as having possessed an adequate poetry, that is, a poetry that "reflected completely the best general culture and intelligence of that age."[8] He adds, however, that the age itself "was a poor time, after all—so the poetry is not and cannot be a first-class one." His own age, in contrast, "is a first-class one—an infinitely fuller richer age than Pope's," but there is no poetry that adequately comprehends the age. Arnold's historical vision here is like that of "The Modern Element." He regards the analytical components of culture as combining more or less randomly with different results at different times. It is in this same letter that he also defines the Elizabethan era as "second-class" and so must have recourse to the miracle of genius to account for the "infinitely *more than adequate* expression" that Shakespeare provides for his age. Just as Arnold

7. *Letters* 2:217 (December 22, 1880).
8. Lowe, "Two Arnold Letters," *Modern Philology* 52 (1955): 263.

will reconsider later in his development the ranking of the Elizabethan era from the perspective of a unified historical progression, so will he also find a historical rationale for the literature of the Augustan age.

For the modern phase of his cultural dialectic Arnold attributes to the French Enlightenment the main influences of expansion, and he attributes to England the main functions of Hebraic counteraction. It is in correspondence with these historical functions that he celebrates France for its critical spirit, and hence for its prose, and celebrates England for its religious and imaginative spirit, and hence for its poetry. "The power of French literature is in its prose writers, the power of English literature is in its poets" (III, 239). The French pole of this duality remains, for the most part, fixed and constant. French literature operates exclusively within the domain of prose and critical reason. French verse is, like that of Dryden and Pope, characterized by the qualities of prose. At the English pole, however, Arnold sets up an internal dialectic. The dominant English tendency is itself qualified and refined through the neoclassical countercurrent of prose and critical reason. As the Puritan moral reaction was "necessary" to world progress, so also the neoclassical literary reaction "was a vital and necessary effort in our literature" (VIII, 317). However, in both instances the reaction, though necessary, created an imbalance of sensibility and so failed of absolute perfection. "Such is the common course and law of progress; one thing is done at a time, and other things are sacrificed to it" (VIII, 318). The Puritan reaction sacrificed everything in life that contributes to beauty, charm, and intellectual dignity. Moreover, it excluded those qualities of poetic imagination that, for Arnold, rightly belong to the religious spirit in its perfected state. Milton, he says, was a poet, not because of, but despite his Puritanism (VIII, 185). On the other hand, the neoclassical writers, in turning to prose and reason, also cut themselves off from the poetic imagination. Because of this dual exclusion, poetry, as natural magic and as a religious evocation of moral life, remained largely dormant in England for over a century. Gray, Arnold thinks, preserved a frail but genuine poetic gift by virtue of his thorough familiarity with Greek literature. It was, however, only with the poetry of Wordsworth that natural religious devotion and the poetic imagination again achieved their proper union.

Neither Puritanism nor neoclassicism, with their limited aims, could attain to the highest spiritual grandeur. However, whereas the civilizing influence of Puritanism appears to Arnold chiefly as an adversative force or a restraining power on Hellenic excess, the neoclassicists marked out for themselves a field of positive literary achievement. Since the main tendency of the age was toward the creation of an adequate prose, its best work is in prose, not verse. Nonetheless, the verse of the period not only furthered the advance of prose but also achieved for poetry a finer sense of compositional order and precision of statement.

> Poetry, or rather the use of verse, entered in a remarkable degree, during that century, into the whole of the daily life of the civilised classes; and the poetry of the century was a perpetual school of the qualities requisite for a good prose, the qualities of regularity, uniformity, precision, balance. This may have been of no great service to English poetry, although to say that it has been of no service at all, to say that the eighteenth century has in no respect changed the conditions for English poetical style, or that it has changed them for the worse, would be untrue. But it was undeniably of signal service to that which was the great want and work of the hour, English prose.
>
> (VIII, 317)

The function of poetry is to call forth in men "their deepest powers of mind and soul," and the poetry of the eighteenth century does not, Arnold thinks, accomplish this (IX, 200). In Gray, Wordsworth, Byron, and Keats, Arnold finds a modern poetry that satisfies these needs, and since he holds that poetry is "more excellent in itself than prose," he ranks the literature of the eighteenth century beneath that of the greater Romantics (VIII, 315). In order, however, to understand Arnold's own literary affinities, we must modify this absolute generic distinction. For the greater part of his literary career Arnold was not a poet but a critic. In his last phase he partially assimilates the spiritual contribution of English Romanticism into his cultural system, but in order to fashion this system he has recourse not to the heart and imagination but to the critical intelligence. When Arnold undertakes his critical mission, the qualities of style and thought he feels to be necessary to himself and his culture at that time place him in closer relation to the neoclassicists than to the Romantics. In both the Augustan and mid-Victorian ages the poetic imagination must give place to a literature of intelligence and critical prose.

In the best of classical literature, Arnold holds, the qualities of poetic genius were fully integrated with the qualities of intelligence. The poetry of Homer and Sophocles could at once satisfy the need for spiritual grandeur and for compositional order. Modern literature, however, has tended to segregate these qualities; it has produced, on the one hand, a literature clear and rational but poetically thin and, on the other hand, a literature richly evocative but chaotic in structure and of dubious intellectual content. English literature of the modern period, the eighteenth and nineteenth centuries, divides itself schematically between the intelligence and the poetic imagination. Arnold highlights the defects of each type of literature by reference to the virtues of the other, but while he responds more emotionally to the poetry of the Romantics, his explicit formulations of a critical and cosmological doctrine more nearly correspond to the ideas of the neoclassicists. The qualities of the critical intelligence—regularity, uniformity, precision, and balance—closely parallel the classical aesthetic criteria that throughout his career Arnold employs as a standard against which he judges and finds wanting the amorphous and fragmentary productions of Romantic expressivism. The different aesthetic standards of neoclassicism and Romanticism reflect different ideas about the structure of the cosmos and the relations between man and nature. In his formulation of a rationalist cosmology Arnold distances himself from the Romantics and reapproaches the neoclassicists.

In the 1853 Preface Arnold sets himself firmly against the subjectivism of Romantic poetry. He denounces the assumption that representational literature should serve as "an allegory of the state of one's own mind" (I, 8); he complains that Romantic poetry concentrates on expressive detail at the expense of a "total impression," and he contrasts the effect produced by the *Iliad* and the *Oresteia* with that produced by works like *Childe Harold* and *The Excursion* (I, 7 and 4). Although he abandons the extreme antimodernism of the 1853 Preface in his later works, he does not abandon his classical aesthetic standards. In the late essay "Literature and Science" Arnold reaffirms the basic ideas in his earliest essay:

> *Fit details strictly combined, in view of a large general result nobly conceived*; that is just the beautiful symmetria prisca of the Greeks, and it is just where we English fail, where all our art fails. Striking ideas we have, and well-executed details we have; but that high symmetry which, with satisfying and delightful effect, combines them, we seldom or never have.
>
> (X, 71)

This is the aesthetic standard of neoclassicism, and Arnold's prose formulation corresponds exactly to the ideal established by Pope in *An Essay on Criticism.*

> In Wit, as Nature, what affects our Hearts
> Is not th'Exactness of peculiar Parts;
> 'Tis not a *Lip*, or *Eye*, we Beauty call,
> But the joint Force and full *Result* of *all.*
> Thus when we view some well-proportion'd Dome,
> (The *World's* just Wonder, and ev'n *thine* O *Rome*!)
> No single Parts unequally surprize;
> All comes united to th'admiring Eyes;
> No monstrous Height, or Breadth, or Length appear;
> The *Whole* at once is *Bold,* and *Regular.*
>
> (LINES 243–52)

In Arnold, as in Pope, the profession of a classical aesthetic involves also the profession of a cosmology fashioned in accordance with the qualities of reason. The relations between the mind and nature consist of the rational recognition of an objective order. For Wordsworth, in contrast, reason acts as a barrier between the imagination and the life of nature. At the end of the *Prelude,* when Wordsworth attempts to figure forth the relations between the imagination and nature, he uses the image of a moon shining through mist into a gulf of the ocean.

> The Moon hung naked in a firmament
> Of azure without cloud, and at my feet
> Rested a silent sea of hoary mist.
>
> . . . .
>
> Not distant from the shore whereon we stood,
> A fixed, abysmal, gloomy, breathing-place—
> Mounted the roar of waters, torrents, streams
> Innumerable, roaring with one voice!
>
> (BK. 14, LINES 39–42 AND 57–60)

This image, which came to Wordsworth with the impact of a revelation, represents to him "the emblem of a mind / That feeds upon infinity." The mind, like a "naked," glowing moon, lights up the shifting vapors of fancy as they mold themselves to the earth's contours and peers into the abyss of primeval being. This is the sort of Romantic sublimity Arnold himself seeks to achieve in such poems as "The Future" and "The Buried Life," but when he turns himself to the pursuit of an intellectual deliverance, he leaves this Romantic aesthetic behind him.

In *Culture and Anarchy* Arnold indicates his shift of alignment by taking from Pope's essay *Peri Bathous* one of his leading ideas. "The learned Martinus Scriblerus well says:—'The taste of the bathos is implanted by nature itself in the soul of man; till, perverted by custom or example, he is taught, or rather compelled, to relish the sublime' " (V, 147). For Pope the sublime is not emotional and inchoate but rational and clearly delineated. In his recurrences to this phrase Arnold himself sometimes substitutes "right reason" for "the sublime" (V, 156). This aesthetic standard corresponds to the ethos that Arnold feels to be most suited to the achievement of human perfection. "To be humanised is to comply with the true law of our human nature: *servare modum, finemque tenere, Naturamque sequi*" (VIII, 286). In "Amiel" Arnold concedes the poetic "charm" of the "fascination of the infinite," but he insists "on the need of limit, the feasibility of performance" (XI, 271 and 272). The poetic equivalent to these ideas is to be found not in Wordsworth but in Pope. In the *Essay on Criticism* Pope, like Wordsworth, employs the image of the ocean to reflect the relations between man and nature, but he focuses on its boundaries, not on its mysterious and unsoundable depths.

Nature to all things fix'd the Limits fit,
And wisely curb'd proud Man's pretending Wit:
As on the *Land* while *here* the Ocean gains,
In *other Parts* it leaves wide sandy Plains.
(LINES 52–55)

Pope is not seeking intimations of infinity but reassurances of order and distinct form. Pope is too much a real poet not to have sought finally a vision of universal comprehensiveness, but when he does so in the *Essay on Man,* he takes for his metaphor not the ocean but a "peaceful lake." The world order is comprehensible as a whole, and the order of things accessible to human recognition mirrors the perfected unity of being and knowing that is God.

> God loves from Whole to Parts: but human soul
> Must rise from Individual to the Whole.
> Self-love but serves the virtuous mind to wake,
> As the small pebble stirs the peaceful lake;
> The centre mov'd, a circle strait succeeds,
> Another still, and still another spreads,
> Friend, parent, neighbour, first it will embrace,
> His country next, and next all human race,
> Wide and more wide, th'o'erflowings of the mind
> Take ev'ry creature in, of ev'ry kind;
> Earth smiles around, with boundless bounty blest,
> And Heav'n beholds its image in his breast.
> (BK. 4, LINES 361–72)

Both the ahistorical universalism and the cosmological quietism of Pope's system are alien to Arnold, but Pope and Arnold nonetheless share a fundamental concern for establishing a rational and humane cosmology in which the motives of human action correspond to the basic principles of the universal order. Pope's system is not, like Arnold's, dialectical, but at bottom Arnold's cultural dualism resolves itself into the same motive that, in Pope, animates all higher human effort. "At the bottom of both the Greek and the Hebrew notion is the desire, native in man, for reason and the will of God, the feeling after the universal order,—in a word, the love of God" (V, 165). Arnold finds the quality of love more aptly expressed in Wordsworth than in Pope, but he segregates Wordsworth's power of poetic evocation from his "philosophy" (IX, 48). Arnold's poetic taste amalgamates classicism and Romanticism, but his philosophy is rationalistic, and his aesthetic doctrine is predominantly neoclassical.

Intellectual history never can, of course, simply repeat itself. Arnold's age of criticism differs from the Augustan both in the extent to which the results of negative lucidity have to be absorbed within any positive, humane doctrine, and in the kinds of theoretical material available for constructive labor. Arnold has an advantage over his neoclassical predecessors in that he can make use of German historical and cultural theories in his efforts to reconstruct or "solve" the universe. The central difference between the views of Arnold and those of the neoclassicists is that none of the eighteenth-century writers provides a theoretical rationale for historical progress. Both Dryden and Johnson possess an acute, concrete sense of the actual development of English literature, but their adherence, on the one hand, to rationalist universalism and, on the other, to the scriptural account of history precludes the development of a world-historical theory of cultural growth. Dryden holds that "mankind is ever the same, and nothing lost out of nature, though everything is alter'd."[9] Johnson is sufficiently affected by the Enlightenment faith in intellectual progress to maintain at one point in his preface to an edition of Shakespeare's plays that the human mind is "gradually gaining upon certainty," but later in the same essay he reverses this judgment. "The opinions prevalent in one age, as truths above the reach of controversy, are confuted and rejected in another, and rise again to reception in remoter times. Thus the human mind is kept in motion without progress."[10]

In Swift, Christian primitivism and militant classicism both entail a degenerative view of history. Arnold's interpretation of dogma as a corruption of the initial intent of the founders of Christianity parallels the idea represented in Swift's allegory of the three brothers in *A Tale of a Tub*, but after the 1853 Preface Arnold never again embraces a degenerative theory of culture as a whole. Whatever failures and setbacks there may be in the cultural progression, each historical phase appears to Arnold as motivated by the instinct for achieving an ultimate perfection. The right reason of Gulliver's Houyhnhnms, in contrast, serves less as a historically progressive goal of human perfection than as an inaccessible satirical norm. Pope, in this respect, does not share Swift's pessimism. The cosmological system in *An Essay on Man* has various, sometimes conflicting historical implications, but its historicist tendencies are subordinated to a static cosmological order and to a perpetual psycho-mythic reenactment of the fall from primitive innocence and the restitution to universal concord. Reason, in the guise of "wit oblique," breaks down the unreflecting unity of man with nature, but unity is then reestablished through the ra-

9. John Dryden, *The Poems of John Dryden*, ed. James Kinsley (Oxford: Oxford University Press, 1958), vol. 4, *Fables Ancient and Modern*, p. 1455.

10. Samuel Johnson, *The Yale Edition of the Works of Samuel Johnson*, ed. E. L. McAdam, Jr., with Donald and Mary Hyde (New Haven, Conn.: Yale University Press, 1958–), vol. 7, *Johnson on Shakespeare*, ed. Arthur Sherbo (1968), pp. 61 and 99.

tional recognition of the static order. In his development of a progressive cultural dialectic Arnold leaves the neoclassicists behind him, but he nonetheless takes from them important elements of his dialectical system. For the Hellenic pole of his dialectic he assimilates Augustan classicism and rationalism, and for the Hebraic pole he assimilates both their English reverence for tradition and the moral reductivism of their religion.

A Literature of Intelligence

Arnold was highly conscious of the influence of the neoclassical writers on his own thinking. His borrowings of phrase and idea begin with his poetry and continue through his latest essays. He was not, however, always equally willing to acknowledge his debts and affinities. In order to gain a just appreciation of the place that the neoclassical writers hold in Arnold's thought, I shall have to range throughout the body of his works, comparing acknowledgments with aspersions, establishing the relative status of the major authors, and examining their influence on Arnold's own writing. To keep the discussion within a manageable scope, I shall limit it to authors within the field of literature proper—to works of imagination and of literary criticism. Taking Arnold's selection from Johnson's *Lives* as a guideline, I shall consider Arnold's relation to the four neoclassical authors included in it—Dryden, Addison, Pope, and Swift—and, finally, to Johnson himself. This selection, it should be noted, does not exhaust the field of eighteenth-century English authors from whom Arnold profited and for whom he professed his esteem. His debts to the eighteenth century extend also to the historical writing of Bolingbroke and Gibbon, the moral theology of the Bishops Butler and Wilson, the aesthetic theory of Reynolds, and the political writings of Burke.[11] Arnold designates Burke as "our greatest English prose-writer" (III, 246), but his intellectual debts to Burke are chiefly in the area

11. Arnold calls Bolingbroke one of the "masters of style" in prose (III, 364), and he complains that Bolingbroke's *Remarks on English History* is "far too little read" (V, 248). He says that Gibbon's "immortal work" tells us all we may reasonably wish to know about the period it covers (V, 259). Arnold eulogizes Wilson in the preface to *Culture and Anarchy*. For Butler, see the essay in volume VIII of the *Complete Prose Works*. Trilling quotes a letter from Arnold to Ernest H. Coleridge in which Arnold acknowledges his obligation to Reynolds. *Matthew Arnold* (1939: reprint ed., Cleveland, Ohio: World Publishing, 1955), p. 159.

of political thought, and the era of Burke's most important political commentary places him outside the neoclassical period. Arnold characterizes him as the main spokesman for the era of concentration that arose in opposition to the French Revolution, and this era marks a sharp break in Arnold's scheme of English cultural history.[12]

Arnold's initial critical response to the plight of Empedocles is to adopt a neoclassical creed of aesthetic unity and thematic universality, and although he later rejects the antimodernism of the 1853 Preface, he retains the rationalist presuppositions of this creed. Arnold's cultural theory develops itself through a dialectical interplay between rationalist universalism and historical progressivism; for the rationalist pole of this dialectic the most important native influence on Arnold is the work of Dryden, Pope, Swift, and Johnson. (This influence merges with that of Lessing and Goethe, and I shall have occasion to note, in this chapter and the next, the points of congruence between these two critical lines.) For the historical pole, the neoclassicists have no highly developed theory, but their practical literary criticism is of great use to Arnold in the formulation of his own theory. Arnold's treatment of Homer, Chaucer, and Shakespeare is largely derivative from that of the neoclassicists, and his treatment of Pope largely derives from that of Johnson. Moreover, in defining the nature of English literature by means of comparing it to the French, Arnold seems simply to have taken over the categories established by Dryden. By examining in some detail Arnold's debts to these writers, we shall be able to demonstrate that for the task of situating English literature within the context of European culture, Arnold owes more to the neoclassicists than to any writers before or after them. At the same time, this detailed examination should provide us with a more specific idea of the way neoclassical aesthetics enter into the formation of Arnold's practical critical judgments.

The least significant figure that Arnold includes in the six *Lives* is Addison. Apart from the example he provides of "a moderation and delicacy" not characteristically English (III, 358), Addison exercises very little influence on Arnold's work. Addison's major effort in practical criticism, the essays on *Paradise Lost*, Arnold holds up as a prime example of inane and formulaic criticism, and he contrasts it to the authenticity of Johnson's re-

12. *Letters* 2:192 and cf. Super, VIII, 247.

sponses (VIII, 173). In aesthetic theory Addison's chief effort is his series of *Spectator* essays, "The Pleasures of the Imagination." Addison derives the three primary types of aesthetic pleasure—the great, the uncommon, and the beautiful—from the different types of sensual perception and their attendant psychological responses. To these primary pleasures, he adds the secondary pleasure of mimetic representation.[13] The sensual, psychological, and mechanical orientation of this aesthetic theory is entirely alien to the moral and rational bent of Arnold's mind. He never mentions Addison's treatise, nor, it might be added, does he ever mention Burke's similarly oriented work, *The Sublime and Beautiful.* Arnold praises Addison chiefly for his character sketches, a genre in which Arnold himself never worked (X, 175).

The main function that Addison serves in Arnold's work is that of a rhetorical decoy. Arnold's single most injudiciously disparaging treatment of the English eighteenth century appears in his 1864 essay "The Literary Influence of Academies," and in this essay he takes Addison as a focal point for his discussion of the relations between style and ideational content. Arnold's purpose in "Academies" is to place a salutary constraint on English self-satisfaction. He begins the essay with a quotation from Macaulay to the effect that the English literature of the last three hundred years is superior to all previous literature. Rather surprisingly, Arnold grants this, but he also recalls "Spinoza's maxim that the two great banes of humanity are self-conceit and the laziness coming from self-conceit" (III, 232). In pursuance of his principle that it is generally better to meditate on one's defects than on one's merits, he sets out to display the limitations of English literature. At the same time, however, he wishes to preserve the English claim to literary preeminence. His solution for this dilemma is to divide literature into two domains, the poetical and the prosaic, and to restrict English sovereignty to the poetical domain. Poetry is governed by genius and imagination, the salient characteristics of the English, and prose is governed by intelligence, the distinguishing quality of the French. In conceding to the English a superiority in the production of works of genius, Arnold can still attribute to them a comparatively poor literature of intelligence. "Our literature, in spite of the genius manifested in it, may fall short in form, method, precision, proportions, arrangement,—all of them, I have

13. See *Spectator* essays nos. 412 and 418.

said, things where intelligence proper comes in" (III, 241). The qualities of intelligence, Arnold holds, can be learned, and it is the function of the French Academy to establish and propagate them. Genius and imagination, however, cannot be learned, and they are inhibited by the authority of established standards. The English, consequently, have no literary academy, but what they gain by their greater freedom must be balanced against their failure to set a high general standard of style and performance in the median range of literary activity, in scholarship and critical prose.

As an outline of general cultural tendencies Arnold's characterization of the French and English in "Academies" is consistent with the views he propounds throughout his career. In this essay, however, he presses his points to an extreme that is both illegitimate and in conflict with his own more circumspect opinions. The conclusion he is aiming at is that the English should strive "to make up our shortcomings," and to do this he feels that they must first admit that their literature does in fact come short. To drive his point home, then, he denies to English literature any significant degree of "intelligence" at all. Just as French poets are actually writers of versified prose, so "many of the celebrated English prose-writers depend wholly for their fame upon the qualities of genius and imagination which they exhibit,—qualities which are the distinctive support of poetry" (III, 239). One of the results of this transgression of boundaries is that English prose tends to an "Asiatic" efflorescence of metaphor and an extravagance of tone. It is "full of hap-hazard, crudeness, provincialism, eccentricity, violence, blundering" (III, 241). To illustrate these qualities he chooses samples from Jeremy Taylor, a seventeenth-century writer, and from Burke, who, though the greatest English prose writer, frequently fails in moderation and urbanity.

In his essays *On Translating Homer,* Arnold had already designated fanciful excess as the characteristic defect of the English intellect, but he had remarked that "our literature of the eighteenth century, the literature of the school of Dryden, Addison, Pope, Johnson, is a long reaction against this eccentricity, this arbitrariness" (I, 140). In "Academies" Arnold passes in silence over the three greater names on this list and takes only Addison as offering a possible qualification of his thesis. Addison's style, he grants, is "Attic," not Asiatic. It is marked by lucidity, measure, and propriety. Despite his urbane manner, however, Addison's matter still betrays an English provinciality. His ideas are "trite" and "commonplace" (III, 247). This is perfectly true, and it enables Arnold to round out his presentation with a neatly balanced antithesis. "In short, where there is no centre like an academy, if you have genius and powerful ideas, you are apt not to have the best style going; if you have precision of style and not genius, you are apt not to have the best ideas going" (III, 248–49). "Academies" is one of Arnold's least creditable performances. For the sake of his rhetorical purpose he allows his "openness" to become dishonesty, and his "flexibility" to become an unscrupulous manipulation of evidence. Arnold does not himself think that the prose of Dryden, Pope, and Johnson is either commonplace in substance or florid in manner. Therefore, he does not discuss or even mention them, and yet he flatly asserts that the whole English eighteenth century is "provincial and second-rate" (III, 240). To refute this conclusion and to build a defense of English neoclassicism, one need not go outside the range of statements made by Arnold himself both before and after "Academies." An examination of Arnold's own evaluations of the writers whom, in "Academies," he does not take into account should help to correct the faulty impression that this essay creates.

Dryden is historically the most remote of the great neoclassicists, but the better qualities of Restoration literature, represented most ably by Dryden himself, find a ready response from Arnold. In his essay on Marcus Aurelius, written less than a year before "Academies," Arnold commends Jeremy Collier's translation of Aurelius by remarking that it "deserves respect for its genuine spirit and vigour, the spirit and vigour of the age of Dryden" (III, 137). Spirit and vigor are close cousins to the "energy" of poetic genius, but they may also be turned to the account of a literature of intelligence. In "The Study of Poetry" Arnold links Dryden and Pope as in similar ways "masters in letters," but he distinguishes Dryden from Pope as being "a man, on all sides, of such energetic and genial power" (IX, 178 and 179). Energy and genius, which in "Academies" Arnold identifies as peculiarly poetic qualities, he later allows, in "The Function of Criticism," to operate in criticism as well, if only that criticism be sufficiently large and original. Dryden's critical genius, like Arnold's, informs his poetic productions as well as his prose, and if it does not suffice to make specifically poetic classics of them, it nonetheless has its own sort of excellence. In the preface to *Merope* Arnold says that "my admiration for Dryden's genius is warm" (I, 64). In a later essay he declares that Dryden "had no real genius for true tragic poetry," but he still calls him a "vigorous rhetorical poet" (IX, 71). Dryden ranges even less than Pope in the region of the grand style, but Dryden's influence on Arnold, unlike that of Milton, is not limited to the moral and aesthetic impact of style. Arnold's criticism of Shakespeare is a lineal descendant of Dryden's, in both its praise and its detraction. In his criticism of Chaucer, Arnold appeals directly to the authority of Dryden, and he draws much of the substance of his commentary from him. Dryden's specific characterizations of Shakespeare and Chaucer provide Arnold with materials for his generalizations about the historical function of the Renaissance and so contribute to Arnold's formulation of those "general ideas" that serve for him as an intellectual deliverance. Dryden's influence on Arnold's criticism begins with Arnold's first published essay, the 1853 Preface, and continues throughout his career. The central idea of "Academies," and a matrix idea for all of Arnold's thought, is the distinction between an English literature of poetic imagination and a French literature of critical intelligence. This distinction appears fully formed in the critical essays of Dryden, and Arnold seems to have drawn his own formulation from Dryden himself.

Johnson identifies Dryden as "the father of English criticism, as the writer who first taught us to determine upon principles the merit of composition."[14] Like all great critics, Dryden worked within a flexible system of general propositions about the nature and function of literature. Without such principles a critic's work remains fragmentary, erratic, and impressionistic. The great virtue of Dryden's criticism, however, and what most renders it a living influence for Arnold, is its empirical character. It may be said of Dryden's criticism, as Arnold says of Johnson's commentary on Milton, "that from rhetoric and convention it is free" (VIII, 173). Dryden judges literary works primarily by their power to please and instruct, and he employs prescriptive rules only insofar as he can discover a rationale for them in these basic purposes. He recognizes, for example, that Shakespeare's drama violates the rules established by French neoclassicist critics, but he subordinates

14. Samuel Johnson, *Lives of the English Poets*, ed. George Birkbeck Hill, 3 vols. (New York: Octagon, 1967), 1:410.

these rules to his own critical perceptions and assigns to Shakespeare the first place in world literature.

> He was the man who of all Modern, and perhaps Ancient Poets, had the largest and most comprehensive soul. All the Images of Nature were still present to him, and he drew them not laboriously, but luckily: when he describes any thing, you more than see it, you feel it too. Those who accuse him to have wanted learning, give him the greater commendation: he was naturally learn'd; he needed not the spectacles of Books to read Nature; he look'd inwards, and found her there.[15]

This is the sort of "positivism" that Arnold praises in "the modern reader," and to which he contrasts the conventionalism of Addison. "Does the work which you praise, he asks, affect me with high pleasure and do me good, when I try it as fairly as I can?" (VIII, 171–72). The helpful critic, Arnold says, is one who, having asked himself this question, "has answered it in a way which agrees, in the main, with what the questioner finds to be his own honest experience in the matter, and who shows the reasons for this common experience."

What Arnold finds to be his own experience in the matter of Shakespeare is very much like what Dryden had found before him. Arnold counsels poets against taking Shakespeare as a model, but like Dryden, he recognizes Shakespeare's preeminence in the "range" and "fertility" of his thought (I, 11). Arnold censures Shakespeare for not rejecting "superfluities," that is, for not limiting his subject and pursuing "the simple and rigorous development of it." In this respect, the negative virtue of restraint, Shakespeare falls beneath the ancients. In his chief works he is like them in that he "has their important action and their large and broad manner," but "he has not their purity of method" (I, 11–12). Dryden, too, complains of Shakespeare's impurity and unevenness, but like Arnold, he sees a greatness of conception that compensates for the defects of method.

> He is many times flat, insipid; his Comick wit degenerating into clenches, his serious swelling into Bombast. But he is alwayes great, when some great occasion is presented to him: no man can say he

15. John Dryden, *The Works of John Dryden*, ed. H. T. Swedenberg (Berkeley and Los Angeles: University of California Press, 1956–), vol. 17, *Prose 1668–1691: An Essay of Dramatick Poesie and Shorter Works*, ed. Samuel Holt Monk (1971), p. 55.

> ever had a fit subject for his wit, and did not then raise himself as high above the rest of the poets.
>
> *Quantum lenta solent, inter viburna cupressi.*[16]

Johnson holds up Dryden's account of Shakespeare as "a perpetual model of encomiastick criticism," and we may take it as evidence for the seminal power of Dryden's critical insight that Johnson and Pope, though working along different lines of interpretation, both take their inspiration from Dryden.[17] Johnson emphasizes the justness of Shakespeare's "representations of general nature," that is, the universal significance of his characters and the coherence of his dramatic design.[18] Pope emphasizes the felicity of Shakespeare's imaginative intuition. In the 1853 Preface Arnold both draws directly from Dryden himself and also recombines the divergent critical lines of Pope and Johnson.

The dominant note of Arnold's criticism of Shakespeare in the 1853 Preface is the Johnsonian emphasis on general nature. There are three things, Arnold says, that the modern poet can learn from the ancients:

> the all-importance of the choice of a subject; the necessity of accurate construction; and the subordinate character of expression. He will learn from them how unspeakably superior is the effect of the one moral impression left by a great action treated as a whole, to the effect produced by the most striking single thought or by the happiest image.
>
> (I, 12)

The "choice of a subject" that Arnold recommends is such as will "most powerfully appeal to. . . . the elementary part of our nature, to our passions" (I, 4). Such passions should have in them "nothing local and casual" (I, 5). It is not the business of the dramatic poet to solicit attention by any appeal "to all our transient feelings and interests" (I, 4). These neoclassical dicta appear to be directly inspired by Johnson's encomium on Shakespeare:

> His characters are not modified by the customs of particular places . . . by the peculiarities of studies or professions . . . or by the accidents of transient fashions or temporary opinions: they are the genuine

16. Ibid., pp. 55–56.
17. Johnson, *Lives*, 1:412.
18. Johnson, *Yale Edition of the Works of Samuel Johnson*, vol. 7, *Johnson on Shakespeare*, p. 61.

progeny of common humanity, such as the world will always supply, and observation will always find. His persons act and speak by the influence of those general passions and principles by which all minds are agitated, and the whole system of life is continued in motion.[19]

Arnold's second and third criteria, accurate construction and the subordinate character of expression, reflect a neoclassical hierarchy of compositional values such as that established by Dryden in the preface to his *Fables Ancient and Modern.*

Now, the Words are the Colouring of the Work, which in the Order of Nature is last to be consider'd. The Design, the Disposition, the Manners, and the Thoughts, are all before it: Where any of those are wanting or imperfect, so much wants or is imperfect in the Imitation of Humane Life; which is the very Definition of a Poem.[20]

Dryden grants that the "Colours" of language "are the first Beauties that arise, and strike the Sight," but in the proper order of artistic values "Expression" takes last place. Arnold, polemicizing against Romantic subjectivism and the Romantic emphasis on richness of expression at the expense of a unified design, insists that dramatic poetry is foremost "an art which imitates actions," and he complains that "we have poems which seem to exist merely for the sake of single lines and passages" (I, 8 and 7). He places a large part of the blame for this fault on the influence of Shakespeare's language. In Shakespeare's own works, however, the gift of "happy, abundant, and ingenious expression" is subordinated to the power of design. His chief excellence as a poet is his "*Architectonicè* in the highest sense; that power of execution, which creates, forms, and constitutes" (I, 9). Arnold attributes the principle of architectonics to Goethe, not Dryden, but the two influences appear to have joined forces in the formulation of Arnold's own classicist doctrine. In applying to Shakespeare the principle of the subordinate character of expression, Arnold again displays a debt to Dryden by way of Johnson's preface to his edition of Shakespeare's plays. Johnson comments on the abundance of "practical axioms and domestick wisdom" to be found in Shakespeare but then cautions against seeking the secret of Shakespeare's excellence in the details of his work:

19. Ibid., p. 62.
20. Dryden, *Poems of John Dryden,* vol. 4, pp. 1448–49.

> Yet his real power is not shewn in the splendour of particular passages, but by the progress of his fable, and the tenour of his dialogue; and he that tries to recommend him by select quotations, will succeed like the pedant in Hierocles, who, when he offered his house to sale, carried a brick in his pocket as a specimen.[21]

Dryden, like Johnson, praises Shakespeare's mimetic faculty, but in his brief encomium he places less emphasis on "the accuracy of construction" than on the felicity of Shakespeare's native intuition. Shakespeare drew his images "not laboriously, but luckily." He reflected nature, but "he look'd inwards, and found her there." It is this intuitive aspect of Shakespeare's genius that most catches the attention of Pope, and it is from Pope that Arnold seems to have borrowed this element of his own characterization of Shakespeare. In the preface to his edition of Shakespeare's plays, Pope remarks that "by a talent very peculiar, something between Penetration and Felicity, he hits upon that particular point on which the bent of each argument turns, or the force of each motive depends."[22] Arnold notes Shakespeare's "strong conception of his subject" and "the genuine way in which he is penetrated with it" (I, 11). *Penetration,* in the quotation from Pope, is a noun representing an active faculty, whereas *penetrated,* in Arnold's statement, is a passive verb. Pope's conception of Shakespeare's power is, however, similar to Arnold's. Pope remarks that "the poetry of *Shakespear* was Inspiration indeed: he is not so much an Imitator, as an Instrument, of Nature; and 'tis not so just to say that he speaks from her, as that she speaks thro' him."[23]

Pope's interest in Shakespeare's "inspiration" and his passive receptivity lend a rather Romantic cast to his commentary, and Arnold apparently recognizes this, for he transfers this part of Pope's Shakespeare criticism to his own commentary on the Romantic poets proper. "In Wordsworth's case," Arnold says, "the accident, for so it may almost be called, of inspiration, is of peculiar importance. . . . It might seem that Nature not only gave him the matter for his poem, but wrote his poem for him" (IX, 51–52). The same quality of passive inspiration, the poet as instrument,

21. Johnson, *Yale Edition of the Works of Samuel Johnson,* vol. 7, *Johnson on Shakespeare,* p. 62.

22. Alexander Pope, *Poetry and Prose of Alexander Pope,* ed. Aubrey Williams (Boston: Houghton Mifflin, 1969), p. 461.

23. Ibid., p. 460.

distinguishes Byron. "When he warms to his work, when he is inspired, Nature herself seems to take the pen from him as she took it from Wordsworth, and to write for him as she wrote for Wordsworth, though in a different fashion, with her own penetrating simplicity" (IX, 235). We may judge of the sweep and vitality of Dryden's critical intelligence from the fact that it thus extends, by way of Pope and Arnold, to the Romantic poets. His literary sensibility does not limit itself to the taste of a single age or the dogma of a single school.

In his criticism of Shakespeare, Arnold derives a substantial part of his perceptions and ideas from his predecessors. He is not, however, merely copying; he is building on a tradition. Whereas Dryden simply remarks, as a given fact, that Shakespeare has provided us with "variety and greatness of characters," Arnold sets this fact within a framework of cultural history.[24]

> Shakspeare's task was to set forth the spectacle of the world when man's spirit re-awoke to the possession of the world at the Renaissance. The spectacle of human life, left to bear its own significance and tell its own story, but shown in all its fulness, variety, and power, is at that moment the great matter.
>
> (III, 381)

Arnold's need to create a new spiritual basis for the modern world requires that his practical criticism adapt itself at all points to the construction of a historical system. Dryden does not attempt cultural criticism on this scale, but he does possess a lucid historical imagination; in combination with his power of seizing at once the essential character of an author, this imagination gives his specific literary judgments the stamp of definitive authority. In his evaluation of Chaucer, Arnold adopts Dryden's opinions, but as in his criticism of Shakespeare, he situates these opinions within a general scheme of cultural history. Contrasting Chaucer with the Romance poets, Arnold identifies him as one of the first modern poets, a poet who has gained a just appreciation of the natural life of man.

> He has gained the power to survey the world from a central, a truly human point of view. We have only to call to mind the Prologue to *The Canterbury Tales*. The right comment upon it is Dryden's: "It

24. Dryden, *Works of John Dryden*, vol. 17, *Essay of Dramatick Poesie*, p. 53.

is sufficient to say, according to the proverb, that *here is God's plenty.*" And again: "He is a perpetual fountain of good sense."

(IX, 174)

Chaucer's purpose is like that of Shakespeare, who had "to exhibit all the kingdoms of human life and the glory of them" (III, 381). The spiritual basis of Chaucer's world is still Christian, and Chaucer does not have to provide a new basis, but by concentrating his attention on the strictly human world, Chaucer, like Shakespeare, provides materials that will contribute to the creation of a new basis. Dryden does not himself theorize about the transition to a post-Christian, neopagan world view, but he grasps the essential character of Chaucer's achievement and so contributes critical materials for Arnold's own theory. Chaucer, Dryden tells us, "follow'd Nature every where; but was never so bold to go beyond her."[25] He was learned in the sciences of his time, but the best part of his learning, like that of Shakespeare, came to him from his humane intuition. "He must have been a Man of a most wonderful comprehensive Nature, because, as it has been truly observ'd of him, he has taken into the Compass of his *Canterbury Tales* the various Manners and Humours (as we now call them) of the whole *English* Nation, in his Age."[26] Chaucer, like Shakespeare, left this spectacle to tell its own story, and the fact that he did so becomes a part of the "story" Arnold tells about the development of modern culture.

Dryden conveys, perhaps more than any other English critic, the vital sense of historical actuality, the sense of origin and development. Johnson, too, has this power, but Johnson, as Arnold says, was the man of an age of prose. Dryden stood on the threshold of this age, and although he turned his own efforts resolutely to its furtherance, he was still close enough to the Elizabethan age of poetry to respond quickly and naturally to the lyric note of poetry. Johnson's fine moral sensitivity and powerful judgment go a long way toward compensating for his relative insensitivity to lyrical qualities. Moreover, his analyses of the logic of poetic imagery are more technically sophisticated than those of Dryden. Nonetheless, in the issue of poetic origins Dryden's critical intuition proves itself truer than that of Johnson. Chaucer's liberty with the final *e* was unknown to Dryden, and he believed, in common with his

25. Dryden, *Poems of John Dryden*, vol. 4, p. 1452.
26. Ibid., p. 1455.

contemporaries, that Chaucer's verse was sometimes unmetrical. He nonetheless sees beyond this supposed technical fault and designates Chaucer as "the Father of *English* Poetry."[27] Johnson disputes this claim on technical grounds, but Arnold vindicates Dryden's judgment.

> Johnson misses the point entirely when he finds fault with Dryden for ascribing to Chaucer the first refinement of our numbers and says that Gower also can show smooth numbers and easy rhymes. The refinement of our numbers means something far more than this. A nation may have versifiers with smooth numbers and easy rhymes, and yet may have no real poetry at all. Chaucer is the father of our splendid English poetry; he is our "well of English undefiled," because by the lovely charm of his diction, the lovely charm of his movement, he makes an epoch and founds a tradition.
>
> (IX, 174–75)

Arnold complains that Dryden himself did not sufficiently praise Chaucer's "exquisite manner and movement" (IX, 178), but Arnold's own praise of Chaucer nonetheless ranges itself in tone and substance under the authority of Dryden.

Dryden's commentary on Chaucer restricts itself to his language and his content. In commenting also on the aesthetic limitations of Chaucer's "manner," Arnold departs from Dryden and at the same time attempts to gain a critical perspective on Dryden's own poetic limitations. Arnold asserts that because Chaucer lacks the "accent" of "high seriousness" he is "not one of the great classics" (IX, 176). Arnold himself refuses to define high seriousness, but his mystification on this point seems unnecessary. The "touchstone" passages he selects from Homer, Dante, Shakespeare, and Milton make it clear that high seriousness is basically the same thing as "the grand style." It may be defined as an intensity of tone—whether it be heroic, religious, tragic, or elegiac—expressed with simplicity and purity of diction and with rhythmic felicity. Chaucer fails of emotional intensity, and Dryden and Pope fall short both in passionate grandeur and in simplicity of manner. Many critics have felt that there is something wrong with Arnold's criterion for high seriousness, particularly in its application to Chaucer. Regarded on its own terms, however, Arnold's denial of this quality to Chaucer seems just. If exception is to be taken, it seems more

27. Ibid., p. 1452.

fruitful to consider the issue as a problem of genre. Arnold's criterion, in effect, excludes comedy or satire of any type from the ranks of the highest classical literature. In the 1853 Preface Arnold devalues comedy on the basis that it uses contemporary materials that are "too much mixed up" with what is "accidental and passing" ever to be able to achieve classic grandeur (I, 7). In "The Modern Element," attempting to make a provision for Aristophanes, he declares that "there is a comic side from which to regard humanity as well as a tragic one" (I, 29), but Arnold himself never much cared for the view offered from this "side" of things. In his 1879 essay "The French Play in London" he shifts the ground of his attack on comedy from its contemporary content to its generic mode. Even while according to Molière the status of a classic writer of comedy, he denies that comedy can ever attain to the significance of tragedy. "Tragedy breasts the pressure of life. Comedy eludes it, half liberates itself from it by irony. But the tragedian, if he has the sterner labour, has also the higher prize" (IX, 72). Arnold's generic devaluation of comic irony, while it helps to explain the secondary rank he assigns to both Chaucer and the neoclassical poets, also gives evidence of the disjunction between his absolute generic standards and his own literary affinities, for Arnold is himself one of the great ironists of English prose. One might note, by the way, that Arnold's severely neoclassical generic categories, in which the representation of contemporary life is confined to the second rank of literature, "to the domain of the comic poet, and of the lighter kinds of poetry" (I, 7), help to account not only for his denial of classical status to Chaucer but also for his defective appreciation of the novel.

In his ranking of Chaucer, Arnold diverges from Dryden, but he takes from Dryden the full measure of his positive evaluation, and he uses this evaluation as the standard by which he judges the verse of Dryden and Pope. Arnold maintains that Chaucer, though not among the greatest of poets, is a true poet. The "lovely charm" of his diction and the musical fluidity of his verse give voice to a sensibility that "has largeness, freedom, shrewdness, benignity" (IX, 177). Chaucer's poetry, like that of Shakespeare and Wordsworth, is a celebration of "life." By testing neoclassical verse against this touchstone quality, Arnold concludes in "The Study of Poetry" that the eighteenth century had, outside of Gray, no real poetry at all. It is, of course, possible to argue that Arnold is wrong, that Dryden and Pope do possess these poetic qualities of shrewdness and benignity; or, even if we grant that the neoclassicists neither display any natural magic nor effectively evoke simple and primary affections and duties, it is still possible to plead for an expansion of the definition of "poetry" so as to include the different merits that they do possess. If, however, we again take Arnold on his own terms, the important thing to notice is that in denying specifically poetic qualities to neoclassical verse, Arnold gives back with one hand what, in "Academies," he had taken with the other. "Form, method, precision, proportions, arrangement"— the qualities by which, in "Academies," Arnold had characterized the French literature of intelligence, are the same qualities by which, in "The Study of Poetry," he characterizes the verse of Dryden and Pope.

> The men of letters, whose destiny it may be to bring their nation to the attainment of a fit prose, must of necessity, whether they work in prose or in verse, give a predominating, an almost exclusive attention to the qualities of regularity, uniformity, precision, balance. But an almost exclusive attention to these qualities involves some repression and silencing of poetry.
>
> (IX, 180)

The "intelligence" displayed in the formal qualities of the verse of Dryden and Pope extends to its ideational content as well. Arnold denies that "the application of ideas to life in the verse of these two men . . . is a powerful *poetic* application," but he grants that it is, taken as prose, "often powerful" (IX, 180).

Arnold's failure, in "Academies," to take account of Dryden is the more egregious in that the distinction he makes there between an English literature of genius and imagination and a French literature of critical intelligence is probably one that he originally borrowed from Dryden. The argument over the comparative merits of French and English literature is one of the leading themes of Dryden's introduction to his translation of the *Aeneid*, a critical work that, in his preface to Johnson's *Lives*, Arnold recommends be read in conjunction with Dryden's biography. Dryden acknowledges his debts to French critics and remarks that "impartially speaking, the *French* are as much better Criticks than the *English*, as they are worse Poets."[28] Dryden suggests, though less categorical-

28. Dryden, *Poems of John Dryden*, vol. 3, p. 1019.

ly than Arnold, that this difference originates in the different intellectual faculties of the two nations. In *An Essay of Dramatick Poesie* Dryden remarks that the plays of Fletcher and Shakespeare, while less regular than the French, display "a more masculine fancy and greater spirit."[29] For Dryden, as for Arnold, this is a matter for patriotic pride. "Let the *French* and *Italians* value themselves on their Regularity: Strength and Elevation are our Standard. I said before, and I repeat it, that the affected purity of the French, has unsinew'd their Heroick Verse."[30] Taken absolutely, the invidious comparison favors the side of the English, but Dryden, like Arnold, believes that it is possible for the English to assimilate the achievements of the French critical intelligence and that to do so would improve not only their criticism but their poetry as well.

> Heroick Poetry is not of the growth of *France*, as it might be of *England*, if it were Cultivated. *Spencer* wanted only to have read the Rules of *Bossu*: for no Man was ever Born with a greater Genius, or had more Knowledge to support it. But the performance of the *French* is not equal to their Skill; and hitherto we have wanted Skill to perform better.[31]

By using the organic metaphor of "growth," Dryden implies what Arnold will explicitly assert: "skill" can be learned, genius is innate. English literature might be capable of trimming and training the exuberance of its fancy, but it is not equally possible for the French to graft imaginative energy onto their prosaic cultivations.

Dryden, even as he ranked the former English literature of genius and imagination above the French literature of precision and regularity, initiated the English age of prose. The finished poet of this age, its "high priest," is Pope. Of all the neoclassical poets Pope is to be the most credited for establishing the qualities of intelligence, that is, precision and propriety, as resources for English verse. Arnold owes more to Pope than he is ever quite willing to concede. His own poetic rhetoric, both in its technique and in its doctrinal assumptions, betrays the influence of Pope, and in his critical doctrines both the aesthetic of a unified design and the rationalist cosmology correspond to theoretical formulations in the didactic verse of Pope. As a writer of verse Pope ranks

29. Dryden, *Works of John Dryden,* vol. 17, *Essay of Dramatick Poesie,* p. 54.
30. Dryden, *Poems of John Dryden,* vol. 3, p. 1055.
31. Ibid., p. 1049.

higher in Arnold's estimation than as a writer of prose. Nonetheless, the quick penetration that distinguishes his poetry operates also in his critical prose, and Arnold feels his influence in this region as well. Arnold takes over insights and phrases from Pope's commentary on Shakespeare, and in his criticism of Homer, Arnold builds on the foundations laid by Pope in the preface to his translation of the *Iliad*. Arnold uses the classical poet as a touchstone by which he judges the neoclassical, but the qualities that Arnold designates as most characteristic of Homer are the same as those Pope had distinguished in his preface. In comparing the different manners of Homer and Pope, Arnold takes his lead from Johnson, who has, in turn, taken his lead on Homer from Pope's preface.

Arnold's judgments on the merits of Pope's poetry vary at different points in his career. He is most appreciative during his first phase, when he is least removed from writing poetry himself and can still feel the benefit of Pope's influence on his own work. He is least appreciative of Pope during his third phase, after he has stopped writing serious poetry and has begun to regard the Romantics as a surrogate for the traditional religion he has not succeeded in preserving. Even during this phase, however, the fluctuating predominance of the Hellenic and Hebraic components of Arnold's mind allow for a divided evaluation of Pope's achievement. Insofar as the poetry of Pope is to be taken as antithetical to that of the Romantics, the Hebraic Arnold disparages his work with a narrow intensity of religious fervor. Insofar, however, as Pope is taken to be an English representative of the modern spirit, a classic of our prose, and an advocate of reason and the will of God, the Hellenic Arnold grants to him both an intrinsic excellence and a useful historical function.

The poetry of Pope figures in Arnold's historical scheme as the English equivalent to the best verse of French neoclassicism, and as a native source it has an impact on Arnold himself more direct than that of Corneille, Racine, and Molière. In "Academies," however, the nature of Pope's achievement as a writer of classical prose in verse is obscured by a distorted historical analogy. As evidence for his claim that intelligence can be learned and propagated while genius cannot, Arnold sets up a comparison between the literature of Elizabethan England and that of France under Louis XIV. The "sequel" to the work of Corneille and Racine,

Arnold says, was the French Enlightenment. The correspondent sequel to the work of Shakespeare and Milton is English neoclassicism (III, 240). By pursuing their steady course of intelligence, the French produced a critical revolution. The English literature of genius, however, degenerated into provinciality. Arnold omits any mention of the greater English neoclassicists not only because it would confute his conclusion but also because it would wreck his whole comparative structure. Both before and after "Academies" Arnold regularly associates, for good and ill, the poetry of Pope with the poetry of seventeenth-century France. In "Maurice de Guérin," when Arnold says that Pope is at a disadvantage with Addison because of his poetic "vehicle," he also says that Racine is similarly at a disadvantage with Bossuet. The alexandrine and the pentameter couplet at once restrain the freedom of prose composition and enforce a rhetorical mode of poetic composition. In "Joubert" Arnold reinforces the analogy between Pope and the French neoclassicists. He quotes Joubert's remark that "Boileau is a powerful poet, but only in the world of half poetry" and adds, "How true is that of Pope also!" (III, 204–205). In these comments we see Arnold's criticism of Augustan poetry shifting its ground from the "age" to the poetry itself, but we also see an alignment of the English poetry of intelligence with the masters of French verse. Arnold never ceases to judge French tragic poetry as essentially unpoetic, but he concedes its historical value in sharpening and refining the understanding of its readers, and what he accords to the French he accords to Pope also. "Pope was in a similar way, though not at all in the same degree, a forming and civilising influence to our grandfathers, and limited their literary taste while he stimulated and formed it" (IX, 74–75). The tendency of Pope's poetic influence is the same as that of Racine, but Pope's influence is lesser in degree, both because it runs counter to the dominant qualities of the English mind, in Arnold's scheme, and because "we English had Shakespeare waiting to open our eyes, whensoever a favourable moment came, to the insufficiencies of Pope. But the French had no Shakespeare to open their eyes to the insufficiencies of Corneille and Racine" (IX, 75).

Dryden had spoken, as an empirical observer, of the tendencies of French and English literature up to his own time. Arnold, by adopting Dryden's observations without adequate modification for the intervening eighteenth century and by too rigidly generalizing

Dryden's categories, loses for them a good deal of their credibility. It seems hardly plausible that poets like Dryden and Pope, who dominated for so long the literature of their nation, should be so entirely alien to the congenital sensibility of that nation. English literature as a whole was not so devoid of intelligence as Arnold maintains in "Academies," nor was the English literature of intelligence so devoid of poetic imagination as he later maintains. The English neoclassicists did not go so far as the French in establishing an exclusively rhetorical and prosaic literature, nor did they repudiate their own poetic heritage. Whereas Voltaire scoffed at the reputation accorded to Shakespeare in England, Dryden, Johnson, and Pope wrote critical appreciations of his work, and Pope and Johnson both published editions of his plays. The coming of a "favourable moment" for a revaluation of the neoclassicists, insofar as it depends on an appreciation of Shakespeare's poetry, owes much to the critical efforts of the neoclassicists themselves.

Arnold firmly, and at times excessively, points out the limitations of rhetorical poetry, but his own poetry has a large obligation to the achievements of the neoclassical writers. In a letter of 1869 Arnold professes a hope that he will eventually achieve as much recognition for his poetry as Tennyson and Browning have already received for theirs. He recognizes that he might be said to have "less poetical sentiment than Tennyson, and less intellectual vigour and abundance than Browning."[32] He remains confident, however, "because I have perhaps more of a fusion of the two than either of them, and have more regularly applied that fusion to the main line of modern development." Arnold's lyric verse is less doctrinally settled and more introspective than the poetry of Pope, but Arnold seldom attains to a Romantic spontaneity of passionate expression or even to the state of passion recollected in tranquillity. He has a few very fine lyric poems and passages, but he is often awkwardly self-conscious, and his efforts to render his verse a vessel for the spontaneous overflow of powerful feelings seldom carry him farther than the embarrassingly frequent reiteration of the expletive "Ah!" If Arnold was nonetheless justified in his hopes, if his poetry on the whole achieves a substantial and lasting worth, this is in good part due to his assimilation of the vigorous intelligence that prevails in neoclassical poetry.[33]

32. *Letters* 2:10.

33. A. Dwight Culler remarks that "the kind of poetry which he tried to

It is during the first phase of his career, while he is still a practicing poet, that Arnold remains most conscious of the poetic merit of Pope's verse. Arnold's most sensitive and generous appreciation of neoclassical poetry, especially that of Pope, appears in his essays *On Translating Homer*, where he says that Pope "had a quick and darting spirit, as he had, also, real nobleness" (I, 142). Arnold quotes an important passage from Pope's translation of the *Iliad*, and although he concurs with Bentley that "you must not call it Homer," he gives high praise to the intrinsic merits of the poetry itself. "Nothing could better exhibit Pope's prodigious talent; and nothing, too, could be better in its own way" (I, 109). Pope departs from Homer in that it is impossible for him to speak plainly and directly. "One feels that Homer's thought has passed through a literary and rhetorical crucible, and come out highly intellectualised; come out in a form which strongly impresses us, indeed, but which no longer impresses us in the same way as when it was uttered by Homer." Locked into the syntactic interplay of the couplet, Pope's style is least suitable for "plain narrative" and for description; since these form the bulk of an epic, Pope's style is not very well adapted to epic verse. However, even restricted as he is by the necessity of rhetoric, Pope is capable of a certain genuine magnificence.

> A literary and intellectualised language is, however, in its own way well suited to grand matters; and Pope, with a language of this kind and his own admirable talent, comes off well enough as long as he has passion, or oratory, or a great crisis to deal with. Even here, as I have been pointing out, he does not render Homer; but he and his style are in themselves strong.
>
> (I, 109)

Arnold's recognition of Pope's strength proceeds from his own experience as a poet; if Arnold's evocation of nature owes something to Wordsworth, the reflective and didactic elements of his poetry owe as much to Pope. For example, in his description of Goethe in the first "Obermann" elegy to Senancour, Arnold, as he often does, employs Pope's method of balanced antithesis. At the

---

produce was that of the imaginative reason, and for this purpose it was necessary to combine with the imagination, which alone was cultivated by the Romantic poets, the opposing faculty of the senses and understanding." *Imaginative Reason: The Poetry of Matthew Arnold* (New Haven, Conn.: Yale University Press, 1966), p. 42.

same time he expresses an attitude toward the proper relations between man and nature that is very similar to the attitude of Pope.

For he pursued a lonely road,
His eyes on Nature's plan;
Neither made man too much a God,
Nor God too much a man.

Pope opens *An Essay on Man* by inviting Bolingbroke to "Expatiate free o'er all this scene of Man; / A mighty maze! but not without a plan." Pope accomplishes his purpose of vindicating the ways of God to man by subordinating human pains and passions to the rational recognition of the cosmic order. For Pope this order entails the assumption of a correspondence between the moral forces in man and the principles by which the universal fabric is maintained. In Arnold's cultural theory this basic humanistic assumption is transmuted into a belief in the correspondence between the constitution of the individual mind and the shape of cultural history, but the moral nature of man is still, as it is for Pope, accessible to rational intuition. In the 1867 poem "Pis-Aller" Arnold, again echoing Pope, takes exception to the belief that man's inner nature is, without the aid of Biblical revelation, an impenetrable mystery.

Nay, look closer into man!
Tell me, can you find indeed
Nothing sure, no moral plan
Clear prescribed, without your creed?

During the first phase of his critical career Arnold, even while disparaging Pope's poetic "vehicle," concedes to him a "genius for didactic poetry" (III, 15). In his third phase, when he is affected with a partisan zeal for the Romantics, he still gives recognition to "Pope's brilliant gift for versification"; he argues, however, that this gift is "exercised within the limits of a form inadequate for true philosophic poetry, and by its very presence excluding it" (IX, 76). In his most extreme declaration against all neoclassical poetry Arnold says that "it was intellectual, argumentative, ingenious; not seeing things in their truth and beauty, not interpretative" ("Thomas Gray," IX, 200). At this point Arnold emphatically overstates his case, and at the same time he exposes the deepest conflict in his critical vision. His distinction implicitly reduces all "interpretation" to a Romantic evocation of sentiment and natural beauty and thus denies the power of "interpretation" to all prose literature, to criticism and to philosophy. This is, in fact, a recurrent tendency throughout Arnold's third phase. His elevation of poetry as a surrogate for religion tinges his treatment of Romantic poetry with something of the fanatical exclusiveness of his Hebraism. In championing Wordsworth's poetry, he sharply asserts that "poetry is the reality, philosophy the illusion" (IX, 48). The purpose of this invidious antithesis is to preserve Wordsworth from the feebleness of his own philosophical pretensions. "But in Wordsworth's case, at any rate, we cannot do him justice until we dismiss his formal philosophy."

Arnold never explicitly abandons his Hellenic ideal of poetry as "a complete magister vitae," the most comprehensive medium of human expression, but he can find no modern poetry that completely answers to this ideal. Goethe, the only poet who even approaches to it, is a greater critic than a poet, and Goethe's "intellectual power," Arnold says, "hurt his poetical operations by its immense predominance."[34] In the first elegy to Senancour, Arnold associates the quality of Goethe's poetic vision with the rationalist cosmology of Pope, but in his third phase, as he defends the English Romantics, Arnold is led to harden the lines of division between intelligence and imagination. By segregating philosophy from poetry and reducing modern English poetry to what he himself believes to be the intellectually impoverished range of Romantic passion, Arnold condemns not only neoclassical verse but, implicitly, the great bulk of his own verse as well; like the verse of Dryden, Pope, and Johnson, it is analytic, homiletic, and didactic.[35]

If Arnold finds no modern English poetry that satisfies his classical ideal, his formulation of this ideal is nonetheless heavily de-

34. *Letters* 1:147 (December 17, 1860). T. S. Eliot notes that Arnold's own poetry is of a "critical" character. *The Use of Poetry and the Use of Criticism* (Cambridge, Mass.: Harvard University Press, 1933), p. 103.

35. From a sympathetic but decidedly Romantic perspective, F. L. Lucas goes so far as to declare that Arnold is "our last great neo-classic." "Matthew Arnold," in *Victorian Literature: Modern Essays in Criticism*, ed. Austin Wright (New York: Oxford University Press, 1961), p. 61. A more carefully qualified appraisal is given by David DeLaura, who holds that, although Arnold lacks "wit" and has not "the Augustan snap of antithesis. . . . Still, in his most austere mood there are detectable elements of neoclassical neatness and precision, as in Empedocles' 'sermon' in Act I." *Matthew Arnold: A Collection of Critical Essays* (Englewood Cliffs, N.J.: Prentice-Hall, 1973), p. 7.

pendent on the critical insights of the English neoclassicists. Arnold's commentary on the *Iliad* appears to derive directly from those of Pope and Johnson, and Arnold identifies the *Iliad* as "the chief work of the Greek world; that work which, whatever the other works of classical antiquity have to give us, gives it more abundantly than they all" (I, 139–40). Pope distinguishes the chief features of Homer's poetry, and Johnson adopts these distinctions in his comparison of Homer and Pope. Arnold assimilates their critical perceptions and uses them in his concept of "the grand style." Arnold's essays on Homer are framed as advice to translators. He singles out four qualities that the translator must at all events seek to imitate:

> that he is eminently rapid; that he is eminently plain and direct, both in the evolution of his thought and in the expression of it, that is, both in his syntax and in his words; that he is eminently plain and direct in the substance of his thought, that is, in his matter and ideas; and, finally that he is eminently noble.
>
> (I, 102)

Pope also emphasizes Homer's "rapidity"; he praises his "pure and noble Simplicity," and he declares that it is "a great Secret in Writing to know when to be plain, and when poetical and figurative, and it is what *Homer* will teach us if we will but follow modestly in his Footsteps."[36] As a poet Pope did not, perhaps, follow Homer modestly enough, but as a critic he, like Arnold, recognizes that the chief difficulty in the translation of Homer is the problem of tone. Pope delineates the two extremes of tonal failure that will provide the framework for Arnold's own discussion:

> Nothing that belongs to *Homer* seems to have been more commonly mistaken than the just Pitch of his Style: Some of his Translators having swell'd into Fustian in a proud Confidence of the *Sublime*; others sunk into Flatness, in a cold and timorous Notion of *Simplicity*. . . . There is a *graceful* and *dignify'd* Simplicity, as well as a *bald* and *sordid* one, which differ as much from each other as the Air of a *plain* Man from that of a *Sloven*.[37]

Arnold expends the greatest part of his critical wit in *On Translating Homer* on Professor F. W. Newman, the latest representa-

36. Alexander Pope, *The Poems of Alexander Pope*, ed. John Butt (London: Methuen, 1961–69), vol. 7, *The Iliad of Homer: Books I–IX*, ed. Maynard Mack (1967), p. 18.
37. Ibid.

tive of the "sloven" school of translators. Arnold criticizes Pope's excess of "ornament," but he does not accuse him of being either bombastic or ignoble.

Arnold finds much to fault in Pope's translation of the *Iliad,* and Johnson accords to it an almost unlimited admiration, but the terms that Arnold employs for his criticism of Pope he derives from Johnson's defense of him. The main thrust of Arnold's critique is that Pope's style lacks "the plainness and directness of Homer's style" and that Pope deviates from "the simplicity with which Homer's thought is evolved and expressed" (I, 111). Johnson had conceded that "Pope's version of Homer is not Homerical; that it exhibits no resemblance of the original and characteristik manner of the Father of Poetry, as it wants his awful simplicity, his artless grandeur, his unaffected majesty."[38] Johnson nonetheless defends Pope's deviations from his original on the basis of historical necessity. "Pope wrote for his own age and his own nation: he knew that it was necessary to colour the images and point the sentiments of his author; he therefore made him graceful, but lost him some of his sublimity." Arnold picks up Johnson's terms and turns them back against Pope. He takes it as a fault that Pope "aims at turning Homer's sentiments pointedly and rhetorically; at investing Homer's description with ornament and dignity," and he holds up Pope as an example of the discrepancy that must arise between Homer and any translation marked by "an artificial evolution of thought and a literary cast of style." Johnson regards the development of an "artificial diction" as an inevitable phase of literary evolution that is not necessarily to be regretted. Accepting this necessity, Johnson concentrates on translation as an adaptation to the taste of the contemporary age. Arnold, in contrast, concentrates on translation as a faithful rendering of the style and manner of the original. The two critics' evaluations of Pope's translation differ accordingly, but the analytical content of the two critiques is much the same. Arnold would almost certainly disagree with Johnson's claim that Pope's *Iliad* is "the noblest version of poetry which the world has ever seen," but the sort of heroic nobility that Pope and Johnson have found in Homer himself nonetheless forms a cornerstone of Arnold's classicism.[39]

In the light of his early comments on Dryden and Pope and the

38. Johnson, *Lives*, 3:238.
39. Ibid., p. 119.

amount of material he borrows from their works, Arnold's failure to take account of them in "Academies" seems, to put it mildly, less than candid. In the omission of Swift, however, Arnold does not appear to have been willfully misrepresenting his views at this time. It seems that Arnold, in the earlier part of his career, did not recognize the importance of Swift in English literature. In the passage from *On Translating Homer* where Arnold speaks of the eighteenth century as a "long reaction" against eccentricity, he does not list Swift among the members of the eighteenth-century "school." Swift does not, in fact, figure in Arnold's work until 1866, when Arnold records in his *Note-Books* that he read *A Tale of a Tub* and copies out a phrase from *The Battle of the Books*: "Furnishing mankind with the two noblest of things, which are sweetness and light."[40] In *Culture and Anarchy* Arnold takes "sweetness and light" (i.e., "beauty and intelligence") as a chapter title; he complains justly enough that Swift possessed too little sweetness, but he denies him nothing of light (V, 99). Having little sense of beauty and a great deal of "intelligence," Swift figures as antithetical to Byron, who, though a great poet, "has no light" (IX, 234). In the essay on Byron, Arnold indicates that it is only light or intelligence that can "lead us from the past to the future." Despite his espousal of an antimodernism more severe even than that of Arnold's 1853 Preface, Swift becomes one of the lights Arnold uses to guide the way into the future.

Arnold catches on to Swift rather tardily, but once he has caught on, he stays by him. In Arnold's later works Swift regularly appears, grouped with other great writers of prose, as an upholder of a standard of excellence against which the style of inferior writers may be judged. On the most superficial level prose style may be considered merely as syntactic technique; and on this level Arnold ranks Swift and Voltaire above Goethe, whose prose "is loose, ill-knit, diffuse" (VIII, 273). Very seldom, however, does Arnold allow for this sort of divergence between manner and matter, or between form and content. In "Academies" he remarks on the importance of "the *ethical* influences of style in language,—its close relations, so often pointed out, with character" (III, 234). Style is an index of intellectual conscience, and sincerity, the instinct for the genuine, is an indispensable component of classical writing. In ex-

40. *NB*, pp. 41 and 580.

plaining why he does not count Emerson as "among the great writers" of the world, Arnold appeals to the character of style and includes Swift in his list of touchstones for detecting it. "Who are the great men of letters? They are men like Cicero, Plato, Bacon, Pascal, Swift, Voltaire,—writers with, in the first place, a genius and instinct for style; writers whose prose is by a kind of native necessity true and sound" (X, 171).

Style is not just a mechanical arrangement of the elements of language. It extends, on the one hand, to the intellectual character of the author and, on the other, to the compositional matter of the subject. Ideas do not exist in isolation one from another. They obtain much of their meaning from the way in which they are arranged and expressed. In "Academies," for the sake of his polemic, Arnold had separated style from "ideas." In order to set up Addison as a representative Attic stylist, Arnold found it necessary to claim that "it is comparatively a small matter to express oneself well, if one will be content with not expressing much, with expressing only trite ideas" (III, 247). Arnold's aim is set on the conclusion that the unwholesome atmosphere of English intellectual life "tends to make even a man of great ability either a Mr. Carlyle or else a Lord Macaulay," that is, either flawed in style or deficient in ideas. This is a false antithesis; Arnold himself notes "that Lord Macaulay's style has in its turn suffered by his failure in ideas," but he supports his rhetorical hypothesis by maintaining that "this cannot be said of Addison's." It can, in fact, be said of Addison's style, and in "A Guide to English Literature" Arnold himself says it very well. Addison's "style cannot equal in varied cadence and subtle ease the style of a man like Plato, because without range and force of thought all the resources of style, whether in cadence or in subtlety, are not and cannot be brought out" (VIII, 249). Addison's style is smooth and clear in part because Addison has a provincial oblivion to disturbing ideas, but for the same reason it is somewhat bland and monotonous. Carlyle, on the other hand, has ideas in abundance, but both his style and his intellectual content are marred by a vehemence and turbulence that may be attributed to a provincial defect of perspective and proportion. The best prose style, avoiding both these extremes, combines intensity of tone and fullness of substance with a lucid mastery of composition. In "Emerson" Arnold takes Swift as one of his touchstone writers for this standard of excellence. However passionate or choleric Swift may be, he controls his materials and so commands a respect that Arnold does not accord to Carlyle.[41]

> Shakespeare, Molière, Swift,—they too had, like Carlyle, the devouring eye and the portraying hand. But they are great literary masters, they are supreme writers, because they know how to work into a literary composition their materials, and to subdue them to the purposes of literary effect. Carlyle is too wilful for this, too turbid, too vehement. (x, 174)

The qualities of precision, authenticity, and compositional mastery render Swift a true "prose classic" (IX, 286). In "Academies" Arnold defines the true classic as an author who is able "to express new and profound ideas in a perfectly sound and classical style" (III, 248). By taking Addison as a representative English prose stylist and then denying that Addison was a classic writer, Arnold is suggesting that English literature has no classic prose, that the English era of prose was, indeed, "provincial and second-rate." Arnold is, however, too much concerned with preserving the best that has been thought and said to rest satisfied with the poverty of this conclusion. In the preface to his selection from Burke's commentaries on *Irish Affairs* Arnold readjusts his ranking of Addison in a way that more accurately reflects his own responses to the English literature of intelligence.

> Our grandfathers were bound to know their Addison, but for us the obligation has ceased; nor is that loss, indeed, a very serious matter. But to lose Swift and Burke out of our mind's circle of acquaintance is a loss indeed, and a loss for which no conversance with contemporary prose literature can make up, any more than conversance with contemporary poetry could make up to us for unacquaintance with Shakespeare and Milton. In both cases the unacquaintance shuts us out from great sources of English life,

41. Kathleen Tillotson shows that some of Arnold's phrases echo Carlyle's, and on this basis she suggests that in Arnold "there is often an affinity with Carlyle's ideas." "Matthew Arnold and Carlyle," *Mid-Victorian Studies* (London: Athlone Press, 1965), p. 231. David DeLaura offers a more detailed and closely reasoned account of the relationship between Arnold and Carlyle, but he too exaggerates the significance of certain verbal echoes and underplays real and basic differences in attitude and thought. His final explanation for Arnold's lasting hostility to Carlyle—Arnold could not forgive Carlyle for having affected him with "empty transcendental prescriptions"—seems just. "Arnold and Carlyle," *PMLA* 79 (1964): 129.

thought, and language, and from the capital records of its history and development, and leaves us in consequence very imperfect and fragmentary Englishmen.

(IX, 286)

In "Academies" Arnold takes passages from Burke as examples of the Asiatic excesses that result from the intrusion of a poetic imagination into the Attic realm of prose. If Burke is, nonetheless, the greatest English prose writer, he owes this distinction in good part to his affiliation with the neoclassical school of prose, to his association, personal and intellectual, with the circle of Johnson, Boswell, and Reynolds.

Between the mid-century deaths of Swift and Pope and the French Revolution, the greatest literary figure in England is Samuel Johnson. From the beginning to the end of his career, Arnold studiously read and reread Johnson, quoted from him, and echoed his phrases. Among the four greatest English neoclassicists, Johnson influenced Arnold most closely. The humane gravity of Johnson's moral vision and his delight in the play of the mind set a comprehensive tonal framework for Arnold's own doctrinal range. The extent and authority of his critical endeavors provide a standard that Arnold himself could scarcely hope to surpass. In his preface to Johnson's *Lives* Arnold handsomely acknowledges the quality of Johnson's influence. He grants that Johnson's neoclassical poetic sensibility and his political and religious conservatism set him at some distance from contemporary needs:[42]

But he was a great man, and great men are always instructive. The more we study him, the higher will be our esteem for the power of his mind, the width of his interests, the largeness of his knowledge, the freshness, fearlessness, and strength of his judgments. The higher, too, will be our esteem for his character.

(VIII, 319)

In his late essay on Emerson, Arnold, thoughtlessly echoing a remark by Coleridge, says that "Johnson lives in Boswell, not by

42. It is interesting to note that the reason Arnold gives for the value of studying Johnson echoes one of his father's general principles, enunciated in Arthur P. Stanley's *Life and Correspondence of Thomas Arnold, D.D.*: "Even on matters of fact, silly and ignorant men, however honest and industrious in their particular subject, require to be read with constant watchfulness and suspicion; whereas *great men are always instructive,* even amidst much of error on particular points" [my italics]. Letter to C. J. Vaughan, February 25, 1835 (New York: Scribner, Armstrong, 1877), 1:356–57.

his works" (X, 174).[43] In other essays of this same period, however, Arnold himself quotes from *Rasselas,* "The Vanity of Human Wishes," and the *Journey to the Western Islands of Scotland.* One might speculate that the critical production of Coleridge might have been less inadequate had he not so smugly repudiated Johnson. For Arnold, at least, Johnson lived by his works, and without this influence, Arnold's own work would have been much the poorer. Arnold regards Johnson, like Dryden, as a public resource, that is, a part of the common critical domain from which ideas may be gleaned freely and with no necessity of specific attribution.

As a post-Romantic Arnold felt that he had a perspective on the nature of poetry superior to that of Johnson, whose position as "the man of an age of prose" often "warped and narrowed" his judgment of poetry (VIII, 319 and 318). In Johnson's view the highest intellectual faculty is reason, and it predominates in poetry as well as in prose. Johnson defines poetry as "the art of uniting pleasure with truth, by calling imagination to the help of reason."[44] Arnold believes that reason predominates in criticism but is in poetry subordinate to the heart and imagination. Arnold approaches most nearly to Johnson's rationalist view of poetry during the first phase of his critical career, when he identifies the modern ideal for literature as "the imaginative reason." He diverges from Johnson's view most widely during his third phase, when he delivers a positive revaluation of the Romantic poets, for the best English poetry of the nineteenth century did not call imagination to the help of reason nor scarcely even call reason to the help of imagination. Despite their differences in poetic doctrine, Arnold still maintains in his third phase that "even on poetry Johnson's utterances are valuable, because they are the utterances of a great and original man" (VIII, 319). Johnson is not, for example, "a satisfying critic of a poet like Milton," but his remarks on Milton, because they are the reflections "of a very acute and robust mind," are often "thoroughly sound" (VIII, 174).

Arnold's poetic taste was more nearly akin to that of Coleridge than to that of Johnson, but Johnson, unlike Coleridge, does not merely provide isolated *aperçus* about literature. He imposes himself as a central authority. Arnold intended his selection from Johnson's *Lives* to serve as a textbook for students of English lit-

43. For Coleridge's remark to this effect, see *Table Talk,* May 15, 1833.
44. Johnson, *Lives,* 1:170 (on Milton).

erature, "a fixed and thoroughly known centre of departure and return" (VIII, 310); while he remarks on Johnson's "defective" criticism of poetry, he expresses a rare diffidence in refusing to impose his own more enlightened views through a supplementary commentary. Taking refuge in the general first-person plural, he suggests that perhaps "we have not Johnson's interest and Johnson's force; we are not the power in letters for our century which he was for his" (VIII, 311).

Johnson is, by his absence, the most conspicuous figure in "Academies." The charges that Arnold there brings against English literature—the extravagance of prose style, the paucity of ideas, and the inferiority of its "journeyman-work"—all find an answer in Johnson. Arnold himself later concedes each of these points to Johnson. As technical analyses his statements on Johnson's prose style are not very satisfactory, but they are distinctly approbatory. Johnson's prose, he says, is "decidedly modern" (VIII, 314). Johnson's words are "often pompous and long," but his Latinate diction does not obscure the structure of his syntax, which "is always plain and modern." Arnold defines a modern prose structure as one that is "opposed to length and involvement" and that enables "us to be clear, plain, and short." This describes well enough the style of Swift and Pope, but Johnson's plainness and clarity do not derive from a short syntactic mode. Johnson supports the length and involvement of his sentences and renders them perfectly lucid by his masterful control of parallelism, subordination, and balanced antithesis. In any case the main point, for Arnold, is that Johnson's style is that of a good, functional prose, "plain, direct, intelligible, serviceable" (VIII, 313).

The formal qualities of Johnson's prose manifest themselves most characteristically in his moral essays, but Johnson adapts his prose perfectly to the sort of journeyman-work to which, in "Academies," Arnold denies the English have any claim. In that essay Arnold maintains that by setting high intellectual standards the French Academy promotes the natural inclination of the French "towards culture, towards clearness, correctness, and propriety in thinking and speaking" (III, 241). Arnold's complaints about the lack, in contemporary England, of any such authority for setting the standards of scholarly activity seem, from the examples he gives, to be justified. As Arnold himself had already said, however, the movement toward propriety in thinking and speaking was the primary tendency of eighteenth-century English literature. Johnson anticipates Arnold when he identifies Dryden's mission as a poet to be the provision of examples "for the establishment of regularity, and the introduction of propriety in word and thought."[45] Johnson himself considers the possibility that an academy like that of the French might "be established for cultivation of our stile," but because he does not "wish to see dependance multiplied," he hopes that "the spirit of English liberty will hinder or destroy" any such attempt.[46] Arnold's own purpose in "Academies" is not to counsel the establishment of an English literary academy. He not only recognizes that it is unlikely the English ever will have one but also declares that "perhaps we ought not to wish to have it" (III, 257). His purpose is, rather, to urge his countrymen "to remember to what shortcomings and excesses, which such an academy tends to correct, we are liable." Johnson was equally concerned with these shortcomings, and he undertakes his own mission of correction at the most fundamental journeyman level: the "harmless drudgery" of making a dictionary. By laboring "to settle the orthography, display the analogy, regulate the structures, and ascertain the signification of English words," Johnson seeks to provide a solid foundation for the cultivation of propriety in English literary activity.[47]

> I have . . . attempted a dictionary of the English language, which, while it was employed in the cultivation of every species of literature, has itself been hitherto neglected, suffered to spread, under the direction of chance, into wild exuberance, resigned to the tyranny of time and fashion, and exposed to the corruptions of ignorance, and caprices of innovation.

In the conclusion of the preface to his dictionary Johnson invites comparison between his achievement and that of the French and Italian academies, and indeed, throughout the latter half of the eighteenth century he served the English as something like a one-man academy, that is, "a sovereign organ of the highest literary opinion" (III, 257). His critical work ranges from the most literal and specific level, that of fixing words, to the most abstract and general, that of evaluating the English poetic tradition. In

45. Ibid., p. 420.
46. Samuel Johnson, *Johnson's Dictionary: A Modern Selection*, ed. E. L. McAdam, Jr. and George Milne (New York: Random House, 1963), p. 27.
47. Ibid., pp. 20 and 3.

"Academies," as evidence for the "second-rate" character of English works of intelligence, Arnold points out that English "books of reference" are inferior to such works written in German or French (III, 242). Later, however, he himself successfully attempts to establish Johnson's *Lives* more firmly as a standard reference work, what he calls a *point de repère* for English literature, and he declares that it is superior to any other production of its kind. "I know of no such first-rate piece of literature, for supplying in this way the wants of the literary student, existing at all in any other language; or existing in our own language for any period except the period which Johnson's six lives cover" (VIII, 310).

Arnold published his edition of Johnson's *Lives* in 1878, but Johnson is not, like Swift, a tardy acquisition to the storehouse of Arnold's critical knowledge. In the 1853 Preface Arnold uses material from Johnson's preface to his edition of Shakespeare's plays. In the preface to *Merope* Arnold takes issue with Johnson's pronouncements in the *Life of Milton* against the "encumbrance" of a chorus. In "The Modern Element" he quotes Johnson's definition of genius from the *Life of Pope* and says that Johnson "nobly describes it" (I, 22–23). In *On Translating Homer* he takes over Johnson's comparison of Pope and Homer; he gives a quote from "The Vanity of Human Wishes" as an example of the nobility to which the couplet can attain (I, 144), and he refers to the style of *Rasselas* as being well-suited "to describe a sage philosophising" (I, 110).

Arnold regards Johnson's style, like that of Swift, as not only a manner of expression but also a quality of thought about culture and literature that can still offer substantial guidance for the modern world. Shortly before writing "Academies" Arnold had asked, "Will Macaulay be saved, in the sweep and pressure of time, for his light's sake, as Johnson has already been saved by two generations, Joubert by one? I think it very doubtful" (III, 210). In "Academies" itself, as we have seen, Arnold defines a true classic as the work of a writer who is able "to express new and profound ideas in a perfectly sound and classical style" (III, 248). This is the standard by which Addison—and through him, by implication, all eighteenth-century prose—is rated as provincial and second-rate. The definition itself, however, appears to owe something of its inspiration to Johnson's discussion of the Metaphysical Poets in his *Life of Cowley*. Johnson takes issue with Pope's definition of wit as that which "oft was *Thought*, but ne'er so well *Exprest*." He complains that Pope's account of wit "depresses it below its natural dignity, and reduces it from strength of thought to happiness of language."[48] Johnson proposes as a "more noble and more adequate conception" his own definition of wit as that "which is at once natural and new, that which though not obvious is, upon its first production, acknowledged to be just." For a poetry that will serve as a primary religious source Arnold will require something that he calls "soul" and that he contrasts to the "wits," but for a "true classic" he does not require in "Academies" more than what Johnson had defined as wit (IX, 202).

The example of Johnson was clearly very much in Arnold's thoughts as he began his own critical career, his campaign against eccentricity, and his search for "the general ideas" that would provide an intellectual deliverance.[49] Johnson was, in fact, so much in Arnold's thoughts that the omission of him from "Academies," although it serves a rhetorical purpose, also seems like a willful clearing of the field by which Arnold seeks to give himself room in which to establish his own critical authority. The main line of Arnold's critical development is, nonetheless, heavily dependent on ideas that, if not entirely original with Johnson, gained the stamp of definitive formulation from him. In the first elegy to Senancour, Arnold's declaration of the inadequate critical perspective of his age takes its phrasing from Johnson's *Life of Pope* and appears as a plea for sympathy from Johnson, who, like Goethe, was a great man of a quieter time. Johnson had remarked that "there is a time when nations emerging from barbarity, and falling into regular subordination, gain leisure to grow wise, and feel the shame of ignorance and the craving pain of unsatisfied curiosity."[50] Arnold answers:

48. Johnson, *Lives*, 1:19.

49. In a letter to Clough (April 22, 1852), Arnold lists four literary projects he would like to undertake. Three of them involve classical scholarship. The fourth, the only one concerned with modern literature, is a "Lives of the English Poets where Johnson ends—and in his method: biographical but above this, critical: presupposing detailed lives of each poet, and contracting the whole." *LC*, p. 121. One may see a partial fulfillment of this intention in Arnold's essays and comments on the Romantic poets.

50. Johnson, *Lives*, 3:239. For the preceding line in Arnold's stanza, "What shelter to grow ripe is ours?", James Simpson points out a possible source in Goethe. *Matthew Arnold and Goethe* (London: Modern Humanities Research Association, 1979), p. 145.

But we, brought forth and rear'd in hours
Of change, alarm, surprise—
What shelter to grow ripe is ours?
What leisure to grow wise?

When Arnold determines to redirect his energies from poetical expression to the attainment of wisdom, he often finds his way under the light shed by Johnson's critical spirit. In explaining why Johnson "has already been saved by two generations," Arnold declares that "truth illuminates and gives joy, and it is by the bond of joy, not of pleasure, that men's spirits are indissolubly held" (III, 210). Johnson, too, holds that "the pleasures of sudden wonder are soon exhausted, and the mind can only repose on the stability of truth."[51] For both Johnson and Arnold the method for attaining truth is historical and comparative. Arnold defines an intellectual deliverance as a "comprehension of this present and past"; it is "to know how others stand, that we may know how we ourselves stand" (I, 20 and 21). Imlac, the philosopher-poet of *Rasselas*, tells us that "to judge rightly of the present we must oppose it to the past; for all judgment is comparative, and of the future nothing can be known."[52] The purpose of culture is to achieve an adequate ideal of human perfection; the basic elements of the synthesis of Arnold's ideal, the union of Hebraism and Hellenism, are reflected in a single sentence from *Rasselas*, which Arnold copies into his *Note-Books*. "Integrity without knowledge is weak and useless, and knowledge without integrity is dangerous and dreadful."[53] In his first phase Arnold fears ignorance more than he fears negative lucidity, and in "Democracy," where he first establishes his ideal of "perfection," he reverses the predicates of these terms. "Culture without character is, no doubt, something

51. Johnson, *Yale Edition of the Works of Samuel Johnson*, vol. 7, *Johnson on Shakespeare*, pp. 61–62. It may help to underline Arnold's neoclassical affinities if we compare this attitude with that adopted by Pater in the "Conclusion" to *The Renaissance*. For Pater, "what is real in our life fines itself down" to "those impressions of the individual mind" that "are in perpetual flight." Pater's frenetic aestheticism abjures the pursuit of those "general laws" that are the chief concern of Johnson and Arnold. "Gathering all we are into one desperate effort to see and touch, we shall hardly have time to make theories about the things we see and touch." *The Works of Walter Pater*, 10 vols. (London: Macmillan, 1900), 1:236, 235, 237.

52. Samuel Johnson, *The History of Rasselas, Prince of Abissinia*, ed. Geoffrey Tillotson and Brian Jenkins (London: Oxford University Press, 1971), p. 80.

53. Ibid., p. 109.

frivolous, vain, and weak; but character without culture is, on the other hand, something raw, blind, and dangerous" (II, 24). The balance suggested here belongs to Arnold's Hellenic phase. In his religious period, when the balance is upset, Arnold does not entirely abandon culture, but the position he assigns to it, relative to "conduct," is perfectly reflected in another *Note-Book* entry from *Rasselas*. "To man is permitted the contemplation of the skies, but the practice of virtue is commanded."[54]

The decisive moment that marks Arnold's return from Hebraism to Hellenism gives evidence, also, of the bond by which he is held to Johnson. Those who awake to the life of the mind, Arnold says, and follow where it leads them find that the only way to salvation is through extensive study and judicious discrimination.

> It leads them to see that it is their business to learn the real truth about the important men, and things, and books, which interest the human mind. For thus is gradually to be acquired a stock of sound ideas, in which the mind will habitually move, and which alone can give to our judgments security and solidity.
>
> (VIII, 170)

This formulation seems to be a combination of statements made by Joubert and Johnson. In "Academies" Arnold bases his whole case for the intellectual poverty of the eighteenth century on the comparison of two quotations, one by Addison and one by Joubert. Addison's statement is an admonition against "reading books of controversy," because these will hinder the achievement of "a fixed and settled habit of faith" (III, 248). Arnold calls this idea "perfectly trite and barren." The problem is not so much that Addison's idea is trite but that it is anti-intellectual. It is exactly opposite in tendency to the statement by Joubert to which Arnold compares it. "L'expérience de beaucoup d'opinions donne à l'esprit beaucoup de flexibilité et l'affermit dans celles qu'il croit les meilleures" (The experience of many opinions gives the spirit much flexibility and confirms it in those it believes to be the best). Only recently before writing "Academies" Arnold had associated Johnson and Joubert as profound moral and critical thinkers. If he had not wished to sacrifice historical accuracy to polemical effect in "Academies," he might have compared the quotation from Joubert with the quotation from Johnson's *Life of Pope* that he later

54. Ibid., p. 108.

copies, twice, in his *Note-Books* and that he does finally quote in his preface to Johnson's *Lives*.

> Johnson, himself, has admirably marked the real line of our education through letters. He says in his life of Pope: "Judgment is forced upon us by experience. He that reads many books must compare one opinion or one style with another; and when he compares, must necessarily distinguish, reject, and prefer." Nothing could be better. The aim and end of education through letters is to get this experience.
>
> (VIII, 311)

A major part of Arnold's own education comes to him through his experience of neoclassical English literature. If he did not do justice to the eighteenth century in "Academies," he amply compensates for this failure in his other works. Dryden, Pope, Swift, and Johnson all do finally receive from him a recognition of their classic status, and a classic for Arnold is a work that contains permanent sources of insight and ennoblement. The neoclassical writers are, moreover, of special interest to Arnold in that they are the first, and in some respects the only, "modern" classics in English. Whatever its limitations in poetic taste and historical theory, the English eighteenth century belongs, as the nineteenth does not, to the mainstream of modern culture. The "element" by which the modern spirit must live, Arnold says, is "the imaginative reason," and the dominant element within the imaginative reason is the critical intelligence. The neoclassical writers believe in reason, they are invested with the critical spirit, and they live in a world of ideas. The essence of an epoch of expansion is a movement of ideas, and its salvation resides in a harmonious ordering of ideas. Johnson's concern for established order and his religious piety characterize him as a force of concentration, but for Johnson, as for Burke, concentration is itself a philosophy, an order of ideas consciously adopted and logically articulated. Johnson's conservatism does not so hinder him but that he too follows the life of the mind. In a late essay Arnold quotes a sentence from Johnson's *Journey to the Western Islands* that could stand as an epigraph to all of Arnold's critical work. "Whatever makes the past, the distant, or the future, predominate over the present, advances us in the dignity of thinking beings" (X, 213).[55]

55. Johnson, *Yale Edition of the Works of Samuel Johnson*, vol. 9, *A Journey to the Western Islands of Scotland*, ed. Mary Lascelles (1971), p. 148.

5 The Shape of History

The Mainstream

For the first half of the eighteenth century the mainstream of modern European literature flows between England and France, but from the middle of the eighteenth century to the middle of the nineteenth century the central current shifts to Germany. The three main critics of modern Europe and its chief intellectual influences are, Arnold says, Voltaire, Lessing, and Goethe (III, 41). The greatest of these is Goethe, and it is Goethe, too, who is the greatest modern poet, that is, the poet most nearly capable of creating a "new spiritual basis." From the death of Goethe to the beginning of Arnold's own career as a cultural critic, the single most important critical and poetic voice in Europe is that of Heinrich Heine, the writer on whom "of all German authors who survived Goethe, incomparably the largest portion of Goethe's mantle fell" (III, 108). Heine is "the man (in spite of his faults) of truest genius that Germany has produced since Goethe" and the poet who "in the European poetry of that quarter of a century which follows the death of Goethe" is "incomparably the most important figure" (III, 182 and 132). In attempting to withdraw himself from the minor current of nineteenth-century English literature and to enter the mainstream of modern European culture, Arnold situates himself as the direct successor of the German critical tradition that extends from Lessing through Goethe to Heine. The one great European critic outside of this line is Voltaire, and for Arnold, Voltaire, however great his ability, serves chiefly as a representative of "negative lucidity" (X, 86). Arnold quotes and approves of Joubert's severe judgment on the corrupting nature of Voltaire's influence, and he remarks that Joubert's opinion is "nearly identical with that of Goethe" (III, 205–206). Goethe's most fundamental objection to the criticism of Voltaire is, like Arnold's, that the world is "nichts damit gedient; es lässt sich nichts darauf gründen. Ja es kann sogar von der grössten Schädlichkeit sein, indem es die Menschen verwirrt und ihnen den nötigen Halt nimmt."[1] Arnold himself never ceases to read and to learn from Voltaire, but he grounds his own sense of a critical mission on the works of the three German writers. From these works, too, he derives the most substantial portion of his cultural theory.

Many of the ideas propounded by these writers were, of course, of wide currency in Arnold's time, and it would be unreasonable to argue for an exclusive derivation. Arnold himself, however, designates these writers as both seminal and authoritative. In several critical instances, as we shall see, he draws directly on Lessing, Goethe, and Heine for the formulation of his key ideas. Thus, while not excluding the possibility of other contributory and confirmatory influences, we may reasonably isolate the three main figures in the German line as constituting the central tradition of cultural theory from which Arnold most immediately derives.

Despite the immense differences of manner and doctrine among these three German writers, they group themselves together in Arnold's mind through a continuity of critical interests and an affinity of philosophical modernism. Arnold describes this community of philosophical outlook in "Spinoza and the Bible." He declares that Spinoza, because of his "noble and lofty character. . . . stands out from the multitude of philosophers, and has been able

1. "[The world is] not at all served by it, nothing can be founded on it. Indeed, it can even be exceedingly harmful in that it confuses people and deprives them of the necessary firmness." (All translations from the German are my own.) Johann Peter Eckermann, *Gespräche mit Goethe in den letzten Jahren seines Lebens*, ed. H. H. Houben (Wiesbaden: F. A. Brockhaus, 1959), pt. 1, October 15, 1825. (All quotations from Eckermann will be drawn from this edition. References will be given only to the part and date of entry.) For a comprehensive statement of Goethe's ambivalence to Voltaire, see *Dichtung und Wahrheit* (*Poetry and Truth*), pt. 3, bk. 11, *Goethes sämtliche Werke. Jubiläums-Ausgabe in 40 Bänden*, ed. Eduard von der Hellen (Stuttgart: J. G. Cotta, 1902), 24:44–47 (hereafter cited as *Jubiläums-Ausgabe* and volume and page number).

to inspire in powerful minds a feeling which the most remarkable philosophers, without this grandiose character, could not inspire" (III, 181–82). The three "powerful minds" whom Arnold selects to demonstrate the significance of Spinoza's influence are Lessing, Goethe, and Heine. Following Heine, Arnold places Spinoza at the center of modern philosophy because Spinoza, rejecting the idea of a divine being external to nature, requires that all divine sanction be derived from natural experience.[2] Arnold stretches a point in including Lessing under this heading, for Lessing's thought retains a theistic element. In characterizing the quality of Spinoza's spiritual influence, however, Arnold is right to include Lessing. Paraphrasing Goethe, Arnold explains the impact of Spinoza on Goethe "and any man like Goethe" in two ways: "First he fills and satisfies his imagination by the width and grandeur of his view of nature," and then directs him to a "joyful activity within the limits of man's true sphere" (III, 177).[3] Although Arnold has little susceptibility to formal metaphysics, he recognizes the main import of Spinoza's thought and aligns his historical and religious commentary with it. In Lessing, Goethe, and Heine, Arnold finds both a confirmation for his Spinozistic naturalism and an inspiration, beyond that of Spinoza, for his large-scale cultural criticism.

In his comments on his German predecessors Arnold's praise for Heine is the most ambivalent, but it is nonetheless from Heine that Arnold derives most of his leading ideas on the elements of culture and the shape of history. Unlike Goethe, Heine does not possess, Arnold thinks, a completely "adequate" modern sensibility, and unlike Lessing he does not propound a vision of history that is unequivocally progressive and purposive. Arnold adopts Heine's dialectical historical scheme, but he superimposes on it Lessing's faith in a teleological progression tending toward the goal of human perfection. To give substance to his own ideal of perfection, Arnold employs, with some distortion, the example offered by Goethe, the most complete and successful representative of modern Hellenism. Arnold gives unreserved acknowledgment to the positive contributions of Lessing and Goethe, and he denounces the mocking irreverence of Heine, but the unresolved conflicts in Arnold's own mind between Hebraism and Hellenism, and

2. See chapter 2 of this study, note 21.

3. For Goethe's appreciation of Spinoza, see *Dichtung und Wahrheit*, pt. 3, bks. 14 and 16 (*Jubiläums-Ausgabe*, 24:216–17; 25:4–10).

between modern poetry and modern criticism, betray how completely he has been comprehended by Heine's prophetic soul. Lessing and Goethe both offer solutions to the modern problem. In Heine, however, the problem remains manifestly unsolved, and though Arnold follows Heine in announcing a new age founded on "joy," he never entirely frees himself from the spiritual plight depicted by Heine. In this chapter we shall first examine the kinds of solutions that Lessing and Goethe provide for Arnold and then consider in what way Arnold, like Heine, remains a victim of the spiritual crisis of modern Europe.

Lessing

In Lessing Arnold finds an exemplary critical production that corresponds closely in doctrinal tendency with his own critical effort. Lessing is of particular importance for Arnold in that he is the only major figure of the continental Enlightenment who combines an outspoken advocacy of the critical modern spirit with a sincere regard for the Christian contribution to European culture. Unlike the English neoclassicists, he directly confronts the problem of an imminent transition to a post-Christian cultural phase, and unlike Voltaire, he concerns himself with creating a vital continuity between past and future. Lessing anticipates Arnold in his belief that literature in the modern world must assume the functions of moral affirmation that had previously been exercised by the institutions of conventional religion. At the same time he remains firmly oriented toward the neoclassical aesthetic principles of universality, objectivity, structural unity, and intellectual clarity. Thus, although Lessing is in no sense a Romantic writer, he nonetheless provides assistance to Arnold in bridging the gap between Arnold's commitment to a neoclassical aesthetics and his religious devotion to Romantic poetry. Arnold first turns to Lessing as a refuge from the intellectual chaos of English Romanticism, and he ultimately derives from him the ideas that enable him to impose a retroactive order on this chaos and to render it historically meaningful.

By tracing the development of Arnold's appreciation of Lessing, we may observe how Arnold's flight from the confusion of English Romanticism transforms itself into a positive crusade for European criticism. At the same time we shall gain some insight into the leading influence that Heine exercises on this transformation, for Arnold, to all appearances, bases his evaluation of Lessing in *Culture and Anarchy* on the commentary of Heine, and Arnold employs this evaluation to define the scope and level of his own critical effort. Arnold first mentions Lessing in 1848 or 1849 in a letter to Clough. Clough had recommended that Arnold read Keats's letters, and the effect of these letters had been anything but salutary. "What a brute you were to tell me to read Keats' Letters. However it is over now: and reflexion resumes her power over agitation."[4] The letters confirm Arnold's feeling that Keats, for lack of intellectual order, has done great harm in English poetry. Keats and Browning "will not be patient neither understand that they must begin with an Idea of the world in order not to be prevailed over by the world's multitudinousness." As an antidote to Keats's tumultuous sensualism Arnold betakes himself to Lessing, and he advises Clough to do the same. "I recommend you to follow up these letters with the Laocoön of Lessing: it is not quite satisfactory, and a little mare's nesty—but very searching." Arnold does not say in what respect Lessing's work is unsatisfactory, and in his 1867 poem "Epilogue to Lessing's Laocoön" he offers no explicit critique of Lessing's essay. The most obvious ways in which the *Laokoon* might disappoint a reader are that it is unfinished and that, though individual passages are distinguished by clarity and vigor, the whole composition is a bit rambling and amorphous. As in other of his critical works Lessing relies heavily for his motive power on a polemical opposition to the mistakes of other critics. Moreover, Lessing keeps a fairly close focus on the technical issue of distinguishing poetry from painting, and he does not attempt in this work to formulate a complete idea of the world. In the *Hamburgische Dramaturgie*, however, Lessing discusses more generally the relations of poetry to the universal order, and Arnold, in his "Epilogue," takes as much from the *Dramaturgie* as from the *Laokoon*. Lessing's most independent and comprehensive formulation of an idea of the world appears in his *Die Erziehung des Menschengeschlechts* (*The Education of the Human Race*), a work to which Arnold refers in a published essay and from which he copies out excerpts into his *Note-Books*. By combining these three works, Arnold can obtain a distinct impression of Lessing's aesthetic, religious, and historical theories. By examining Arnold's

4. *LC*, p. 96.

response to these works, we shall be able to determine the significance that Lessing has for Arnold.

Despite its limited aims and fragmentary character, the *Laokoon*, like all of Lessing's work, is animated by the conviction that life and art are accessible to rational comprehension. It is on the basis of this conviction that Lessing elevates poetry above painting, for he holds that the purpose of all art is to interpret the world, not merely to depict its sensual surface, and he believes that in the power of interpretation poetry has the advantage. Lessing attempts to allow to both arts their proper sphere. He maintains that painting depicts spatial relations and that poetry relates a succession of events in time. He grants, moreover, that painting can render a more vivid concrete impression than poetry. He nonetheless insists that "die Poesie die weitere Kunst ist; dass ihr Schönheiten zu Gebothe stehen, welche die Malerey nicht zu erreichen vermag."[5] Whereas painting is restricted to the representation or at most the intimation of events, poetry draws its power from an ideational realm that transcends the limitations of actual space and time. Poetry draws its advantages "aus dem unendlichen Felde unserer Einbildungskraft, aus der Geistigkeit ihrer Bilder, die in grösster Menge und Mannigfaltigkeit neben einander stehen können, ohne dass eines das andere deckt oder schändet, wie es wohl die Dinge selbst, oder die natürlichen Zeichen derselben in den engen Schranken des Raumes oder der Zeit thun würden."[6] The *Geistigkeit* of poetic images derives not only from their quantitative superiority and their greater freedom of arrangement but also from their power to disclose the inner nature of things. Lessing quotes a masterly floral description by Haller, and he locates its power not in its pictorial qualities but in "die Entwickelung der innern Vollkommenheiten, welchen die äussere Schönheit nur zur Schale dienet."[7] The didactic purpose of Lessing's essay is to

5. "Poetry is the broader art; . . . it commands resources of beauty which are inaccessible to painting." Gotthold Ephraim Lessing, *Sämtliche Schriften*, ed. Karl Lachmann, 3d ed. by Franz Muncker (Stuttgart: G. J. Göschen, 1886–1924), 9:61 (hereafter cited as Lessing and volume and page number).

6. . . . "out of the limitless field of our imagination, out of the spirituality of its images, which can stand next to one another in the greatest abundance and variety without concealing or harming one another, which is what would happen with the things themselves, or their natural signs, in the narrow boundaries of space and time." Lessing, 9:44–45.

7. . . . "the unfolding of the inner perfections, for which the external beauty serves only as a shell." Lessing, 9:103–104.

designate the true sphere of poetry and so to discourage the proclivity of poets for mere description. It is not certain that in 1847 Arnold had already read the *Laokoon*, but it is an attitude like that of Lessing, a disdain for merely external beauty, that inspires his complaint to Clough about Tennyson dawdling with the "painted shell" of the universe.

When Lessing speaks of poetry as developing the inner perfection of beautiful things, he approaches Arnold's idea of "natural magic." For the most part, however, Lessing's tendency, as a true son of the Enlightenment, is to concentrate on the other side of poetic interpretation, the moral criticism of human life. In *Laokoon* Lessing does not explicitly declare the particularly moral character of his views on poetry, but he gives some indication of his orientation by signaling his affiliation with Pope.

> Der männliche Pope sahe auf die mahlerischen Versuche seiner poetischen Kindheit mit grosser Geringschätzung zurück. Er verlangte ausdrücklich, dass wer den Namen eines Dichters nicht unwürdig führen wolle, der Schilderungssucht so früh wie möglich entsagen müsse.

Lessing quotes Pope's declaration about himself: "That not in Fancy's maze he wander'd long, / But stoop'd to Truth, and moraliz'd his song." Lessing remarks that Pope seems to have regarded the issue "mehr auf der moralischen als kunstmässigen Seite," but he takes Pope's moral standard as corroboration for his own more technically artistic view of the question.[8] In his other works it is often difficult to distinguish between ideas of moral content and ideas of artistic structure.

In his "Epilogue to Lessing's Laocoön" Arnold represents Lessing's essay as providing the initial stimulus for a discussion that proceeds independently of Lessing. However, in his distinctions about the nature of literature, and especially in his conclusions about its religious function, Arnold continues to draw on Lessing. The discussion begins as a dialogue in which Arnold and an unnamed friend attempt to define the nature and limits of poetry and painting. Arnold does not say exactly what transpires in this part

8. "Pope in his maturity looked back with great scorn on the painterly efforts of his poetic childhood. He explicitly maintained that anyone who wished to bear the name of a poet in no unworthy fashion must renounce the lust for description as early as possible."

. . . "more from the moral than from the artistic side." Lessing, 9:106.

of the discussion, and the substance of the poem consists of Arnold's response to the question posed by his friend:

Why music and the other arts
Oftener perform aright their parts
Than poetry? why she, than they,
Fewer fine successes can display?

This question presents itself initially as simply an issue of quantity. Italian poetic masters have been fewer in number than great Italian painters, and the quantity of great verse, such as the "nobly perfect" poetry of Goethe and Wordsworth, has been inferior to the quantity of great music by such masters as Mozart, Beethoven, and Mendelssohn. The solution that Arnold proffers for this problem is to oppose quality to quantity. He declares that poetry is in itself more excellent than the other arts and presents greater difficulty in the attainment of mastery.

Beethoven, Raphael, cannot reach
The charm which Homer, Shakespeare, teach.
To these, to these, their thankful race
Gives, then, the first, the fairest place;
And brightest is their glory's sheen,
For greatest hath their labour been.

In the question that he has posed Arnold departs from Lessing, but the basic topic is still the nature and limits of poetry and the other arts. By introducing music to the discussion Arnold supplements Lessing's classical emphasis on mimesis with an element of Romantic expressivism, but he nonetheless remains within the bounds of neoclassical aesthetics in that he regards art as a representation of the intelligible, not as an intimation of the ineffable. Arnold's theoretical dependence on Lessing is most evident in his treatment of painting, but it appears as well in his effort to distinguish poetry from both painting and music with only one theoretical term, *movement*. The painter, Arnold says, can display only the surface of things and only one moment in time. "In outward semblance he must give / A moment's life of things that live." Like Lessing, Arnold assumes that this surface is interesting chiefly for its narrative content, the story it suggests. The moment caught in a painting must bring to mind a meaningful sequence of events, or what Lessing designates as a *Handlung*. "Then let him choose his moment well, / With power divine its story tell." Music, unlike painting, not only intimates a progression but is itself extended through time. If it lacks the power to depict the "aspect" of things in an objective fashion, it has in the subtle and varied expression of feeling its own range of special effectiveness. "What power of passion, wealth of change!" In music, however, as in painting, Arnold regards only that part that is translatable into literary terms. The formal aesthetic qualities of both painting and music have significance for him only as means to the quasi-literary purposes of representation and expression.

By bringing painting and music within the framework of literary theory Arnold can concede that they both fulfill their limited aims more perfectly than poetry and can still claim for poetry a more complete form of artistic composition. The poet must be "painter and musician too! / The aspect of the moment show, / The feeling of the moment know." Like Lessing, Arnold concedes that the representation of physical reality can never be so vivid in poetry as in painting, and he admits further that in the expression of feeling poetry does not "explore / So deep as the musician's lore." The poet, however, not only combines the functions of painting and music, he also exercises an interpretative power exclusively his own.

> But, ah! then comes his sorest spell
> Of toil—he must life's *movement* tell!
> The thread which binds it all in one,
> And not its separate parts alone.
> The *movement* he must tell of life,
> Its pain and pleasure, rest and strife;
> His eye must travel down, at full,
> The long, unpausing spectacle.

Within the single word *movement* Arnold conflates two rather different meanings. On the literal level the word signifies the temporal progression of life from its "primal source" to the "solemn silence of its close." On a more abstract level it signifies the relation of all the parts of life, not only chronologically but thematically. The main distinction is not between the static and the dynamic, as it would be in a comparison of painting and music, but between the fragmentary and the complete. For Arnold sensation and feeling provide only the disorganized materials of experience. Painting and music give shape to these materials, but they do not situate them within a comprehensive idea of the world.

In his essay "On Poetry" Arnold takes up this issue again, and he leaves no doubt that the contrast he intends is between the merely sensual and the intellectual. "Compare poetry with other efforts of the human spirit. . . . Compare it with art. It is more intellectual than art, more interpretative. Along with the plastic representation it utters the idea, it thinks" (IX, 62). This seems an awkward construction to place on the word *movement*, but from what follows in his poem, it is clearly what he intends to convey. Very few people, he says, ever achieve a comprehensive vision of their own existence. Poorly endowed with natural faculties and constantly beset by "pain," "terror," and "distress," they live and die in a chaos of bewildering sensations. Their oppressive plight, however, does not prevent them from rising to some poor approximation of the fragmentary artistic consciousness represented by painting and music.

Sometimes a momentary gleam
They catch of the mysterious stream;
Sometimes, a second's space, their ear
The murmur of its waves doth hear.
That transient glimpse in song they say,
But not as painter can pourtray—
That transient sound in song they tell,
But not, as the musician, well.

The contrast here is between popular culture (song) and the superior work of professional painters and musicians. In the passage that immediately follows this, however, there is an implied distinction between poetry and the other arts:

And when at last their snatches cease,
And they are silent and at peace,
The stream of life's majestic whole
Hath ne'er been mirror'd on their soul.

The painter and the musician, like the multitude, can bring only isolated pieces of experience into their aesthetic formulations. It is the poet alone who is capable of reflecting "life's majestic whole."

In his ambiguous use of the word *movement* Arnold has attempted to combine the distinction between painting and poetry with the additional distinction between music and poetry. In the concluding section of the poem, however, Arnold drops the literal distinction between static and dynamic artistic media and retains only the abstract sense of movement as a thematic relation among the separate parts of life. The idea of a temporal progression of experience is subordinated to the idea of a completeness and unity of poetic vision. Arnold accomplishes this transition through a mutation in his metaphor of water; the image of a stream changes into an image of rain. The poet, who has been represented as wandering along "the life-stream's shore," now appears as standing motionless in an atmosphere that is saturated, as it were, with divinity.

> They speak! the happiness divine
> They feel, runs o'er in every line;
> Its spell is round them like a shower—
> It gives them pathos, gives them power.

In this metaphoric shift from a temporal progression to a mystical unity Arnold implicitly shifts the source of poetry from actual human experience to a religious intuition transcending that experience. Arnold had intimated earlier in the poem that the burden of the poet's song is not his own privileged state of existence but the experience of the multitude, those whom "He follows home, and lives their life." If, however, the poet restricted his attention to the temporal progression of these lives, "From change to change and year to year," he would scarcely be able to compose any "majestic whole," for the experience of the many is mean and narrow, not to say ludicrous. "They faint, they stagger to and fro." Arnold's artistic tact in this poem may be defective, but his argument is meant to be taken seriously. Poetry is the highest form of art because it rises above both sensual reality and personal passion and articulates a religious vision of the world. It is through his transcendent intuition that the poet both enables himself to rejoice and attains the power of "cheering souls."

Arnold's belief in the religious function of literature finds corroboration in the *Hamburgische Dramaturgie*. In the preface to *Merope* Arnold makes much use of Lessing's discussion in the *Dramaturgie* of the modern treatments of Merope. He sometimes takes exception to Lessing's opinions, but his attitude toward Lessing, "the great German critic" (I, 40), is one of high respect. The *Dramaturgie* concerns itself specifically with the drama, but Lessing also establishes general principles that easily extend themselves to all creative literature. Objecting to the dubious moral content of *Richard III*, he maintains that the poet must construct his works in such a way that they reflect the wisdom and goodness that prevail in the universal order. "Das Ganze dieses sterblichen Schöpfers sollte ein Schattenriss von dem Ganzen des ewigen Schöpfers seyn; sollte uns an den Gedanken gewöhnen, wie sich in ihm alles zum Besten auflöse, werde es auch in jenem geschehen."[9] In its starkest signification this principle would require the kind of poetic justice prevalent in the eighteenth century, for example, the kind that inspired the rewriting of *King Lear* so as to leave Cordelia with a reward commensurate to her merit. Interpreted more broadly, however, Lessing's principle requires only that the artist begin with an idea of the world and that this idea enable us to rejoice. For Lessing "joy" is itself necessarily a moral experience. He regards it as self-evident that the purpose of all poetry is to strengthen our sense of humanity, "dass sie die Triebe der Menschlichkeit nähren und stärken; dass sie Liebe zur Tugend und Hass gegen das Laster wirken solle."[10]

Since the reward of virtue and the punishment of vice appeal not so much to love as to self-interest, we may infer that to fulfill his didactic intent properly the poet should appeal more directly to disinterested moral and aesthetic values. Lessing himself implies this conclusion in his distinction between the works of genius and a merely mechanical sort of naturalistic representation.

> Absicht.—Mit Absicht handeln ist das, was den Menschen über geringere Geschöpfe erhebt; mit Absicht dichten, mit Absicht nachahmen, ist das, was das Genie von den kleinen Künstlern unterscheidet. . . . die Absicht uns zu unterrichten, was wir zu thun oder zu lassen haben; die Absicht uns mit den eigentlichen Merkmahlen des Guten und Bösen, des Anständigen und Lächerlichen bekannt zu machen; die Absicht uns jenes in allen seinen Verbindungen und Folgen als schön und als glücklich selbst im Unglücke, dieses hingegen als hässlich und unglücklich selbst im Glücke, zu zeigen.[11]

9. "The whole of this mortal creator should be a microcosm of the whole of the eternal creator; should accustom us to the thought that just as everything resolves itself for the best in that, so will it in this." Lessing, 10:120.

10. . . . "that it should nourish and strengthen the impulses of humanity; that it should produce a love for virtue and a hatred of vice." Lessing, 10:118.

11. "Intention.—To act with intention is what elevates men above the inferior creatures; to compose with intention, to imitate with intention, is what distinguishes the genius from the petty artists. . . . the intention to instruct us in what we are to do or refrain from doing; the intention to make us acquainted with the actual characteristics of good and evil, of the becoming and the fool-

Arnold, like Lessing, believes that "the right function of poetry is to animate, to console, to rejoice—in one word, to *strengthen*" (VIII, 1); the kind of strength he has in mind is very similar to what Lessing means by *Menschlichkeit*, a reverential regard for "the primary duties and affections." Lessing believes that it is by working in this fashion, by becoming a "school of the moral world," that the theater may assume a leading place in the progress of civilization.[12] In order for the Germans to construct a literature that satisfies this purpose, Lessing recommends that they ally themselves with the literature of the English. Arnold confirms this judgment in that he believes that the distinguishing feature of English poetry is "the energetic and profound treatment of moral ideas" (IX, 46). The "application of ideas to life" finally resolves itself for Arnold, as for Lessing, into the question "How to live?"

At the beginning of his career Arnold regards Lessing as an alternative to the sensual and emotional turbulence of Romanticism. After modifying his attitude toward the greater Romantics, Arnold does not repudiate Lessing; instead, he adapts the Romantic poets to the moral framework of Lessing's aesthetic and historical theory. In his first phase Arnold distances himself from Wordsworth, Keats, and Byron in part because they provide him with no adequate perspective on the tendencies of world history. The perspective that he himself attains, however, enables him to revaluate the Romantic poets and to assign them a place of central importance for the modern spirit. As early as *Culture and Anarchy* Arnold proclaims that poetry is destined "to transform and govern" religion (V, 100), and he comes finally to believe that poetry must not only govern but replace religion. Lessing's argument that the theater must serve as the school of the moral world anticipates this development in Arnold's thought, for Lessing, like Arnold, considers religion to be essentially moral in origin and purpose. Lessing and Arnold both hope to preserve for literature the fervor and reverence that attend religious beliefs. It is in accordance with this hope that Lessing constructs his theory of religious history as a progressive revelation of a humane cosmology. This cosmology, Lessing says, is founded in the "ewigen unendlichen

---

ish; the intention to depict the former to us in all its combinations and consequences as beautiful and happy even in misfortune, and the latter, in contrast, as ugly and unhappy even in good fortune." Lessing, 9:327.

12. Lessing, 9:188.

Zusammenhange aller Dinge," and Arnold calls it "the universal order which seems to be intended and aimed at in the world" (V, 93).[13]

Arnold first alludes to Lessing's theory of religious history in "The Bishop and the Philosopher" (1862). All works on religion, Arnold says, must satisfy at least one of two requirements, either to "edify the little-instructed" or to "inform the instructed" (III, 43). As a contrast to this standard Arnold points to a recent collection of essays and reviews on religious subjects. Some of these pieces, he says, not only fail to inform or edify but are positively impudent. He excepts from this censure one piece on the *Education of the World,* but he still finds it at fault in that it "offers to the instructed nothing which they could not have found in a far more perfect shape in the works of Lessing" (III, 53). Although Arnold does not here give any more detailed account of Lessing's *Erziehung des Menschengeschlechts,* he copies into his *Note-Books* seven significant excerpts from this work, and the historicist character of Lessing's religious ideas informs all of Arnold's own cultural theory. Lessing's work conforms to what Arnold declares in "The Function of Criticism" to be "the very essence of the religious problem, as now presented" (III, 279). For its solution this problem requires "a fresh synthesis of the New Testament *data,*— not a making war on them, in Voltaire's fashion, not a leaving them out of mind, in the world's fashion, but the putting a new construction upon them." Lessing's solutions are not completely satisfactory, but they continue to provide inspiration for Arnold's own fresh synthesis. Arnold does not accept Lessing's assumption that there is a benevolent deity guiding the destiny of the human race, and he does not attempt to preserve, as Lessing does, the idea of personal immortality. He does, however, follow Lessing in treating history as a process of "education" in which the experience of the race is something analogous to the development of the individual from childhood to maturity.

Lessing's basic thesis in the *Erziehung* is that the Biblical revelation is not one and whole from beginning to end but progressive, and he finds a rationale for this fact in the analogous limitations of individual and cultural development. Just as the individual is capable of learning only in graduated stages, so too the race has had to come to moral knowledge one step at a time. "Und so wie

13. . . . "eternal, infinite connectedness of all things." Lessing, 10:120.

es der Erziehung nicht gleichgültig ist, in welcher Ordnung sie die Kräfte des Menschen entwickelt; wie sie dem Menschen nicht alles auf einmal beybringen kann: eben so hat auch Gott bey seiner Offenbarung eine gewisse Ordnung, ein gewisses Mass halten müssen."[14] The first two main stages of development are the original idea of a national God who offers concrete rewards and punishments for obedience and the monotheistic God who offers immortality for moral behavior. For the third and final stage Lessing prophesies a condition in which men will be motivated solely by a disinterested recognition of the intrinsic excellence of virtue. Arnold, having rejected the idea of a God who "sits outside" the world and watches its operation, preserves from Christianity "the idea that the world is in a course of development, of *becoming*, towards a perfection infinitely greater than we now can even conceive" (V, 83). In religious terms Arnold formulates this thesis as the gradual revelation of God through history. It is wrong, he says, to regard the Bible as a fixed system of dogma that must be either adopted or rejected as it stands. Instead, one must be able to "watch the God of the Bible, and the salvation of the Bible, gradually and on an immense scale discovering themselves and *becoming*" (VI, 152).

In the earlier phases of his religious thinking Arnold draws from this thesis of gradual revelation the implication that the Bible contains many truths as yet undiscovered (VI, 87). Later, having himself reduced Biblical doctrine to a moral message "so simple that it did not require science" (VIII, 343), Arnold can still maintain that "the way, truth, and life have been found in Christianity, and will not now be found outside of it" (X, 232). Arnold had attempted to use the historical power of Christianity as a proof for its continuing influence. This argument is logically unsound, and Lessing does not employ it; however, he does suggest other reasons why Christianity may be considered both of supreme historical value and of continuing benefit to civilization. The New Testament has, he declares, "seit siebzehnhundert Jahren den menschlichen Verstand mehr als alle andere Bücher beschäftiget; mehr als alle andere Bücher erleuchtet, sollte es auch nur das Licht

14. "And just as to education it is no matter of indifference in what order the powers of man are developed; as all cannot be imparted at once: so also was it necessary to God, in his revelation, to maintain a certain order and sense of proportion." Lessing, 13:416.

seyn, welches der menschliche Verstand selbst hineintrug."[15] Arnold is not always willing to grant that the centuries of "varying, amplifying, and adorning" the basic teachings of Christ have been of positive value (V, 166). He does, however, consistently maintain that the moral force of Christianity has for two thousand years worked "a divine cure" for sin and misery (VIII, 330), and he follows Lessing in attempting to preserve this beneficent influence by "insisting on the natural truth of Christianity," that is, the valid moral basis in Christian doctrine (VI, 143). Lessing, like Arnold, explains the fabulous and mythic elements of the Biblical narrative as moral doctrine adapted to the primitive mentality of a sensual and superstitious people. In one of the passages that Arnold copies out from the *Erziehung* Lessing sets the pattern for the kind of moral retranslation that Arnold will systematically apply to all Christian doctrine. Lessing begins at the beginning, with original sin, which he explains as an allegorical representation of a historical fact, "dass der Mensch auf *der ersten und niedrigsten* Stufe seiner Menschheit, schlechterdings so Herr seiner Handlungen nicht sey, dass er moralischen Gesetzen folgen könne."[16]

For the individual and for the race the goal of education is the attainment of moral maturity, the power of commanding oneself to act in accordance with the dictates of moral reason. Since Lessing regards the entire historical progression as a necessary series of preparatory stages for the achievement of this goal, he believes that the individual must retain within himself each successive stage of cultural development. Interpreted literally, this theory implies a mystical unity of all the individuals within the history of civilization. Lessing boldly confronts the mystical implications of his theory, and to account for them he advances the hypothesis of metempsychosis. He suggests that not only the race but every individual within it may finally achieve perfection and that to do so the individual is reincarnated in every cultural epoch. "Warum könnte jeder einzelne Mensch auch nicht mehr als einmal auf dieser Welt vorhanden gewesen seyn? . . . Warum sollte ich nicht

15. . . . "for seventeen hundred years occupied the human understanding more than any other book; more than any other book it has enlightened, even if the light was only that which the human understanding itself brought to bear on it." Lessing, 13:429.

16. . . . "that on *the first and lowest* level of his humanity man simply had too little mastery over his own actions to enable him to follow moral laws." Lessing, 13:431.

so oft wiederkommen, als ich neue Kenntnisse, neue Fertigkeiten zu erlangen geschickt bin?"[17] For Arnold the analogy between the individual and the race has less drastically literal consequences, but Arnold also requires that the individual recreate within himself, by means of culture, the experience of the race. Men are born in a state of ignorance, sensuality, and egoism. To escape this condition, they must assimilate the "centuries of probation and discipline" that constitute the Christian interregnum (V, 169). The soul that perfects itself through the preservation of culture has no expectation of personal survival, but it does participate, temporally, in "the eternal order." Though unwilling to abandon what Arnold calls "the materialistic future state," Lessing also characterizes the millennium as a time when men will love virtue for its own sake.

> Sie wird gewiss kommen, die Zeit der Vollendung, da der Mensch, je überzeugter sein Verstand einer immer bessern Zukunft sich fühlet, von dieser Zukunft gleichwohl Bewegungsgründe zu seinen Handlungen zu erborgen, nicht nöthig haben wird; da er das Gute thun wird, weil es das Gute ist, nicht weil willkührliche Belohnungen darauf gesetzt sind, die seinen flatterhaften Blick ehedem bloss heften und stärken sollten, die innern bessern Belohnungen desselben zu erkennen.[18]

Lessing's ideal of human perfection is egalitarian. He assumes that all men can achieve the same state of moral enlightenment. Lessing's egalitarianism, joining with that of Heine, sways Arnold's thinking, but it never entirely overcomes Arnold's tendency to cultural elitism. Lessing himself makes allowance for the different capacities of different men, but he renders these differences as merely differences in rate of progress, not as absolute distinctions of ultimate potential. In Lessing's scheme transitions from one spiritual stage to another occur gradually, and some individuals

17. "Why could every single person also not have been present in this world more than once? . . . Why should I not return as often as I am capable of achieving new knowledge and new abilities?" Lessing, 13:435.

18. "It will certainly come, the time of consummation, when no matter how convinced the understanding may be of an ever better future, man will nonetheless have no need to borrow from this future the motives for his behavior; when he will do the good because it is good, not because there are attached to it those arbitrary rewards that are meant only to fix and strengthen his flighty gaze so that it may recognize the inner, better rewards of the good itself." Lessing, 13:433.

naturally advance more rapidly than others. In accordance with his belief that relatively imperfect religious ideas are necessary and proper for less mature minds, he warns against any too hasty propagation of advanced religious doctrines. "Hüte dich, du fähigeres Individuum . . . es deine schwächere Mitschüler merken zu lassen, was du witterst, oder schon zu sehn beginnest."[19]

In "The Bishop and the Philosopher" Arnold hardens Lessing's lines of division between the critical elite and popular culture. The higher levels of enlightenment not only are not yet but never will be accessible to the majority of men. "Knowledge and truth, in the full sense of the words, are not attainable by the great mass of the human race at all" (III, 44). Arnold identifies poetry as the highest form of human utterance, and he maintains that poetry appeals primarily to the heart and imagination, but he nonetheless relegates these faculties to those lower orders who are incapable of achieving any critical understanding. "The great mass of the human race have to be softened and humanised through their heart and imagination, before any soil can be found where knowledge may strike living roots." Arnold denounces all criticism that by directing itself toward enlightening the masses will "impede the working of influences which advance this softening and humanising process." It is only for the enlightened few that he will allow a free scope of disinterested inquiry. Arnold's doctrine of two cultures, the popular and the elite, aroused sharp protest, and in a later essay he denies that he had intended any such division. He complains that he "had been misrepresented as wishing to make religious truth the property of an aristocratic few, while to the multitude is thrown the sop of any convenient fiction" (III, 65). With allowance made for polemical effect, this is in fact something very like what he had advocated, and although his resentment seems genuine, his defense is unconvincing.

Arnold felt the force of the objections brought against his position in "The Bishop and the Philosopher," and his response to these objections, combined with the influence of Heine's democratic convictions, color his general evaluation of Lessing in *Culture and Anarchy*. In his last decade Arnold will return to an outspoken elitism, but in *Culture and Anarchy* he argues for the necessity

19. "Take care, you more capable individual . . . that you do not let your weaker fellow-student perceive what you suspect, or already begin to see." Lessing, 13:429.

of a widespread critical enlightenment. He argues that culture and religion are at one in their belief that salvation is not individual but generic, that "individual perfection is impossible so long as the rest of mankind are not perfected along with us" (V, 94 and 215). It is only fair to note that, if this position seems to entail a tacit retraction of Arnold's elitism, the democratic ideal of *Culture and Anarchy* continues the line of thought Arnold had taken in "Democracy" and "A French Eton" before "The Bishop and the Philosopher." There is, nonetheless, a real conflict between the democratic and elitist tendencies, and Arnold's evaluation of Lessing in *Culture and Anarchy* reads like a criticism of his own position in "The Bishop and the Philosopher." In his allusion to Lessing's *Erziehung* Arnold had implied that the essay was "strong meat for men," not "milk for babes" (III, 53). Later he objects to any such invidious distinction among the materials of culture, no matter how well-meaning the distinction may be. "Plenty of people will try to give the masses, as they call them, an intellectual food prepared and adapted in the way they think proper for the actual condition of the masses" (V, 112). In contrast to this method, real culture "seeks to do away with classes; to make the best that has been thought and known in the world current everywhere" (V, 113).

To exemplify this democratic view of culture, Arnold chooses four men: Saint Augustine, Abelard, Lessing, and Herder. The inclusion of Augustine and Abelard reinforces the idea of the progressive unity of Western thought and thus gives evidence of Arnold's own debt to Lessing. The terms in which Arnold formulates his democratic standard, however, appear to derive from Heine's eulogy of Lessing in *Die romantische Schule*. Arnold declares that "the great men of culture are those who have had a passion for diffusing, for making prevail, for carrying from one end of society to the other, the best knowledge, the best ideas of their time" (V, 113). The great men of culture serve as popularizers, in the best sense, of specialized scholarly and philosophical knowledge. They have sought "to divest knowledge of all that was harsh, uncouth, difficult, abstract, professional, exclusive; to humanise it," that is, to make it generally accessible, but without diluting it or modifying its essential principles. Arnold calls this "the *social idea*; and the men of culture are the true apostles of equality."

Heine, too, maintains that Lessing's work, as the founder of a new German literature, is directed toward the "social idea."

> Alle Richtungen des Geistes, alle Seiten des Lebens, verfolgte dieser Mann mit Enthusiasmus und Uneigennützigkeit. Kunst, Theologie, Altertumswissenschaft, Dichtkunst, Theaterkritik, Geschichte, alles trieb er mit demselben Eifer und zu demselben Zwecke. In allen seinen Werken lebt dieselbe grosse soziale Idee, dieselbe fortschreitende Humanität, dieselbe Vernunftreligion, deren Johannes er war und deren Messias wir noch erwarten.[20]

By syntactic apposition Heine suggests a virtual equation between the social idea, or the idea of a progressive humanity, and rational religion. A similar association of ideas appears in Arnold, who praises Lessing and Herder for having "broadened the basis of life and intelligence," and for having worked powerfully "to make reason and the will of God prevail" (V, 113).

What Arnold says of Lessing's critical mission applies to himself as well, and insofar as Arnold adopts Heine's characterization of Lessing, it is Heine who defines for Arnold the nature and purpose of Arnold's own cultural criticism. Arnold does not mention Heine at this point in *Culture and Anarchy,* but it seems fairly certain that his evaluation of Lessing is directly inspired by Heine. We may take as evidence for this thesis the fact that Arnold links the names of Lessing and Herder as exponents of the social idea. "Such were Lessing and Herder in Germany, at the end of the last century; and their services to Germany were in this way inestimably precious." Arnold appears to have read very little, if any, of Herder at this time. Herder's *Metakritik* of Kant appears on an early reading list, but there is no certain evidence that Arnold actually read it.[21] Herder's *Ideen* appears on his reading lists for 1866 and 1867,

20. "This man pursued all tendencies of the spirit and all sides of life with the same enthusiasm and disinterestedness. Art, theology, antiquities, poetry, dramatic criticism, history—he handled them all with the same zeal and to the same end. There lived in all of his works the same great social idea, the same forward-marching sense of humanity, the same religion of reason, of which he was the John the Baptist, and the Messiah of which we still await." Heinrich Heine, *Sämtliche Schriften,* ed. Klaus Briegleb, 6 vols. in 7 (Munich: Karl Hanser, 1968–76), 3:371 (hereafter cited as Heine and volume and page number). (If the title of the work referred to is not cited in the text, it will be included in the note in parentheses.)

21. See Kenneth Allott, "Matthew Arnold's Reading-Lists in Three Early Diaries," *Victorian Studies* 2 (1959): 262.

but he does not mark it as having been read, and then only in part, until 1868 and 1869. Arnold never mentions Herder before this one passage in *Culture and Anarchy*, and he mentions him again after this only once, again in association with Lessing (VII, 333).[22] He copies nothing from Herder into his *Note-Books* and never quotes him in his published works. The association, then, of the names of Lessing and Herder on an equal footing scarcely seems to reflect Arnold's own experience of their work. It seems, rather, to reflect a large confidence in the reliability of Heine's judgment. After commenting on Lessing, Heine mentions Herder's name as that of "eines anderen Schriftstellers, der in demselben Geiste und zu demselben Zwecke wirkte und Lessings nächster Nachfolger genannt werden kann."[23]

Arnold's impression of the kind of response these two writers must evoke from a German appears to be based on the response they actually do evoke from Heine.

> Generations will pass, and literary monuments will accumulate, and works far more perfect than the works of Lessing and Herder will be produced in Germany; and yet the names of these two men will fill a German with a reverence and enthusiasm such as the names of the most gifted masters will hardly awaken.
>
> (V, 113)

"The most gifted literary master" of whom Arnold is thinking is most probably Goethe. Heine freely acknowledged Goethe's preeminent rank among German writers, but as much as he admired and honored Goethe, he could not love him. Lessing, he knows, is not so gifted a writer, but it is of Lessing that he says, "dass er in der ganzen Literaturgeschichte derjenige Schriftsteller ist, den ich am meisten liebe."[24] Herder receives less attention from Heine, but as a spiritual influence, by virtue of his character, he belongs with Lessing.

22. Arnold mentions Lessing, Herder, and Goethe as models for "any competent tribunal" on questions of Biblical criticism. Ironically enough, the point in question is whether Jesus really believed in the immortality of the soul. All three of the German critics do believe in this, and Lessing argues that the main historical significance of Christ is to have taught this doctrine. See Lessing, 13:428.

23. . . . "another writer, one who worked in the same spirit and to the same end and who may be named Lessing's closest successor." Heine, 3:372.

24. . . . "that he is in the whole of literary history the writer I love the most." Heine, 3:372.

> Die Literaturgeschichte ist die grosse Morgue wo jeder seine Toten aufsucht, die er liebt oder womit er verwandt ist. Wenn ich da unter so vielen unbedeutenden Leichen den Lessing oder den Herder sehe mit ihren erhabenen Menschengesichtern, dann pocht mir das Herz. Wie dürfte ich vorübergehen, ohne Euch die blassen Lippen zu küssen![25]

As an Englishman Arnold has not Heine's emotional interest in the origins of a German national literature. Very seldom, moreover, does Arnold risk himself in this kind of passionate lyrical fancy, but his own sober prose reads like a commentary on it.

In both Heine and Arnold there is a deep strain of patriotic feeling. The love they bear for their native literature, however, hinders neither of them from exposing the follies and limitations of their countrymen, and they are both firm in placing their primary loyalties above and beyond national boundaries. With Lessing, as they both remark, German literature begins, but Lessing also sets the pattern in Germany for a transnational, European literature. Heine defines this cosmopolitan ideal in contrast to the narrow Germanism of the Romantic school, and Arnold, taking issue with Carlyle, follows Heine in depicting the German Romantics as a minor current that diverges from the mainstream (III, 107–108).

> Es begann die schäbige, plumpe, ungewaschene Opposition gegen eine Gesinnung die eben das Herrlichste und Heiligste ist was Deutschland hervorgebracht hat, nämlich gegen jene Humanität, gegen jene allgemeine Menschen-Verbrüderung, gegen jenen Kosmopolitismus, dem unsere grossen Geister, Lessing, Herder, Schiller, Goethe, Jean Paul, dem alle Gebildeten in Deutschland immer gehuldigt haben.[26]

The greatest writer in this group, and the most immediate source for Arnold's own cosmopolitan ideal, is Goethe. In his essay on

25. "Literary history is the great morgue where everyone seeks out his dead, those whom he loves or to whom he is related. When, among so many insignificant corpses, I see there Lessing or Herder with their noble human visages, then my heart throbs. How might I pass by without kissing your pale lips!" Heine, 3:372–73.

26. "There began the shabby, gross, unwashed opposition against an attitude that is, in fact, the most splendid and holy Germany has ever brought forth, namely, against that sense of humanity, against that general human brotherhood, against that cosmopolitanism to which our great spirits—Lessing, Herder, Schiller, Goethe, Jean Paul—to which all cultivated people in Germany have always paid homage." Heine, 3:379.

Wordsworth, Arnold describes Goethe as "the critic who, above all others, may count as European" (IX, 432). In the same essay, when Arnold reiterates his own cosmopolitan creed, he appeals to the authority of Goethe.

> Let us conceive of the whole group of civilised nations as being, for intellectual and spiritual purposes, one great confederation, bound to a joint action and working towards a common result; a confederation whose members have a due knowledge both of the past, out of which they all proceed, and of one another. This was the ideal of Goethe, and it is an ideal which will impose itself upon the thoughts of our modern societies more and more.
>
> (IX, 38)

Arnold had propounded this ideal as early as "The Modern Element." The formulation he gives to it in his essay on Wordsworth is nearly identical with that in "The Function of Criticism" (III, 284) and appears to be a paraphrase from two passages in Goethe. In one of the *Maximen und Reflexionen* that Arnold copies into his *Note-Books* Goethe declares that art and science have no patriotic character and that they both "können nur durch allgemeine freie Wechselwirkung aller zugleich Lebenden, in steter Rücksicht auf das was uns vom Vergangenen übrig und bekannt ist, gefördet werden."[27] In this statement Goethe enunciates a general principle without reference to the historical context. In Eckermann's *Gespräche* he emphasizes the peculiarly modern character of this principle. "National-Literatur will jetzt nicht viel sagen, die Epoche der Welt-Literatur ist an der Zeit, und jeder muss jetzt dazu wirken, diese Epoche zu beschleunigen."[28] Arnold accepts this commission, and he makes it a salient point of his cosmopolitan program to establish Goethe himself as not only "the manifest centre of German literature" (III, 107–108) but as the central figure in the literature of all modern Europe.

Goethe

Arnold's praise of Goethe is as emphatic as his praise of Sophocles or Shakespeare. Goethe is "the greatest poet of modern times,

27. . . . "can be furthered only through a general, free mutual influence among all people living at the same time, and with a constant regard for what remains and is known to us from the past." *NB*, p. 164.

28. "National literature is not now of much significance; the time has come for the epoch of world literature, and everyone must work to precipitate this epoch." Eckermann, pt. 1, January 31, 1827.

the greatest critic of all times" (I, 8). This evaluation seems straightforward enough, but when he is pressed to give a more specific appraisal of Goethe's achievement, Arnold finds himself strangely embarrassed. By 1877 Arnold had for thirty years quoted from Goethe more often than from any other writer, but he had never devoted an entire essay to him. When he finally does come to write a whole essay, he chooses not to attempt a complete and independent evaluation but only to synopsize and comment on the lengthy and severely critical analysis of Goethe given by Edmond Scherer. In a letter to his sister, Arnold expresses relief at not being obliged to construct his own critique. "Considering how much I have read of Goethe, I have said in my life very little about him; to write an article in general about him would be an alarming task; I am very glad to be limited by having only to speak of my Frenchman's talk of him."[29] Arnold does not himself explain the reason for his alarm; it would appear from his essay that, although he still venerates Goethe, he is able neither to substantiate the claims he had made earlier about the spiritual significance of Goethe's poetry nor to say exactly what it is in Goethe's criticism that has proved of such profound importance. Arnold had always considered the chief virtue of Goethe's poetry to be its critical intelligence, and though he concurs with most of Scherer's derogatory judgments about Goethe's larger creative efforts, he still insists on Goethe's value as a critic. He does not, however, attempt to define the signal features of Goethe's critical doctrines. Goethe wrote no one major theoretical work, and Arnold argues that "it is not principally in his published works, it is in the immense Goethe-literature of letter, journal, and conversation . . . that the elements for an impression of the truly great, the truly significant Goethe are to be found" (VIII, 275). For Arnold this vast body of epigrams, insights, and detached observations adds up to an image of Goethe as "our greatest modern man," that is, the most successful exemplar of a life devoted to the pursuit of culture.

Goethe's letters and conversations do not, however, add up to a single coherent and fully articulated theoretical framework. For the matrix ideas that shape his theory of culture Arnold owes more to Heine than to Goethe. Heine schematizes cultural history as an alternation of Hebraism and Hellenism, and it is Heine who identifies the modern problem as the creation of a new spiritual basis

29. *Letters* 2:165–66 (December 1877).

by means of a union between Hebraism and Hellenism. Heine himself, however, tends toward an ironic repudiation of both cultural poles, and in Goethe, Arnold finds a more simply positive, constructive standard of criticism.

> Alles opponierende Wirken geht auf das Negative hinaus, und das Negative ist nichts. . . . Wer recht wirken will, muss nie schelten, sich um das Verkehrte gar nicht bekümmern, sondern nur immer das Gute tun. Denn es kommt nicht darauf an, dass eingerissen, sondern dass etwas aufgebaut werde, woran die Menschheit reine Freude empfinde.[30]

Arnold enlists himself under this banner of idealistic affirmation, and he sanctions negative criticism only insofar as it is clearly subordinated to the realization of human perfection. The idealism of Heine does not preclude an ironic impulse that sometimes takes mastery and concludes in a vision of cosmic absurdity. Consequently, Arnold tries to minimize the scope of Heine's influence and to align himself as much as he can with Goethe.

Goethe's presence in Arnold's work is all-pervasive but amorphous. The antimodernism of the 1853 Preface, the modernism of the first critical phase, the resurgence of Hebraism, and then again the advocacy of general culture—all receive corroboration from fragments of Goethe's commentary, and at each point this corroboration involves in some degree a distortion of Goethe's actual views.[31] Of all these phases the most distinct image of Goethe in

30. "All oppositional effort aims at the Negative, and the Negative is nothing. . . . Whoever wants genuinely to have an effect must never scold, must not fret himself at all with the perverse, but only always do the good. For what really matters is not that something is demolished, but that there be something built about which mankind can feel pure joy." Eckermann, pt. 1, February 24, 1825.

31. In an essay that has until recently served as the standard critical work on Arnold's relations to Goethe, James Bentley Orrick maintains that Arnold's conception of Goethe "did not influence his mode of thought quite as much as his mode of thought influenced his conception of Goethe." *Matthew Arnold and Goethe* (1928; reprint ed. London: Wm. Dawson and Sons, 1966), p. 52. This thesis is sound, but Orrick himself has little sympathy for Arnold's "mode of thought" and no sense of its development. His jaundiced view of Arnold as a narrow, unintelligent moralist and his boundless admiration for Goethe render him unable to discern with any precision the points of connection and disparity between their ideas. Orrick's essay has now been superseded by James Simpson's *Matthew Arnold and Goethe* (London: MHRA, 1979). Simpson's interpretation of Arnold himself is not strikingly original, but he provides a careful, judicious sifting of Arnold's references and allusions to Goethe. His section on the differences in the social and political views of Goethe and Arnold is superb.

Arnold's writing remains that of the early poetry and the 1853 Preface. Arnold's classicism validates itself by appeal to the authority of Goethe, and the Hellenic ideal that Arnold propounds in the early essays and in *Culture and Anarchy* models itself in part after the description of Hellenism in Goethe's essay on Winckelmann. Arnold himself, however, situates this ideal within a teleological scheme of cultural progress, and he associates his Hellenism with the modern spirit of democratic social change. The Hellenism of Goethe, in contrast, is of a more purely aesthetic character, and Goethe does not attempt to develop a teleological rationale for the shape of history. In his religious phase Arnold draws support from Goethe's adherence to natural religion, but Goethe's religious thought is not, like Arnold's, predominantly moralistic. Goethe's apothegmatic moral statements, which form a large proportion of the entries from Goethe in Arnold's *Note-Books*, concern themselves primarily with the necessity of self-discipline, the discipline of the artist and the student.[32] Finally, Arnold's determination in his last decade to fuse poetry with religion runs directly counter to Goethe's purist aestheticism. Arnold is seldom willing to recognize any divergence between his own opinions and those of Goethe. He makes promiscuous, indiscriminate use of Goethe's gnomic utterances, and in tracing the course of Goethe's influence on Arnold, we shall observe that Arnold frequently twists the intent of Goethe's phrases to suit his own purposes. The diffuse, desultory character of Goethe's criticism lends itself to this kind of treatment, but the treatment is nonetheless an abuse. The consequence of this abuse is that Arnold ultimately renders himself incapable of giving any very firm or precise critique of Goethe's thought.

In the early 1850s Arnold had read some of Heine, but he had not yet made any public profession of Heine's critical importance, nor perhaps had he yet recognized his importance. Even so, there is a striking similarity in the images of Goethe that are sketched out by Heine and Arnold. The evaluative emphasis, however, is somewhat different. Heine admires Goethe's regal composure, but he also resents it. Moreover, Heine is, as Arnold calls him, a "Paladin of the modern spirit," and he cannot but resent Goethe's ab-

32. A similar point is made by David J. DeLaura in *Hebrew and Hellene in Victorian England: Newman, Arnold, and Pater* (Austin: University of Texas Press, 1969), p. 190. I would disagree, however, with DeLaura's contention (p. 189) that "Goethe played a notably small part in the development of Arnold's Hellenism in the sixties."

straction from the problems of social change (III, 112). For Arnold at this time, Goethe's detachment from the malaise of the modern spirit presents itself first as a desirable but inaccessible condition and then, in the 1853 Preface, as a model to be emulated.[33] Since during this period Arnold himself wishes to withdraw from the turmoil of the modern world, he does not share Heine's resentment of Goethe, but when he later commits himself to modernism, his attempt to adapt Goethe to his own new attitudes will stand in conflict with the image of Goethe that he has developed in parallel with Heine. For Heine, Goethe epitomizes a whole epoch of German literature, the *Kunstperiode,* in which the artist concerns himself exclusively with creating a perfect world of aesthetic objects, or what Heine calls "eine unabhängige zweite Welt." The *Goetheaner* who propound this aesthetic creed regard the artist virtually as a god, and they consider the real world as merely a source of material for artistic composition. Heine is himself a worshiper in the temple of art, but he declares that it is a mistake "die Kunst selbst als das Höchste zu proklamieren, und von den Ansprüchen jener ersten wirklichen Welt, welcher doch der Vorrang gebührt, sich abzuwenden."[34] Despite his resistance to the idea of aesthetic supremacy, Heine himself depicts Goethe as a Greek god, an artist who embodies in his person and manner, as well as in his art, the composed grandeur of the ancient aesthetic ideal. "Überall . . . sehen wir ihn klug, schön, liebenswürdig, eine holdselig erquickende Gestalt, ähnlich den ewigen Göttern. . . . Um seinen Mund will man einen kalten Zug von Egoismus bemerkt haben; aber auch dieser Zug ist den ewigen Göttern eigen, und gar dem Vater der Götter, dem grossen Jupiter."[35] Heine's own passionately in-

33. James Simpson quotes a passage from *Wilhelm Meisters Wanderjahre* in which Goethe remarks that "fate has exalted the poet above. . . . the conflicting tumult of the passions." *Matthew Arnold and Goethe,* p. 26. Throughout his discussion, Simpson emphasizes the influence of personal feelings on the development of Arnold's thought. The preeminent significance Simpson attributes to the affair with Marguerite seems to me inordinate.

34. . . . "an independent second world."

". . . to proclaim art itself as the highest, and to turn oneself away from the claims of that first actual world, to which however precedence rightly belongs." Heine, 3:393 (*Die romantische Schule*).

35. "Everywhere . . . we see him clever, beautiful, amiable, a most charmingly invigorating figure, similar to the eternal gods. . . . People claim to have noticed a cold trait of egoism around his mouth; but this trait also belongs to the eternal gods, and indeed to the father of the gods, the great Jupiter." Heine, 3:404–405 (*Die romantische Schule*).

volved nature, his "glühendes Enthusiastenherz," recoils from Goethe's "kalte Behaglichkeit," but he nonetheless grants that Goethe is "der grösster Kunstler in unserer Literatur."[36]

In the "Memorial Verses" for Wordsworth, Arnold, like Heine, pictures Goethe as an embodiment of Olympian detachment. Goethe, "Physician of the iron age," recognized the spiritual distress of his time but took refuge from it in the more nearly perfect world of artistic composition.

He look'd on Europe's dying hour
Of fitful dream and feverish power;
His eye plunged down the weltering strife,
The turmoil of expiring life—
He said: *The end is everywhere,*
Art still has truth, take refuge there!
And he was happy, if to know
Causes of things, and far below
His feet to see the lurid flow
Of terror, and insane distress,
Of headlong fate, be happiness.

For Arnold the dispassionate clarity of Goethe's vision represents, if not happiness, at least composure, and it seems to him that this state of mind is no longer attainable. In the first elegy to Senancour, Arnold declares that "Goethe's course few sons of men / May think to emulate." Goethe owes his composure both to the possession of a spirit uniquely lucid and "sane" and to the good fortune of being born in a more settled period of history.

For though his manhood bore the blast
Of a tremendous time,
Yet in a tranquil world was pass'd
His tenderer youthful prime.

Arnold never comes to believe that it would be possible for himself, as an artist, "Goethe's wide / And luminous view to gain." However, in the 1853 Preface he believes that as a critic he may imitate Goethe's aesthetic detachment from the strife and travail of the modern world.

36. His "glowing enthusiast's heart" recoils from Goethe's "cold composure," but he nonetheless grants that Goethe is "the greatest artist in our literature." Heine, 1:455 ("*Die deutsche Literatur* von Wolfgang Menzel"), and 3:395 (*Die romantische Schule*).

The classicist antimodernism of Arnold's 1853 Preface draws on the aesthetic doctrines both of Goethe and of the English eighteenth century. Arnold does not acknowledge his debt to the English neoclassicists, perhaps because he feels that they are not modern enough to serve as authorities for his own antimodernism. He is entirely willing, however, to acknowledge the influence of Goethe. He alludes to Goethe's idea of *architectonicè*; he paraphrases Goethe's definition of the two types of dilettante, those who disregard form and those who regard nothing but form; and he appeals directly to Goethe's authority as support for his disparagement of the contemporary world. Anticipating the indignant rejoinders that will be roused by his essay, he declares that "he who possesses the discipline I speak of will content himself with remembering the judgments passed upon the present age, in this respect, by the men of strongest head and widest culture whom it has produced; by Goethe and by Niebuhr" (I, 14). Arnold's inability to resolve the spiritual problems he has explored in his poetry appears to have left him in a state of passive acquiescence to the attitudes that have enabled Goethe to transcend doubt and frustration. The man who possesses a classical discipline will rely upon Goethe and Niebuhr because "he feels assured in his own mind that their aims and demands upon life were such as he would wish, at any rate, his own to be; and their judgment as to what is impeding or disabling such as he may safely follow."

The derivative character of Arnold's essay goes a long way toward validating his profession of docility, but Arnold's submission is not quite so complete as he claims. Whereas Goethe says only that it is difficult under modern conditions to write good poetry, Arnold suggests that it is altogether impossible, and Arnold includes Goethe's own poetry in his censure. Nonetheless, the terms in which Arnold establishes his invidious comparison of ancient and modern literature appear to be directly inspired by Goethe. In Eckermann's *Gespräche* Goethe complains of readers who ignore the action of a poem and judge the work solely on the basis of what Arnold calls "attractive accessories." "Dies Gedicht ist schön, sagen sie, und denken dabei bloss an die Empfindungen, an die Worte, an die Verse. Dass aber die wahre Kraft und Wirkung eines Gedichts in der Situation, in den Motiven besteht, daran denkt niemand."[37] Poets, moreover, succumb to the superficiality of their

37. "This poem is beautiful, they say, and thereby think merely of the

readers and write to please them. Goethe, like Arnold, suggests two related reasons for this inadequacy of modern poetry and modern readers of poetry: first, the tendency of modern literature to concern itself with the inner nature of man rather than with external events; and second, the pettiness of these events in the contemporary world. Commenting on a contemporary poet, Goethe remarks that "er leidet an der allgemeinen Krankheit der jetzigen Zeit, an der Subjektivität."[38] Goethe maintains that the object, *Gegenstand,* is of primary importance in literature, and he suggests that the problem with modern literature is that it has no worthy objects to imitate.

> Alles Talent ist verschwendet, wenn der Gegenstand nichts taugt. Und eben weil dem neuern Künstler die würdigen Gegenstände fehlen, so hapert es auch so mit aller Kunst der neuern Zeit. Darunter leiden wir alle; ich habe auch meine Modernität nicht verleugnen können.[39]

Later in Eckermann's *Gespräche* he modifies this judgment and renders the inadequacy of literary objects dependent on the spiritual condition of the public. The standard he employs to judge of modern taste is, as for Arnold, that of Periclean Athens.

> Die Zeit, in welcher Äschylus, Sophokles und Euripides schrieben, war freilich eine ganz andere: sie hatte den Geist hinter sich und wollte nur immer das wirklich Grösste und Beste. Aber in unserer schlechten Zeit, wo ist denn da das Bedürfnis für das Beste? Wo sind die Organe es aufzunehmen?[40]

Arnold reiterates these notions, and he even reproduces the ambiguity that arises from ascribing the faults of modern litera-

---

sentiments, of the words, of the verses. But that the true power and effect of a poem consists in the situation, in the subject, nobody thinks about that." Eckermann, pt. 1, January 18, 1825.

38. "He suffers from the general sickness of the present time, from subjectivity." Eckermann, pt. 1, January 29, 1826.

39. "All talent is squandered if the object is worth nothing. And it is just because worthy objects are lacking to the more recent artist that all art of the recent time goes so wrong. We all suffer from this; I also have been unable to repudiate my modernity." Eckermann, pt. 1, November 3, 1823.

40. "The period in which Aeschylus, Sophocles and Euripides wrote was, to be sure, of another order altogether: They had the spirit behind them and always wanted only the truly greatest and best. But in our bad time, where is there then any need for the best? Where are the organs to receive it?" Eckermann, pt. 1, December 20, 1826.

ture, on the one hand, to a defect of great objects and, on the other, to a defect of taste in the reading public. Speaking in the voice of noble-minded modern poets, he declares that an age devoted to "the great ideas of industrial development and social amelioration" offers nothing worthy of poetic imitation (I, 13). The poets for whom Arnold speaks maintain that "the elements they need for the exercise of their art are great actions, calculated powerfully and delightfully to affect what is permanent in the human soul," and "that an age wanting in moral grandeur can with difficulty supply such, and an age of spiritual discomfort with difficulty be powerfully and delightfully affected by them." In this statement Arnold clearly suggests that not only are there no great subjects for poetic imitation, but even if there were, no one would appreciate them. In the very next paragraph, however, he recommends that if the poet will only take his material from the heroic past he will find an audience to respond to his work. He will "enable others, through his representation of it, to delight in it also." Finally, though, Arnold gives the impression of having abandoned all hope for contemporary literature. Even taking the ancient poets as a guide, it may be "impossible for us, under the circumstances amidst which we live, to think clearly, to feel nobly, and to delineate firmly" (I, 15). The conscientious poet will constrain his creative efforts to classicist imitations, not so much in the expectation of attaining to "the mastery of the great artists," but only so that he may transmit to his successors "the practice of poetry, with its boundaries and wholesome regulative laws, under which excellent works may again, perhaps, at some future time, be produced" (I, 15).

In his diagnosis of the modern plight and in his comparison of ancient and modern literature, Arnold places himself under the tutelage of Goethe. When, however, he categorically condemns all modern poetry, including Goethe's own, he steps beyond the bounds of Goethe's authority, and he does not acknowledge this divergence. Arnold names Goethe as the greatest modern poet, but he does not advise that Goethe's poetry be taken, like that of the ancients, as a model. He holds up *Hermann und Dorothea*, one of Goethe's poems that Goethe himself most favored, as an example of the triviality of modern topics, and he mentions *Faust* as an example of the structural debility that results from excessive subjectivity. "*Faust* itself, judged as a whole, and judged strictly as a poetical work [i.e., judged structurally], is defective: its illustrious author . . . would have been the first to acknowledge it; he only defended his work, indeed, by asserting it to be 'something incommensurable' " (I, 8). Goethe does indeed describe *Faust* as something incommensurable, but he certainly does not intend by this to concede that the work is "defective."[41] Goethe uses the word *inkommensurabel* to signify a grandeur that is unique and not answerable to explicit general principles. "Der Faust . . . ist doch ganz etwas Inkommensurabeles, und alle Versuche, ihn dem Verstand näherzubringen, sind vergeblich."[42] It is with a similar signification that Goethe declares, with reference to his scientific studies, that "die Natur sei inkommensurabel, und bei den grossen Irregularitäten sei es sehr schwer das Gesetzliche zu finden."[43] When he applies the word *incommensurable* to Byron's poetic talent, he intends the word to signify the highest possible praise. "Er ist ein grosses Talent, ein *geborenes* und die eigentlich poetische Kraft ist mir bei niemanden grösser vorgekommen als bei ihm."[44] Goethe is willing to concede that he has himself suffered from his modern circumstances, but he regards his poetic production as of the highest order. He believes, like Arnold, that the Greeks provide the finest prototype of aesthetic excellence, but he is by no means ready to condemn all of modern literature by comparison. His classicism, like that of Dryden and Johnson, concludes not in a withdrawal from present reality but in an affirmation of it. "Man spricht immer vom Studium der Alten; allein was will das anders sagen, als: richte dich auf die wirkliche Welt und suche sie auszusprechen; denn das taten die Alten auch, da sie lebten."[45] Arnold proclaims himself Goethe's disciple, but he turns Goethe to suit his own

41. Other evidence in support of this contention is adduced by James Simpson, *Matthew Arnold and Goethe*, pp. 73–74.

42. "Faust is, however, entirely something incommensurable, and all attempts to bring it closer to the understanding are futile." Eckermann, pt. 2, January 3, 1830.

43. "Nature is incommensurable and in regard to the great irregularities it is very difficult to find that which accords to law." Eckermann, pt. 1, March 22, 1824.

44. "He is a great talent, a born talent, and the specifically poetic power seems to me greater in no one than in him." Eckermann, pt. 1, February 24, 1825.

45. "People are always talking about the study of the ancients; only, what does that signify other than: address yourself to the actual world and seek to express it; for that is what the ancients also did in their lifetime." Eckermann, pt. 1, January 29, 1826.

needs, and this maneuver includes turning Goethe against himself.

If one were to subtract from the 1853 Preface everything that derives from Aristotle, the English neoclassicists, and Goethe, there would be very little left that Arnold might call his own; moreover, that little would scarcely be to his credit, for he departs from his sources chiefly by rendering their classicist ideas more rigid and extreme than they would themselves approve. In defense of Arnold we should remark that this was his first attempt at formal prose composition—he mentioned to Clough the trouble it gave him—and that, however supercilious and dogmatic it may appear, Arnold's strict classicism is not so much a finished doctrine as a program of therapy. He confesses that he has turned to the classical poets because they seem to offer him "amid the bewildering confusion of our times . . . the only sure guidance, the only solid footing" (I, 14). In the works that follow the 1853 Preface Arnold ceases to employ the classical ideal as a standard by which he may condemn the modern world and justify his retreat from it. He employs it instead as a standard of an accessible excellence, and for this sort of classicism Goethe serves more legitimately as an authority.[46] "Im Bedürfnis von etwas Musterhaftem müssen wir immer zu den alten Griechen zurückgehen, in deren Werken stets der schöne Mensch dargestellt ist."[47]

In the development of his Hellenic ideal Arnold continues both to draw on Goethe's ideas and to modify them for his own purposes. There are many passages scattered throughout Goethe's writing that contribute to Arnold's Hellenism, but the most important source appears to be the essay on Winckelmann, especially the section "Antikes." Goethe attributes the excellence of classical art to a unity of sensibility that it is difficult in the modern world to reapproximate. "Noch fand sich das Gefühl, die Betrachtung nicht zerstückelt, noch war jene kaum heilbare Trennung in der gesunden Menschenkraft nicht vorgegangen." The Greeks achieved this unity of sensibility, Goethe says, by holding themselves close to immediate, objective reality. Despite their relative disregard for

46. Helen C. White notes that in his essay "Literarisches Sansculottismus" Goethe defines the conditions under which a "classical" literature can arise, and that his formulation corresponds closely to that of Arnold in "The Modern Element." "Matthew Arnold and Goethe," *PMLA* 36 (1921): 450.

47. "In the need for something exemplary we must always go back to the ancient Greeks, in whose works a beautiful humanity is constantly represented." Eckermann, pt. 1, January 31, 1827.

the subjective side of experience, they were able to bring all the human faculties to bear on their artistic works. A man may achieve great things through the use of specialized capabilities, "aber das einzige, ganz Unerwartete leistet er nur, wenn sich die sämtlichen Eigenschaften gleichmässig in ihm vereinigen."[48] Anyone who attains to this condition of perfected performance delights in *das harmonische Behagen* (the harmonious ease) of his own existence. This passage from *Winckelmann* appears to be one of the main sources for Arnold's definition of perfection in *Culture and Anarchy*. Perfection "is a harmonious expansion of *all* the powers which make the beauty and worth of human nature, and is not consistent with the over-development of any one power at the expense of the rest. Here culture goes beyond religion, as religion is usually conceived by us" (V, 94).[49] Culture goes beyond religion, but it does not exclude religion, and Arnold differs from Goethe in that he identifies Hellenism, at its best, as a unification of religious and intellectual, moral, and aesthetic capabilities. Goethe says that the ancients felt "ihre einzige Behaglichkeit innerhalb der lieblichen Grenzen der schönen Welt" and that the temperamental and aesthetic perfection of the Greeks is accessible only to a heathen sensibility.[50] In Arnold's judgment this restriction of attention to the beautiful world is a feature of late Hellenistic paganism, not of Hellenism proper.

The difference between Arnold's and Goethe's opinions on the nature of Greek literature becomes apparent as early as the preface to *Merope*. In discussing the effects of Greek tragedy Arnold takes issue both with Goethe's biographer, G. H. Lewes, and with Goethe himself. Lewes maintains that "the Greek Drama is distinguished by its absence of repose; by the currents of passion being for ever kept in agitation" (I, 59). Goethe, conversely, emphasizes the calm

48. "Feeling and observation still found themselves unfragmented, that scarcely curable split in healthy human power had not yet taken place."

"But the unique, the totally unexpected, he accomplishes only when all of the faculties unite themselves equally in him." *Jubiläums-Ausgabe*, 34:13 and 11–12. Also see *Dichtung und Wahrheit*, pt. 3, bk. 12 (*Jubiläums-Ausgabe*, 24:81).

49. Edward Alexander and James Simpson both note a contributory influence for this idea from Wilhelm von Humboldt. *Matthew Arnold and John Stuart Mill* (London: Routledge and Kegan Paul, 1965), p. 244; *Matthew Arnold and Goethe*, p. 115.

50. . . . "their sole composure within the charming borders of the beautiful world." *Jubiläums-Ausgabe*, 34:12 and 14.

and composure of Greek tragedy. Arnold says that Goethe is not wrong in thinking "that there is repose in tragedy" but that Goethe "errs from Greek practice in the mode in which he tries to produce that repose." Taking *Iphigenie auf Tauris* for evidence, Arnold argues that Goethe produces repose "by inculcating it; by avoiding agitating matter; by keeping himself in the domain of the soul and conscience, not in that of the passions." Sophocles, however, "produces it by exhibiting to us the most agitating circumstances under the conditions of the severest form." This antithesis describes the tragic work itself. In "The Modern Element" Arnold describes a similar antithesis in the mind of the tragic dramatist. Sophocles is "a man who has mastered the problem of human life, who knows its gravity, and is therefore serious, but who knows that he comprehends it, and is therefore cheerful" (I, 35). Arnold's formula for a balance between agitation and composure seems to echo Heine's description of the heroic spirit evident in the statues of antique gods. Heine declares that this spirit consists "nicht, wie unsre Ästhetiker meinen, in einer ewigen Ruhe ohne Leidenschaft, sondern in einer ewigen Leidenschaft ohne Unruhe."[51] The kind of aesthetic power that Heine and Arnold discover in ancient art is something very different from Goethe's idea of a *harmonisches Behagen* that creates *ein reines, freies Entzücken* (a pure, free delight). Ironically, Arnold will ultimately describe Heine himself as an advocate of "the religion of pleasure" and will associate him with the one-sided aestheticism of late paganism (III, 229). Although Arnold takes issue with Goethe's view of Greek tragedy and agrees with Heine, he never criticizes Goethe in the general way that he criticizes Heine; nonetheless, the accusations that Arnold levels against Heine's pagan sensibility could often with more justice be leveled against Goethe.

In "The Modern Element," when Arnold reverses his 1853 evaluation of the kind of material the modern world offers to a creative mind, he does not make appeal to Goethe, nor when he sets about constructing a historical framework for the theory of culture does he find much support in Goethe's critical work. He nonetheless reserves for Goethe a foremost place in the vanguard of the modern spirit. In order to do so, however, he has recourse to

51. . . . "not, as our aestheticians believe, in an eternal rest without passion, but rather in an eternal passion without unrest." Heine, 2:498 (*Reisebilder* [*Travel Sketches*], "Die Stadt Lucca").

a distortion nearly opposite in character to that of the 1853 Preface. Whereas Arnold had previously represented Goethe as sanctioning his withdrawal from the actual world, in the essay on Heine, Arnold represents Goethe as working quietly but deliberately for the process of political and social liberation. Arnold quotes a passage from Goethe's essay "Ein Wort für junge Dichter" ("A Word for Young Poets") in which Goethe identifies himself as a "liberator." Goethe says that through his work the Germans have come to realize that all judgment is based on individual experience. "I can clearly mark where this influence of mine has made itself felt; there arises out of it a kind of poetry of nature, and only in this way is it possible to be original" (III, 110, Arnold's translation). Arnold grants that this might seem to be "a lame and impotent conclusion to Goethe's declaration that he had been the liberator of the Germans." He maintains, however, that this appearance is misleading, for Goethe's "naturalism" is "absolutely fatal to all routine thinking." Consequently, "nothing could be more really subversive to the foundations on which the old European order rested." As a description of the effect Goethe's influence may ultimately have had, Arnold's statement may have some validity. When, however, Arnold goes further and implies that Goethe's own conscious intention was subversive, he gives an impression of Goethe that is transparently at variance with the evidence of Goethe's own stated opinions.

Arnold attempts to establish a connection between Goethe's poetry of nature and the polemical writing of Heine.

> Heine is noteworthy, because he is the most important German successor and continuator of Goethe in Goethe's most important line of activity. And which of Goethe's lines of activity is this?—His line of activity as "a soldier in the war of liberation of humanity." . . . Nevertheless the process of liberation, as Goethe worked it, though sure, is undoubtedly slow. . . . Heinrich Heine was in 1830 in no humour for any such gradual process of liberation from the old order of things as that which Goethe had followed. His counsel was for open war.
>
> (III, 108, 110, 111)

There is here an implied contrast between the "open war" practiced by Heine and a supposed covert warfare practiced by Goethe. This implication is, if not intentionally deceptive, at least willfully self-deluding. For Goethe "freedom," in a political context, means nothing more than the liberty to operate within the traditional, divinely appointed social order. "Der Bürger ist so frei wie der Adelige, sobald er sich in den Grenzen hält, die ihm von Gott durch seinen Stand, worin er geboren, angewiesen."[52] Goethe's naturalism works toward dissolving Christian dogma, but it has no subversive intent toward the existing order of society.[53] At one point in Eckermann's *Gespräche*, Goethe speaks of a gradual social amelioration, but he also declares that social conflicts will, in one form or another, be eternal, and he concludes from this observation that everyone should just stay in his own place. "Der Schuster bleibe bei seinem Leisten, der Bauer hinter dem Pflug und der Fürst wisse zu regieren."[54] Arnold never mentions these comments, which he had undoubtedly read, nor does he mention Goethe's remark that the conflict of aristocracy and democracy has "kein allgemein menschliches Interesse."[55] In "Democracy," "A French Eton," and "Heinrich Heine" Arnold defines the modern spirit largely as a commitment to democratic social progress. When, therefore, he speaks of "the modern spirit, as this spirit manifests itself in Goethe's works or Heine's," he is making an improper use of Goethe's prestige to advance his own beliefs (III, 120).[56]

52. "The burgher is as free as the nobleman, as soon as he holds himself within the bounds that have been designated for him by God through the rank into which he has been born." Eckermann, pt. 1, January 18, 1827.

53. This distinction is also marked by W. A. Bruford in "Goethe and Some Victorian Humanists," *Publications of the English Goethe Society* 18 (1949): 51. Bruford deftly relates Goethe's political quietism to the social and spiritual character of his age.

54. "Let the shoemaker stay by his work, the peasant behind the plow, and let the prince know how to rule." Eckermann, pt. 1, February 25, 1824. To be fair, one should note that later on in Eckermann (pt. 3, January 4, 1824), Goethe denies that he is unequivocally "a friend of the established order." He recommends that the aristocracy make timely reforms so as to avoid revolutionary unrest. To counsel an aristocratic policy of enlightened self-interest is, however, hardly subversive, and René Wellek is certainly correct in objecting against Arnold's claim that Goethe is on the whole "an enemy of the old order." *A History of Modern Criticism 1750–1950 in Five Volumes* (New Haven, Conn.: Yale University Press, 1955–1965), 4:175. For an extended analysis of this issue, see James Simpson, *Matthew Arnold and Goethe*, pp. 109–110. Also see Charles D. Wright, "Matthew Arnold on Heine as 'Continuator of Goethe,'" *Studies in Philology* 65 (1968): 693–701.

55. . . . "no generally human interest." Eckermann, pt. 1, October 25, 1823.

56. This passage in which Arnold attempts to link together the political views of Goethe and Heine is correctly regarded by most commentators as a distortion of Goethe. Ilse-Maria Tesdorpf reads it as a distortion of Heine,

While drawing out the supposed connection between Goethe and Heine, Arnold notes that "Heine himself would hardly have admitted this affiliation" (III, 109). By putting the matter in this fashion Arnold implies in himself the possession of an insight, superior to that of Heine, that enables him to descry subterranean affinities. Actually, Heine gives an analysis of Goethe and of his own relations to Goethe that is far more precise and accurate than that which is given by Arnold. Heine locates the point of connection between himself and Goethe in their adherence to the pantheistic naturalism of Spinoza. In this sense they are both "modern," or as Arnold would say, "scientific." In identifying the "imaginative reason" as the faculty by which the modern world must live and in designating Goethe as the chief modern exemplar of the imaginative reason, Arnold bases his judgment on Heine's description of Goethe. Heine depicts the pantheism of Goethe's poetry as a synthesis of the sensual pagan understanding and the imaginative sentiment of Christianity.

> Das Heidentum des Goethe ist wunderbar modernisiert. Seine starke Heidennatur bekundet sich in dem klaren, scharfen Auffassen aller äusseren Erscheinungen, aller Farben und Gestalten; aber das Christentum hat ihn zu gleicher Zeit mit einem tieferen Verständnis begabt, trotz seines sträubenden Widerwillens hat das Christentum ihn eingeweiht in die Geheimnisse der Geisterwelt. . . . Der Pantheismus des Goethe ist also von dem heidnischen sehr unterschieden. Um mich kurz auszudrücken: Goethe war der Spinoza der Poesie.[57]

This is the modern spirit as it actually "manifests itself in Goethe's work or Heine's." There is, however, a distinction to be drawn between the "naturalism" of Goethe and that of Heine. Goethe concentrates his attention, as Heine says, on art, science, and individual feelings; he remains detached from modern historical

---

but her reading conflicts with the explicit content of the passage. *Die Auseinandersetzung Matthew Arnolds mit Heinrich Heine* (Frankfurt: Athenäum, 1971), p. 75.

57. "The paganism of Goethe is marvellously modernised. His intense pagan character manifests itself in the clear, sharp comprehension of all external appearances, all colors and shapes; but at the same time Christianity has gifted him with a deeper understanding; in spite of his bristling antipathy, Christianity has initiated him into the mysteries of the spirit-world. . . . The pantheism of Goethe is thus very different from the pagan. In a word: Goethe was the Spinoza of poetry." Heine, 3:618 (*Geschichte der Religion und Philosophie in Deutschland* [*History of Religion and Philosophy in Germany*]).

developments. Heine contrasts this detachment with his own historical absorption, and he bases this contrast on a difference of philosophical perspective.

> Nein, Gott manifestiert sich nicht gleichmässig in allen Dingen, wie Wolfgang Goethe glaubte, der dadurch ein Indifferentist wurde, und statt mit den höchsten Menschheitsinteressen, sich nur mit Kunstspielsachen, Anatomie, Farbenlehre, Pflanzenkunde und Wolkenbeobachtungen beschäftigte: Gott manifestiert sich in den Dingen mehr oder minder, er lebt in dieser beständigen Manifestation, Gott ist in der Bewegung, in der Handlung, in der Zeit, sein heiliger Odem weht durch die Blätter der Geschichte, letztere ist das eigentliche Buch Gottes.[58]

For Heine, as for Arnold, the issue of highest human concern is spiritual and social progress, and Heine is right in contrasting this concern with Goethe's historical *Indifferentismus.* Goethe makes various, conflicting statements on the nature and significance of historical change, but like the English neoclassicists, his main tendency is to seek the real and true in what is universal and permanent, not in what undergoes any essential transformation in the progress of time. In one of his *Note-Book* entries Arnold quotes Goethe's remark that "die Religion selbst, wie Zeit, wie Leben und Wissen, in stetem Fortschritt und Fortbildung begriffen ist."[59] In Eckermann's *Gespräche,* however, Goethe says that "die Welt bleibt immer dieselbe . . . die Zustände wiederholen sich, das eine Volk lebt, liebt und empfindet wie das andere."[60] The dominant pattern for both natural and historical change in Goethe's thought is that of repetition within a stable order. In a letter to Clough, written in 1848, Arnold remarks that the political events in France "must be disheartening to the believers in progress—or at least in

58. "No, God does not manifest himself equally in all things, as Wolfgang Goethe believed, who because of his belief became an indifferentist, and instead of occupying himself with the highest human concerns, occupied himself only with the playthings of art, anatomy, the theory of colors, botany, and the observation of clouds: God manifests himself in things to a greater or lesser degree, He lives in this perpetual manifestation, God is in movement, in action, in time, his holy breath blows through the leaves of history, which latter is the actual book of God." Heine, 3:394 (*Die romantische Schule*).

59. "Religion itself, like time, like life and knowledge, is caught up in continual progress and further development." *NB,* p. 126.

60. "The world remains always the same . . . conditions repeat themselves, one people lives, loves and feels just as another does." Eckermann, pt. 1, January 18, 1825.

any progress but progress en ligne spirale which Goethe allows man—tho: from him I scarcely understand this concession."[61] The concession is not of much import, however, for in the passage from the *Farbenlehre* to which Arnold alludes, Goethe emphasizes not the progressive but the circular aspect of the spiral.

> Der Kreis, den die Menschheit auszulaufen hat, ist bestimmt genug, und ungeachtet des grossen Stillstandes, den die Barbarei machte, hat sie ihre Laufbahn schon mehr als einmal zurückgelegt. Will man ihr auch eine Spiralbewegung zuschreiben, so kehrt sie doch immer wieder in jene Gegend, wo sie schon einmal durchgegangen. Auf diesem Wege wiederholen sich alle wahren Ansichten und alle Irrtümer.[62]

Goethe recognizes that the character of individual experience can be significantly modified by the age in which one lives—Arnold takes the term *Zeitgeist* from Goethe's essay "Homer noch einmal" —but he regards culture as a means by which the individual may rise above the vagaries of historical circumstance. Like Alexander Pope, Goethe seeks for himself a perspective from which all change is subsumed within a transcendent unity of nature.

> WENN im Unendlichen dasselbe
> Sich wiederholend ewig fliesst,
> Das tausendfältige Gewölbe
> Sich kräftig ineinander schliesst,
> Strömt Lebenslust aus allen Dingen,

61. *LC*, p. 80.

62. "The circle through which mankind has to run its course is definite enough, and regardless of the great period of motionlessness, which barbarianism effected, mankind has already more than once completed its course. One may wish to ascribe to it also a spiral movement, but it nonetheless turns ever again in that region through which it has already gone once before. In this way all true outlooks and all errors repeat themselves." *Jubiläums-Ausgabe*, 40: 120–21. Also see *Dichtung und Wahrheit*, pt. 2, bk. 7, where Goethe remarks that history appears to present us only with "a vacillation within a necessarily closed circle." *Jubiläums-Ausgabe*, 23:74. The poem that follows below is from *Zahme Xenien*, VI (*Jubiläums-Ausgabe*, 2:97):

> WHEN in infinity the very same thing
> Flows eternally, occurring over and over again,
> The thousandfold vault
> Powerfully closes in upon itself,
> The joy of life wells out of all things,
> The smallest just as the greatest star,
> And all urgency, all struggle
> Is eternal rest in God the Lord.

Dem kleinsten wie dem grössten Stern,
Und alles Drängen, alles Ringen
Ist ewige Ruh in Gott dem Herrn.
(ZAHME XENIEN, POEM 6)

We may illustrate the differences in the historical viewpoints of Goethe and Arnold by comparing the different use that they make of the terms "expansion" and "concentration." Arnold may have picked these terms up from *Dichtung und Wahrheit* (pt. 2, bk. 8); if so, he radically modifies the signification that Goethe had given to them. Goethe uses the terms allegorically to explain the Biblical myth of the Fall. For Goethe the Fall represents a cosmic truth, the proposition that "die ganze Schöpfung nichts ist und nichts war als ein Abfallen und Zurückkehren zum Ursprünglichen." Salvation, the return to God as the origin of creation, repeats itself throughout eternity. It is a process that "durch die ganze Zeit des Werdens und Seins sich immer wieder erneuern muss."[63] Within this scheme *Expansion* characterizes the spirit striving back to God. *Konzentration* characterizes the Satanic party, with which Goethe associates egoistic self-absorption and the "heaviness" of matter. Arnold may have taken from this dichotomy the ideas of a creative expansion and an uncreative self-absorption. In Arnold's theory, however, expansion and concentration do not represent mythic forces within an eternal cosmic process. They represent categories of cultural development within an actual historical progression. They do not, moreover, constitute absolute good and evil; they receive a relative valuation according to their necessary historical function. Arnold suggests, for example, that the epoch of concentration initiated by the English Puritans gave a "necessary and salutary" check to the expansive thrust of the Hellenic Renaissance. "If Hellenism was defeated, this shows that Hellenism was imperfect, and that its ascendancy at that moment would not have been for the world's good" (V, 175 and 174). For Arnold, as for Heine, history is "das eigentliche Buch Gottes" (the actual book of God). Expansion and concentration serve as complementary forces of cul-

63. "The whole creation is nothing and was nothing but a falling away [from] and a turning back to its origin. . . . [a process that] through the entire time of becoming and being must ever again renew itself." *Jubiläums-Ausgabe*, 23:166. Arnold's use of this passage is mentioned in passing by Walter Fischer, "Matthew Arnold und Deutschland," *Germanisch-Romanische Monatsschrift* 4 (1954): 126.

tural progress. In Goethe's formulation this dichotomy negates historical change by subsuming it within a repetitive universal process.

From Goethe's ahistorical perspective, large-scale political and social events such as the French Revolution appear primarily as intrusions on his own carefully cultivated *harmonisches Behagen*. In "The Function of Criticism" Arnold mentions that Goethe reproached the French Revolution for having "thrown quiet culture back," and he himself calls the Revolution "the greatest, the most animating event in history" (III, 264 and 265). Arnold tries to keep a foot in both camps, but he does not succeed in his attempt to connect Goethe's modernist naturalism with the progressive historical orientation of the modern spirit. In "A French Critic on Goethe" Arnold himself identifies the dominant note of Goethe's thought as an ahistorical classicism. " '*Die Gestalt dieser Welt vergeht*; und ich möchte mich nur mit dem beschäftigen, was bleibende Verhältnisse sind.' 'The fashion of this world passeth away; and I would fain occupy myself only with the abiding.' There is the true Goethe" (VIII, 276). This viewpoint satisfies only part of Arnold's own needs, and in his effort to construct a bridge between classicist universalism and the modern consciousness of historical change, Goethe can be of little assistance to him. Arnold knows this, but he is nonetheless reluctant to admit that there is any conflict between Goethe and himself with respect to actual social change in the modern world.

The combination of naturalism and universalism in Goethe's thought imposes itself on Arnold as constituting an authoritative power of judgment. By establishing Goethe as the greatest modern critic, however, Arnold places himself in an awkward position, for his own critical opinions are often quite different from those of Goethe. Arnold deals with this difficulty for the most part either by avoiding confrontation or by misreading Goethe so as to reduce or eliminate the disparity between them, and Arnold employs these tactics not only in the more nebulous regions of general theory but in practical criticism as well. The kinds of distortion that arise from his efforts to bring Goethe's opinions into alignment with his own make themselves most glaringly apparent in his treatment of Byron. Arnold claims that in Goethe's judgment on Byron—if we will but make some small adjustment to compensate for the excessive praise caused by the influence of Byron's contemporary popularity—"we shall have a judgment on Byron, which comes, I think, very near to the truth, and which may well command our adherence" (IX, 226). Arnold's contention that his own judgment on Byron is substantially the same as that of Goethe evinces a remarkable lack either of candor or of discretion. Their general evaluations of Byron's merit are quite disparate, and their attitudes toward Byron's involvement in social change are diametrically opposed to one another. In Arnold's view Byron's social involvement compensates for his defects of intelligence and artistry; in Goethe's view this involvement appears as the fatal flaw in the finest artistic sensibility the world had ever seen.

Goethe maintains that Byron's poetry is superior, in most respects, to that of all other English poets. Arnold quotes Goethe's statement to this effect, and he tries, unsuccessfully, to explain it away.

> Die Engländer . . . mögen auch von Byron halten, was sie wollen, so ist doch so viel gewiss, dass sie keinen Poeten aufzuweisen haben, der ihm zu vergleichen wäre. Er ist anders als alle übrigen und meistenteils grösser.[64]

Arnold argues that in making this statement Goethe "was not so much thinking of the strict rank, as poetry, of Byron's production; he was thinking of that wonderful personality of Byron which so enters into his poetry" (IX, 227). Goethe does, elsewhere, speak of Byron's eminent personality, but in the passage just quoted he speaks simply and unequivocally of Byron as a poet. Goethe recommends that Eckermann learn to read English most particularly so that he may read Byron, and he maintains that Byron has more raw poetic power than any other writer. "Die eigentlich poetische Kraft ist mir bei niemanden grösser vorgekommen als bei ihm."[65] In the essay on Heine, Arnold makes a similar remark, but he leaves out the idea of a particularly poetic power. He calls Byron "the greatest natural force, the greatest elementary power, I cannot but think, which has appeared in our literature since Shakspeare"

64. "The English . . . may think of Byron however they like, but this much is certain, that they have no other poet to show who might be compared to him. He is different from all the others and for the most part greater." Eckermann, pt. 1, March 26, 1826.

65. "The specifically poetic power seems to me greater in no one than in him." Eckermann, pt. 1, October 19, 1823, and February 24, 1825.

(III, 132). Since, for Arnold, Byron's power is chiefly a power of personal passion, the comparison with Shakespeare is misleading and betrays the ill-assimilated influence of Goethe. Arnold does not repeat this comparison of Byron and Shakespeare in any later essay, and in his essay on Wordsworth he expresses agreement with Edmond Scherer's opinion that "Byron's talent is oratorical rather than poetical" (IX, 431). In the essay on Byron, Arnold modifies this judgment. The influence of Goethe, joining with Arnold's memory of his own youthful enthusiasm for Byron, induces him to grant that when Byron is inspired "his verse then exhibits quite another and a higher quality from the rhetorical quality" (IX, 234). Whereas he had only recently said that Scherer's remarks were "words of truth and soberness," he now says that "it would be most unjust to label Byron, as M. Scherer is disposed to label him, as a rhetorician only" (IX, 431 and 234). Arnold does not, however, either raise his estimate of Byron to the height of Goethe's nor admit the disparity between them. He quotes Goethe's declaration that Byron is the greatest "talent" of the century, but he argues that there is an implicit distinction to be made between "talent" and "genius"; "while talent gives the notion of power in a man's performance, genius gives rather the notion of felicity and perfection in it; and this divine gift of consummate felicity by no means, as we have seen, belongs to Byron and to his poetry" (IX, 226). This distinction is entirely of Arnold's own making. Goethe himself says of Byron that "alles, was er produzieren mag, gelingt ihm."[66]

As Arnold suggests, Goethe does make a distinction between Byron's potential and his ultimate success; indeed, without this qualification Goethe would be forced to conclude that Byron was the greatest poet of all time. The reason that he gives for this qualification, however, is not what Arnold makes it out to be. Arnold and Goethe agree that Byron was defective in the power of critical reflection and that "inspiration" takes the place of reflection in his poetry. Arnold falsely contends, however, that Goethe, like Arnold himself, considers this defect of reflective power to be the cause of artistic failures in Byron's work. "Goethe lays his finger on the cause of all these defects in Byron, and on his real source of weakness both as a man and as a poet. 'The moment he reflects, he

66. "In everything he wishes to produce he succeeds." Eckermann, pt. 1, February 24, 1825.

is a child,' says Goethe" (IX, 227). Actually, Goethe speaks of this defect only in regard to Byron's critical judgment, and he isolates Byron's purely "poetic" power from his weakness as a critic. The quotation to which Arnold alludes refers to Byron's source study of *Faust*. Evidently miffed at Byron's attributions, Goethe remarks, "Lord Byron ist nur gross, wenn er dichtet, sobald er reflektiert, ist er ein Kind."[67] In Goethe's opinion the real source of Byron's weakness is not his defect of critical intelligence but his defect of social conformity. Goethe says that Byron, by detaching himself from the traditional and the patriotic—"vom Herkömmlichen, Patriotischen"—both ruined himself personally and stunted his supreme poetic talent. "Lord Byron ist an seiner polemischen Richtung zugrunde gegangen."[68] In the essay on Heine, Arnold partially combines this judgment with his own opinion that Byron failed as a poet because he had no adequate "intellectual equipment." He says that Byron "inevitably shattered himself to pieces against the huge, black, cloud-topped, interminable precipice of British Philistinism" (III, 132). The implication that Arnold intends is that Byron, because he lacked "culture" and "ideas," wasted himself in ineffectual opposition to British society. This is already very different from Goethe's contention that Byron weakened himself by cutting himself off from the spiritual resources of patriotism; in the essay on Byron, when Arnold modifies this judgment, he renders his own opinion exactly opposite to that of Goethe. Byron has no "light," but he derives a compensatory inspiration from his outrage at the "system of established facts and dominant ideas which revolted him" (IX, 232). Comparing the insubstantial content of Shelley's poetry with the political substance of Byron's, Arnold expresses an appreciation of Byron that provides a reverse mirror image of Goethe's.

67. "Lord Byron is only great when he writes poetry; as soon as he reflects he is a child." Eckermann, pt. 1, January 18, 1825. Charles D. Wright also notes Arnold's distortion of Goethe's intent in this reference. "How Matthew Arnold Altered 'Goethe on Poetry.'" *Victorian Poetry* 5 (1967): 60.

68. "Lord Byron was ruined by his polemical tendency." Eckermann, pt. 1, February 24, 1825, and pt. 2, February 11, 1831. Goethe's judgment on Byron applies a general principle and expresses an attitude that he maintained with unusual consistency. For example, at the beginning of part 2, book 7 of *Dichtung und Wahrheit*, where he proposes to survey the condition of literature in Germany during his youth, he says he will speak first "about the two hereditary enemies of all comfortable life and all cheerful, self-sufficient, poetic art: about satire and criticism." *Jubiläums-Ausgabe*, 23:53.

> He threw himself upon poetry as his organ; and in poetry his topics were not Queen Mab, and the Witch of Atlas, and the Sensitive Plant—they were the upholders of the old order, George the Third and Lord Castlereagh and the Duke of Wellington and Southey, and they were the canters and tramplers of the great world, and they were his enemies and himself.
>
> (IX, 233)

The choice of these topics, which fill Arnold with admiration and appear to him as the main source of Byron's strength, fill Goethe with apprehension, discomfort, and disapproval. Arnold mentions that Goethe perceived in Byron "the constant state of warfare and combat, the 'negative and polemical working,' which makes Byron's poetry a poetry in which we can find so little rest" (IX, 227). A few pages later, however, he falsely associates Goethe's admiration for Byron's personality with his own belief that this personality found its finest expression in a revolt against "the old order" (IX, 231 and 232). As a preparation for this false association Arnold has already deflected Goethe's objection to Byron's polemical activity into the sphere of metaphysics and art. Goethe "saw the *Hang zum Unbegrenzten,* the straining after the unlimited, which made it impossible for Byron to produce poetic wholes such as the *Tempest* or *Lear*" (IX, 227). Goethe does not, however, make any such connection between Byron's straining after the unlimited and a failure of artistic composition. He complains, rather, that Byron's titanism did not restrain itself from the world of social propriety ("Staat und Kirche blieben nicht unangetastet"), and contrary to Arnold, he maintains that Byron's actual artistic production was thoroughly successful.[69] Goethe finds in Byron something like what Arnold finds in Sophocles, a balance between passion and artistic control, but he can tolerate this passion only so long as it is kept within the bounds of social submission. "Seinem stets ins Unbegrenzte strebenden Naturell . . . steht jedoch die Einschränkung, die er sich durch Beobachtung der drei Einheiten auflegte, sehr wohl. Hätte er sich doch auch im Sittlichen so zu begrenzen gewusst!"[70]

69. ("State and church did not remain untouched"). Eckermann, pt. 1, February 24, 1825.

70. "The constraint that he placed on himself through observation of the three unities is very becoming to his disposition to be striving constantly into the limitless. Would that he had also known to limit himself thus in the realm of morals!" Eckermann, pt. 1, February 24, 1825.

Goethe's evaluation of Byron may serve as a test case for Arnold's claim that Goethe, as the finest critic of modern European literature, provides a reliable guide and authority for Arnold's own judgments. In a passage, later deleted, from the magazine publication of his essay on Wordsworth, Arnold quotes Goethe's dismissal of Hugo's *Hernani*, and he says that Goethe is the critic, above all others, "whose judgment on the value of a work of modern poetry is the judgment which will, we may be almost sure, at last prevail generally" (IX, 432). In the same passage Arnold paraphrases, as an example of a false and disproportionate criticism, Taine's comment on Byron: "Byron is the supreme and incomparable expression of the English genius after eight centuries of preparation." As we have seen, however, Goethe himself remarks that Byron is incomparable to the other English poets. The disproportionate praise that Goethe gives Byron may be attributed in part to the notorious difficulty critics have in judging foreign poets, especially contemporaries, but then, Goethe's judgment of his German contemporaries also appears to have been less than authoritative. Heine remarks that Goethe so consistently elevated second-rate writers above their superiors that it became a seal of mediocrity to be praised by him. "Goethe hatte Angst vor jedem selbständigen Originalschriftsteller und lob und pries alle unbedeutende Kleingeister; ja er trieb dieses so weit, dass es endlich für ein Brevet der Mittelmässigkeit galt, von Goethe gelobt worden zu sein."[71] Heine estimates Goethe's artistic merit at a rate that Arnold himself would consider almost excessive, but Heine does not, like Arnold, find it necessary to support his own opinions by meretriciously associating them with those of Goethe. Heine declares himself still in suspense awaiting a modern literary messiah. Arnold is too impatient to wait, and when the actual Goethe does not satisfy his needs, he fabricates an idol who does.

The conservative strain in Goethe's thought, which causes Arnold some difficulty during his first critical phase, would seem to be of more account to him during his religious period, and Arnold himself takes it to be so. He employs as an epigraph to *God and*

71. "Goethe became anxious before every self-reliant, original writer, and he praised and commended all insignificant petty spirits; indeed, he went so far in this that it finally amounted to a certificate of mediocrity to be praised by Goethe." Heine, 3:390 (*Die romantische Schule*).

the Bible a statement by Goethe that though political in reference may easily be translated into religious terms. "Im Prinzip, das Bestehende zu erhalten, Revolutionärem vorzubeugen, stimme ich ganz mit ihnen [den Monarchisten] überein, nur nicht in den Mitteln dazu. Sie nämlich rufen die Dummheit und die Finsternis zu Hilfe, ich den Verstand und das Licht."[72] Just as Goethe hopes to preserve the old political order on rational grounds, so Arnold hopes to preserve the moral essence of Christianity through the exercise of critical reason. Arnold's religious writings are sprinkled with quotations from Goethe, and up to a certain point Goethe and Arnold are in real agreement on the validity of natural religion and the use of conventional religion as "poetry." Arnold takes from Goethe the phrase about superstition being the poetry of life: "Der Aberglaube ist die Poesie des Lebens" (VI, 212, from the *Maximen*). He appeals to Goethe's authority for his assertion that the Bible is "not only a national book, but the Book of the Nations" (V, 256), and he concurs with Goethe in taking Spinoza as a guide for the right use of the Bible. Arnold copies into his *Note-Books* Goethe's comment on the effect of making the Bible generally accessible. "Mir ist klar: schaden wird sie wie bisher, dogmatisch und phantastisch gebraucht; nutzen wie bisher, didaktisch und gefühlvoll aufgenommen."[73] In another *Note-Book* entry Arnold translates a passage from *Dichtung und Wahrheit* that well describes the sentiments of natural religion.

> Universal, Natural Religion needs, properly speaking, no Faith: for the conviction that a great, producing, ordering, and guiding Being hides himself as it were behind Nature, in order to make himself comprehensible to us:—such a conviction impresses itself on every man.[74]

72. "In the principle of conserving the existing, hindering the revolutionary, I entirely agree with the monarchists, only not in the means to this end. That is to say, they call to aid stupidity and darkness, I call on understanding and light." Friedrich von Müller, *Goethes Unterhaltungen mit dem Kanzler Friedrich von Müller*, ed. C. A. H. Burkhardt, 3d edition (Stuttgart: J. G. Cotta, 1904), p. 71 (September 18, 1823). Arnold rearranges and misquotes slightly. The sense remains unaffected.

73. "To me it is clear: used dogmatically and fantastically it will be harmful, as it has been heretofore; and it will be helpful as it has been heretofore if it is taken didactically and feelingly." *NB*, p. 142. This maxim characterizes Goethe's own use of the Bible as he describes it in *Dichtung und Wahrheit*, pt. 3, bk. 15 (*Jubiläums-Ausgabe*, 24:228).

74. *NB*, p. 450.

Goethe and Arnold are at one in retaining a belief in some animating and ordering power superior to individual men. They part company, however, in their beliefs about the way this power manifests itself. Goethe limits true religion to two types, and neither of these types describes Arnold's conception of what religion should be. "Es gibt nur zwei wahre Religionen, die eine die das Heilige, das in und um uns wohnt, ganz formlos, die andere die es in der schönsten Form anerkennt und anbetet. Alles was dazwischen liegt ist Götzendienst."[75] Arnold marks this *Note-Book* entry with the comment "Judea . . . Greece," but Goethe's two categories are not equivalent to Hebraism and Hellenism as Arnold understands them. Arnold's Hebraism consists not in the adulation of an amorphous animative source but in a strict regard for an eternal and absolute moral order. "Righteousness tendeth to life," and Arnold's Hebraic God is but the poetic personification of righteousness. Moreover, high Hellenism in Arnold's view consists not in aesthetic delight alone but in the union of an aesthetic and intellectual enlightenment with a Hebraic fervor for righteousness. The Hellenic Greeks arrived "at the idea of a comprehensive adjustment of the claims of both the sides in man, the moral as well as the intellectual" (V, 179). Thus the difference of opinion that emerges between Goethe and Arnold over the nature of Greek tragedy reappears here as a difference of religious thought. The quotation from Sophocles that Arnold gives at the end of "Pagan and Mediaeval" as an example of the "imaginative reason," he alludes to again in "Bishop Butler" as a summation of religious principle. " 'Oh! that my lot may lead me in the path of holy innocence of word and deed, the path which august laws ordain, laws that in the highest empyrean had their birth, of which heaven is the father alone. . . .' " (III, 231 and VIII, 46).

On the surface Arnold and Goethe seem at one in their belief that religion must be subsumed in art. There is, however, a deep gulf between Arnold's religious attitudes and the purist aestheticism of Goethe. Whereas Arnold believes that art must assume the moral functions of religion and so become religion, Goethe believes

75. "There are only two true religions, the one which acknowledges and worships the holiness that lives in and around us, entirely formless, and the other which acknowledges and worships holiness in the form of the most beautiful sort. Everything that lies in between is idolatry." *NB*, p. 147 (from *Maximen und Reflexionen*).

that art is sufficient unto itself and that religion, as Arnold understands it, is unnecessary. Goethe explicitly repudiates "die falsche Tendenz solcher Künstler, welche die Religion zur Kunst machen wollen, während ihnen die Kunst Religion sein sollte." Religion does not stand on an equal footing with art. "Sie ist bloss als Stoff zu betrachten, der mit allen übrigen Lebenstoffen gleiche Rechte hat."[76] For Arnold, in contrast, religion is "the deepest thing in human life" (X, 252), and art can attain to high seriousness only by submitting itself to the needs and motives of religion. The "false tendency" that Goethe repudiates describes precisely what Arnold tries to do in his last two decades; moreover, despite the frequency of his quotations from Goethe on religion, Arnold recognizes that there is a conflict between them. In *Literature and Dogma* Arnold takes exception to Goethe's statement that "he who has art and science, has also religion" (VI, 177). This attitude, the readiness to call "all high thought and feeling by the name of religion," actually serves to exclude Hebraism from the world altogether, to reduce religion to a name, and to absorb it within the province of aesthetics. In "Theodore Parker" Arnold quotes "Goethe's wise epigram" that man " 'calls the best he knows, *God,*' " and he remarks that "the manner in which a man translates and expresses to us the best he knows must determine his claim to spiritual leadership of the highest order" (V, 83). Although Arnold never denies to Goethe this high order of spiritual leadership, Goethe's God is different from Arnold's, and this difference extends itself throughout the whole range of their thought on aesthetics, history, and the function of literature in the modern world.

It is, then, no wonder that when Arnold comes finally to give a general evaluation of Goethe, he finds himself at something of a loss. From the beginning of his career he has placed Goethe on a pedestal from which Goethe overshadows his own work, and yet the aesthetic, historical, political, and religious character of Goethe's thought is often at variance with his own. In his essay on Emerson, quoting from Carlyle's translation of *Wilhelm Meisters Lehrjahre,* Arnold says that this poetic eloquence represents "the great Goethe,

76. . . . "the false tendency of such artists, who want to turn religion into art, while art serves for them as religion."

"It is to be regarded merely as material, which stands on an equal footing with all other materials from life." Eckermann, pt. 1, May 2, 1824.

and the true one," and he contrasts this Goethe, the figure for whom he had in his youth felt such reverence, with "the stiff, and hindered, and frigid, and factitious Goethe who speaks to us too often from those sixty volumes of his" (X, 167). Arnold is unwilling to deny his own youthful enthusiasm, but neither is he willing to trust to it as a basis for his mature critical opinion. In the letter to his sister, written while he was preparing his essay on Goethe, Arnold remarks that Carlyle's criticism of Goethe was vitiated by an injudicious admiration. Taking Carlyle's failure as a warning, he hopes to avoid this fault and to achieve an authoritative judgment. "On looking back at Carlyle, one sees how much of *engouement* there was in his criticism of Goethe, and how little of it will stand. That is the thing—to write what will *stand*. Johnson, with all his limitations, will be found to *stand* a great deal better than Carlyle."[77]

By following Scherer's lead, Arnold can introduce a critical note into his own evaluation and then, while granting the justness of Scherer's reservations, can nonetheless plead for a warmer tone of appraisal. Arnold does not know, however, on what this greater warmth may be made to depend, and he takes refuge from analysis in a metaphor from painting. "Tone and perspective are somehow a little wrong; the distribution of colour, the proportions of light and shade, are not managed quite as they should be" (VIII, 275–76). In specific and explicit judgment, however, Arnold aligns himself with Scherer. Working through Goethe's artistic productions one by one, Arnold sometimes rates a particular piece a little more or a little less highly than Scherer does, but he concludes in substantial agreement with Scherer's contention that " 'Goethe is truly original and thoroughly superior only in his lyrical poems (the *Gedichte*), and in the first part of *Faust*' " (VIII, 269 and cf. 273). In *Celtic Literature* Arnold, who was probably misled by Heine's excessively coherent interpretation of *Faust I*, had contrasted Byron's obscure "Titanism" with "the consistent development and intelligible motive of Faust" (III, 373).[78] In his essay on Goethe, Arnold returns to his original opinion and concurs with Scherer that *Faust*, despite the excellence of episodes and detached scenes, is structurally defective and cannot produce a "single, powerful total-impression" (VIII, 273). This leaves only the lyric poems

77. *Letters* 2:166–67 (December 1877).
78. See Heine, 3:400 (*Die romantische Schule*).

by which Arnold might justify his earlier claim that Goethe had written "our only first-rate body of contemporary poetry" (III, 380). Arnold does not altogether renounce his former estimate of Goethe's poetry, but he suggests a reason why his opinion, which he is reluctant to abandon, may well be wrong. "His preciousness and importance as a clear and profound modern spirit, as a master-critic of modern life, must communicate a worth of their own to his poetry, and may well make it erroneously seem to have a positive value and perfectness as poetry, more than it has" (VIII, 275).

What Arnold most values in Goethe's poetry is its critical spirit or its intelligence, and this Goethe's poetry undoubtedly does possess.[79] However, a good deal of what Arnold takes from Goethe's critical thought Arnold has himself placed there. Perhaps Arnold has some suspicion that this may be so, for he makes no effort to explain or describe what he means by Goethe's "criticism of life." He merely lists the works where it is to be found and leaves us to define it for ourselves. Arnold praises Scherer for giving a "double judgment" of Goethe, but a double judgment is not necessarily a balanced judgment, and Arnold's own critique is not so much judiciously moderated as simply uncertain. Goethe had been of immense benefit to Arnold as a source of stimulating ideas, as an example of a poet who unites verbal power with a critical intelligence, and as a model of universal culture. Nonetheless, Arnold is not at all conscientious in determining accurately what Goethe himself actually thought. Goethe was of use to Arnold, but however helpful Arnold may be in other respects, Arnold is not of much use, finally, as a critic of Goethe.

Heine

Arnold's evaluation of Goethe fails in "justness of spirit" because Arnold attributes to Goethe a significance greater than he

79. At least at times Goethe himself would have agreed with this assessment. In part 3, book 11 of *Dichtung und Wahrheit,* he says, "I honor rhythm and rhyme, through which poetry first becomes poetry, but the actually deep and fundamentally effective, the truly educative and furthering, is that which is left over from a poet when he is translated into prose." And also in part 2, book 7: "For the inner content of an object that has been fashioned is the beginning and end of art." *Jubiläums-Ausgabe,* 24:56 and 23:79. Clearly, for Goethe a poem must not only be but mean, and it must (in these formulations) primarily mean. At other times, however, as when he defends *Faust,* he takes refuge in an aestheticism inaccessible to the prerogatives of critical reason.

can substantiate. His evaluation of Heine fails of justness for the opposite reason that Arnold is ultimately unwilling to attribute to Heine the significance warranted by Heine's influence on Arnold himself.[80] In his 1863 essay on Heine, Arnold objects strenuously to Heine's moral character, but he also designates him as the founder of a new epoch in European literature. From the evidence of Arnold's *Note-Books*, it appears that he wrote his essay on Heine in the same year he completed his poem "Heine's Grave." The image that Arnold draws of Heine in this poem blends the idea of mocking frivolity with the idea of archetypal, Satanic evil. Arnold situates "Heine's Grave" among his elegiac poems, but the placement is deceptive; the poem is not so much a dirge as an exorcism, that is, an attempt to purge Heine from Arnold's own soul.[81] In his ambivalence toward Heine, Arnold once again betrays the conflict in his own mind between his commitment to criticism and his instinctive need for a religious salvation, for Heine embodies both the appeal and the threat of a complete liberty of historical vision. Heine both fascinates and terrifies Arnold, because more than any other writer of his time, he gives evidence of what Cardinal Newman in the *Apologia pro Vita Sua* bitterly decries, "the wild living intellect of man."[82] Rather than confront the conflict in his own mind, Arnold finally resolves his perplexity over Heine by factitiously depicting him as an advocate of a one-sided paganism, as a sensibility limited to "the senses and the understanding" (III, 226).

Arnold's ultimate repudiation of Heine frees him from the burden of conscious intellectual dependence and alleviates his fear of

80. The most detailed study of Arnold and Heine is that of Ilse-Maria Tesdorpf, *Die Auseinandersetzung* (see n. 56 this chapter). The chapters on Heine and Arnold in Stanton L. Wormley's *Heine in England* (Chapel Hill: University of North Carolina Press, 1943) and Solomon Liptzin's *The English Legend of Heinrich Heine* (New York: Block, 1954) are both perfunctory paraphrases of Arnold. As Tesdorpf notes (p. 31), Elsie M. Butler, in her essay "Heine in England and Matthew Arnold," *German Life and Letters* 9 (1956): 157–65, is more concerned to defend Heine from Arnold's adverse criticism than to define the nature of Heine's influence on Arnold.

81. The same point is made in A. Dwight Culler's *Imaginative Reason: The Poetry of Matthew Arnold* (New Haven, Conn.: Yale University Press, 1966), p. 246, but in Culler's treatment Heine appears less as a dangerously seductive influence than as an easily suppressed annoyance.

82. Cardinal John Henry Newman, *Apologia pro Vita Sua*, ed. A. Dwight Culler (Boston: Houghton Mifflin, 1956), p. 233.

suffering under the anguish of Heine's spiritual suspension. Heine remains, nonetheless, the primary formative influence on Arnold's cultural theory.[83] Heine provides, as Goethe does not, a real source for Arnold's political modernism, and it is from Heine that Arnold derives the idea that there are in human nature two basic impulses: one toward moral deliverance and the other toward intellectual deliverance. This dichotomy, already at work in "The Modern Element," governs Arnold's thinking throughout his early essays and appears in *Culture and Anarchy* as forming "the very ground and cause" of all human action (V, 162). Between "The Modern Element" and *Culture and Anarchy* the main place in which Arnold develops his idea of the religious spirit and associates this spirit with the poetic imagination is in his essay "Pagan and Mediaeval Religious Sentiment." This essay is also the place where Arnold restricts Heine's range to the Hellenistic side of culture. The ideas in this essay, however, derive almost entirely from Heine. The religious criteria by which Arnold judges Heine and finds him wanting, Arnold takes from Heine himself. By limiting his own vision to a willful optimism, or at worst to a pious severity, Arnold excludes Heine's world-embracing irony, but he does not exclude the conflicts that are the source of Heine's irony. Insofar as Arnold's vision remains perplexed by the division of his loyalties between the religious imagination and the critical intelligence, he remains in thrall to the ghost of Heine.

Arnold first comes across Heine in 1848. His initial response of glib deprecation betrays something of the British insularity from which Heine will later help to free him.

> I have just finished a German book I brought with me here: a mixture of poems and travelling journal by Heinrich Heine, the most famous of the young German literary set. He has a good deal of power, though more trick; however, he has thoroughly disgusted me. The Byronism of a German, of a man trying to be gloomy, cynical, impassioned, *moqueur*, etc., all *à la fois*, with their honest bonhommistic

83. Ilse-Maria Tesdorpf also argues that Arnold drew his philosophy of history from Heine. *Die Auseinandersetzung*, p. 153. Her collocation of key passages from Heine and Arnold is instructive, particularly since she rightly presupposes in both Arnold and Heine a concern for "system." The usefulness of her analysis of these passages is diminished in that she oversimplifies both Heine and Arnold, fabricates strict contrasts between them, and then charges Arnold himself with deforming Heine's ideas. See pp. 158 and 167–68.

> language and total want of experience of the kind that Lord Byron, an English peer with access everywhere, possessed, is the most ridiculous thing in the world.[84]

Arnold's own thinking at this time is too immature for him to recognize what value Heine might have for an intellectual deliverance. Arnold's comments limit themselves to Heine's manner, and he judges this manner to be pretentious. Since he is himself not yet able to define the modern malaise with any precision, he is unable to judge properly of a poet who so effectively gives voice to it. Arnold senses something of the complexity of Heine's poetic temper, but he regards it in the way that a French neoclassicist would regard Shakespearean tragicomedy—as an impure mixture of genres. "I see the French call this Heine a 'Voltaire au clair de lune,' which is very happy." If we make allowance for the derogatory intent, this description is in fact quite apt. It accords with Heine's own self-depiction, and it is on this basis, the union of Enlightenment wit with the Romantic imagination, that Arnold will later most highly commend Heine's poetry.

By 1861 Arnold has begun to modify his former opinion of Heine. In a letter to Clough he says of Tennyson that "I care for his productions less and less and am convinced both Alfred de Musset and Henri Heine are far more profitable studies, if we are to study contemporaries at all."[85] Understandably enough, Musset does not long retain Arnold's interest, but by 1863 his rather grudging concession to Heine has been replaced by a tone of emphatic admiration. In "Heinrich Heine," when Arnold declares his intention "to mark Heine's place in modern European literature, the scope of his activity, and his value" (III, 117), he chooses the *Reisebilder*, the same work he had derided in his 1848 letter, as a representative sample of Heine's ability.[86] "Prose and verse, wit and seriousness, are mingled in it, and the mingling of these is characteristic of Heine, and is nowhere to be seen practiced more naturally and happily than in his *Reisebilder*." Arnold quotes several passages at length, and he selects one in particular to dis-

84. *Letters* 1:10–11.

85. *LC*, p. 154.

86. On the basis of publication evidence Tesdorpf notes that Arnold's first reference to this work can be only to the first two parts, "Die Harzreise" and "Die Nordsee." *Die Auseinandersetzung*, p. 11. These first two parts are not altogether of the same high quality as the later parts, but the characteristics Arnold chooses first to blame and then to praise are present in both.

play Heine as "the born poet he is,—full of delicacy and tenderness, of inexhaustible resource, infinitely new and striking" (III, 123). Arnold inverts his previous complaint about Heine's mixed manner and renders it as praise. Heine is "so effective a writer," he says, "because he unites so much wit with so much pathos" (III, 115). Arnold also renews the comparison with Byron, but this time in Heine's favor. Because of their intellectual poverty, Byron and Shelley, in contrast to Heine, "did not succeed in their attempt freely to apply the modern spirit in English literature" (III, 121).

When Arnold designates Heine as an advocate of the modern spirit, he gives the appearance of applying a broad, general idea to Heine as a specific instance. In truth, however, Heine's own work, more than that of any other writer, gives the pattern for the modern spirit as Arnold conceives it; in describing the character of Heine's modernism, Arnold defines as well the task he has set for himself as a "liberator." Because they are "children of light" and "invokers of reason against custom," the "representatives of the modern spirit" necessarily regard themselves as members of "the party of change, the would-be remodellers of the old traditional European order" (III, 112).[87] In his essay Arnold takes less account of Heine's relation to the European than to the English social system, and when he depicts Heine's career as "a life and death battle with Philistinism," he is thinking of the battle that he himself must wage (III, 111). He points out that Heine's political modernism did not expend itself in "direct political action," for such action is not "the true function of literature," and "Heine was a born man of letters." His agitation against the old order "took the character of an intrepid application of the modern spirit to literature" (III, 118 and 119). Arnold assigns the same kind of position to himself. In a letter of 1863 he says that "in this concluding half of the century the English spirit is destined to undergo a great transformation. . . . I shall do what I can for this movement

87. Tesdorpf takes as the starting point of her study of Arnold and Heine the differences in the political backgrounds to their work, and she concludes that their political views actually stand in complete contrast to one another. She argues that there is a deep gulf between Heine's concern for political freedom and Arnold's concern for inner freedom. On this basis she asserts that Arnold's use of Heine depends on a fruitful but thorough misunderstanding of him. *Die Auseinandersetzung*, pp. 29, 8, 30, 61. The oppositions here are exaggerated. The presentation of Arnold's political conservatism is one-sided in the extreme, and likewise, Heine's political radicalism is stripped of every qualification and ambiguity.

in literature; freer perhaps in that sphere than I could be in any other."[88] We may gain some sense of how closely Arnold identifies himself with Heine at this point by comparing a passage in this letter with a passage from the *Reisebilder* that Arnold translates in his essay. Heine likens himself to a loyal court jester, Conrad von der Rosen, who has joined his exiled king, an allegorical image for the German people. Asked how he would be recompensed for his fidelity, the jester replies, "Ach! lieber Herr, lasst mich nicht umbringen."[89] Arnold freely translates this as "Ah, dear master, by not leaving me to die in a ditch!" (III, 117). In his letter Arnold echoes his own translation of this passage. He foresees "the risk always before me, if I cannot charm the wild beast of Philistinism while I am trying to convert him, of being torn in pieces by him; and, even if I succeed to the utmost and convert him, of dying in a ditch or a workhouse at the end of it all." The "Philistinism" against which Heine campaigned in Germany was much more of a "wild beast" than the English breed, and Arnold in 1863 anticipated a struggle much more severe than it actually turned out to be. There is nonetheless a real connection between the two types of Philistine in that they both display an obstinate resistance to "modern ideas."

It is in part by means of Heine's commentary on the British that Arnold is able to define the nature of his own life-long battle, and in "Heine's Grave" Arnold acknowledges this debt. He remarks on Heine's hostility to England and grants it to be just, "for we / Heavy and sad, for her sons, / Long since, deep in our hearts, / Echo the blame of her foes." Arnold echoes Heine not only deep in his heart but in his published essay, where he paraphrases Heine's critique of unreflective English liberalism.

> What he hated in the English was the "ächt britische Beschränktheit," as he calls it,—the *genuine British narrowness*. In truth, the English, profoundly as they have modified the old Middle-Age order, great as is the liberty which they have secured for themselves, have in all their changes proceeded, to use a familiar expression, by the rule of thumb.
>
> (III, 112–13)

This pragmatic method, "which saved them from the necessity of recurring to general principles," has rendered the English "of all

88. *Letters* 1:240.
89. "Ah! dear master, do not allow me to be destroyed." Heine, 2:605.

people the most inaccessible to ideas and the most impatient of them." In his "Englische Fragmente" Heine had made the same charge. "Die Konzessionen, die dort den Liberalen gemacht worden, sind dieser mittelalterlichen Starrheit nur mühsam abgekämpft worden; und nie aus einem Prinzip, sondern aus der faktischen Notwendigkeit, sind alle modernen Verbesserungen hervorgegangen."[90] A Philistine, Arnold says, is someone who values "practical conveniences" over "reason, the idea" (III, 113). This distinction is the basis of Heine's objection to the English parliamentary system. "Selten in ihren parlamentarischen Verhandlungen ist es den Engländern möglich ein Prinzip auszusprechen, sie diskutieren nur den Nutzen oder Schaden der Dinge."[91]

Unlike the liberals, Heine does not limit his modernism to a concern for concrete social improvements. He seeks, like Arnold, an intellectual deliverance, a complete and independent vision of the past and present.

> To the ideas with which the burning questions of modern life filled him, he made all his subject-matter minister. He touched all the great points in the career of the human race, and here he but followed the tendency of the wide culture of Germany; but he touched them with a wand which brought them all under a light where the modern eye cares most to see them, and here he gave a lesson to the culture of Germany,—so wide, so impartial, that it is apt to become slack and powerless, and to lose itself in its materials for want of a strong central idea round which to group all its other ideas.
>
> (III, 119)

The strong central idea to which Arnold alludes is an idea that he himself adopts: the belief in the central historical significance of the French Revolution and the rational validity of its principles. "Ich spreche von der französischen Revolution, jener Weltepoche, wo die Lehre der Freiheit und Gleichheit so siegreich emporstieg aus jener allgemeinen Erkenntnisquelle, die wir Ver-

90. "The concessions that have been made there to the liberals have only with great effort been wrung from this medieval rigidity; and no modern reforms have ever derived from a principle, but only from actual necessity." Heine, 2:597.

91. "Seldom in their parliamentary affairs is it possible for the English to express a principle; they discuss only the use or harm of things." Heine, 2:583.

nunft nennen."[92] In the *Einleitung zu Kahldorf über den Adel* Heine draws a series of detailed parallels between the history of modern German philosophy and the history of the French Revolution. The comparisons, though clever, are somewhat fanciful. The ground idea, however, is that the consequence of modern philosophical speculation is to have rendered man a free agent, subject to no authority higher than that of his own reason. For Heine the Revolution represents the practical manifestation of this philosophical consequence, and Arnold accepts this association. In "The Function of Criticism" he elevates the French Revolution above that of the English because "it appeals to an order of ideas which are universal, certain, permanent. 1789 asked of a thing, Is it rational? 1642 asked of a thing, Is it legal?" (III, 264). There is, Arnold holds, a necessary moral relation between idea and practice, and like Heine, he finds this relation exemplified in a conjunction of German culture and French politics. He does not, like Heine, draw a parallel between, say, Kant and Robespierre or Fichte and Napoleon. Instead, he situates the conjunction of French practice and German ideas in Heine's own writing. "It is because he thus operates a junction between the French spirit, and German ideas and German culture, that he founds something new, opens a fresh period" (III, 120). Arnold rightly regards himself as the continuer of Heine in the effort to establish a doctrinal synthesis between high culture and democratic progressivism.

Arnold's approbation of Heine reaches its apex in the middle of his essay. At the end of the essay Arnold abruptly performs an about-face, criticizes Heine with a discordant harshness, and sets limits to Heine's importance that are in conflict with the tendency of his former statements. Arnold's concluding remarks begin a process of narrowing and reducing that will continue in "Pagan and Mediaeval" and in *Culture and Anarchy*, but Arnold has already said enough to give us a critical perspective on his later evaluations. Arnold utterly condemns Heine's character and his personal life, and he draws from this moral censure a conclusion of intellectual import. "He died, and has left a blemished name; with his crying faults,—his intemperate susceptibility, his un-

92. "I am speaking of the French Revolution, that world-epoch when the doctrine of freedom and equality so triumphantly arose out of that general source of understanding that we call reason." Heine, 2:598 (*Reisebilder*, "Englische Fragmente").

scrupulousness in passion, his inconceivable attacks on his enemies, his still more inconceivable attacks on his friends, his want of generosity, his sensuality, his incessant mocking,—how could it be otherwise?" (III, 131). Only one of these personal faults has any bearing on Heine's usefulness as a cultural theorist and a pattern of intellectual deliverance. "His incessant mocking" derogates from the Sophoclean serenity that Arnold has posed to himself as a goal. Arnold does not, however, immediately draw this connection. He segregates intellectual and moral deliverance and denies to Heine only the latter. "To his intellectual deliverance there was an addition of something else wanting, and that something else was something immense; the old-fashioned, laborious, eternally needful moral deliverance" (III, 132). Morality is, Arnold thinks, essential to any "true dignity of character," and it is apparently because Heine was lacking in this dignity that Arnold limits the significance of his work. "He is not an adequate interpreter of the modern world. He is only a brilliant soldier in the Liberation War of humanity." "Adequacy" is in part an intellectual quality, and this sort of adequacy Heine possesses. "In his head fermented all the ideas of modern Europe." The other part of adequacy is a spiritual (that is, a moral and emotional) quality. In "The Modern Element" Arnold says that Lucretius and Vergil lacked the strength, and Horace the seriousness, to be adequate interpreters of their world (I, 33, 35, 36). Heine lacks "moral balance" and "nobleness of soul and character" (III, 132). Insofar as this criticism is literary and not merely personal, what it amounts to is that Heine fails to sustain a consistent tone of reverence and gravity. Arnold will later say that Heine's most serious fault is "that he could reverence so little" (III, 182), and in his essay he concedes to Heine every poetic merit except that of moral gravity. Heine is "a man of genius, who finds in verse his freest and most perfect expression" (III, 123). He combines in his verse the finest qualities of European literature. "The wit and ardent modern spirit of France Heine joined to the culture, the sentiment, the thought of Germany. This is what makes him so remarkable; his wonderful clearness, lightness, and freedom, united with such power of feeling, and width of range" (III, 122).

Since Arnold grants so much to Heine and yet denies that he is adequate, we may conclude that even in his first critical phase Arnold's expectations of poetry are largely governed by his religious needs. To confirm this thesis, we may compare Arnold's evaluation of Heine with his evaluation of Wordsworth. In his essay on Heine, Arnold criticizes Wordsworth for retreating from the modern spirit, but it is nonetheless by reference to a Wordsworthian standard of poetry that Arnold finds Heine to be inadequate. In his essay on Wordsworth, Arnold isolates Wordsworth's peculiar superiority by distinguishing him from two other groups of poets. Neoclassical poets—Arnold lists Voltaire, Dryden, Pope, Lessing, and Schiller—"never, or scarcely ever, attain the distinctive accent and utterance of the high and genuine poets" (IX, 48). The second group, in which Arnold includes Burns, Keats, and Heine, "have this accent,—who can doubt it? And at the same time they have treasures of humour, felicity, passion, for which in Wordsworth we shall look in vain." Therefore, when Arnold declares that Wordsworth is superior to these poets because "he deals with more of *life* than they do," he does not mean to signify a greater range or complexity of life, but a more profound, religious veneration of life. Heine is capable of religious enthusiasm, but his intellectual vivacity, his wit, and his involvement in the spiritual turmoil of the modern world all render him incapable of a sustained Wordsworthian solemnity. By retreating from the modern spirit Wordsworth enabled himself to enjoy the calm simplicity of introspective sentiment and so rendered his poetry a surrogate to Arnold for conventional religious devotion. The value of religion, Arnold says, is the "beauty and rest" and the "grace and peace" that it gives, and he considers Wordsworth "the purest and most poetic" voice of the century because he "gives us so much to rest upon" (VIII, 84; X, 189; IX, 43).

Heine's poetry is brilliant, but it is not restful and it is seldom edifying. Heine himself suggests a defense for his failure to sustain an earnest tone. "Das Leben ist im Grunde so fatal ernsthaft, dass es nicht zu ertragen wäre ohne solche Verbindung des Pathetischen mit dem Komischen."[93] Nonetheless, Heine takes cognizance of the dubious spiritual quality of his own temperament, but he makes a plea for sympathetic understanding. "Es ist nun mal nicht zu leugnen, dass die Spottlust, die Freude am Widerspruch der Dinge, etwas Bösartiges in sich trägt, statt dass der Ernst mehr

93. "Life is at bottom so disagreeably serious that it would be unbearable without such a blending of the pathetic with the comic." Heine, 2:282 (*Reisebilder*, "Ideen: Das Buch Le Grand").

mit den besseren Gefühlen verwandt ist—die Tugend, der Freiheitssinn und die Liebe selbst sind sehr ernsthaft. Indessen, es gibt Herzen, worin Scherz und Ernst, Böses und Heiliges, Glut und Kälte sich so abenteuerlich verbinden, dass es schwer wird darüber zu urteilen."[94] Arnold does not, however, find it hard to judge, and as his religious needs become more insistent, his judgments become progressively less sympathetic.

Arnold is right that Heine had little power of sustained reverence. If we concede that this power is a necessary component of adequacy, then we may grant that Heine is not "an adequate interpreter of the modern world." However, insofar as "interpretation" is taken to mean the power of theoretical formulation, Arnold's mature interpretation of the modern plight and his solution for it are almost completely dependent upon those of Heine. At the end of the essay on Heine, Arnold suggests that Heine's scope is limited to the advocacy of political modernism, but in the body of his essay he has already intimated that Heine's cultural vision is of a much broader scope.

> He has excellently pointed out how in the sixteenth century there was a double renascence,—a Hellenic renascence and a Hebrew renascence,—and how both have been great powers ever since. He himself had in him both the spirit of Greece and the spirit of Judaea. . . . By his perfection of literary form, by his love of clearness, by his love of beauty, Heine is Greek; by his intensity, by his untamableness, by his 'longing which cannot be uttered,' he is Hebrew.
>
> (III, 127–28)

This is the closest Arnold ever comes to admitting that his own dichotomy of Hebraism and Hellenism derives from Heine. The passage in *Der Doktor Faustus,* which Arnold alludes to here, comments specifically on the Renaissance. Nonetheless, in Heine's major theoretical works (*Die romantische Schule,* the *Geschichte der Religion und Philosophie in Deutschland,* and the essay on Ludwig Börne) Arnold found this dichotomy presented as the two basic cultural prototypes and used to outline the shape of Western

94. "It is simply not to be denied that the delight in mockery, the joy at the contradiction of things, bears in itself something of maliciousness, whereas earnestness is more related to the better feelings—virtue, the sentiment of freedom, and love are themselves very earnest. Nonetheless, there are hearts in which jest and earnestness, evil and holiness, ardor and coldness mingle themselves so strangely that it becomes difficult to make a judgment about it." Heine, 2:508 (*Reisebilder,* "Die Stadt Lucca").

cultural history[95]—as it will later appear in Arnold's own work. "Alle Menschen sind entweder Juden oder Hellenen, Menschen mit ascetischen, bildfeindlichen, vergeistigungssüchtigen Trieben, oder Menschen von lebensheiterem, entfaltungsstolzem und realistischem Wesen."[96] In explaining the enmity that Ludwig Börne, a political radical, felt for Goethe, Heine ascribes to these two character types an innate temperamental aversion that has manifested itself on a world-historical scale of cultural conflict.

> Ein Hader, welcher, alt wie die Welt, sich in allen Geschichten des Menschengeschlechts kund gibt und am grellsten hervortrat in dem Zweikampfe, welchen der judäische Spiritualismus gegen hellenische Lebensherrlichkeit führte, ein Zweikampf, der noch immer nicht entschieden ist und vielleicht nie ausgekämpft wird: der kleine Nazarener hasste den grossen Griechen, der noch dazu ein griechischer Gott war.[97]

Like Arnold, Heine considers the Renaissance a reawakening of Hellenism, and like Arnold, he maintains that Christianity is not different from, but only an extension of, the spiritualist tendency

95. Tesdorpf contends that Arnold probably did not read *Ludwig Börne. Die Auseinandersetzung*, p. 43. Her main evidence is that the title does not appear on his reading lists. However, several entries for Heine list only his name, or his name and a subject-area, but not the specific works to be read. See *NB*, pp. 566, 571, 572. Tesdorpf also presents evidence that, contrary to R. H. Super's annotational attribution, Arnold did not paraphrase a certain passage from *Ludwig Börne*. Nonetheless, Arnold read a good deal of Heine that he did not directly paraphrase. On the whole, it seems unlikely that in the period of intensive reading preparatory to his essay on Heine, Arnold would not have read the work on Börne. Moreover, the similarity of certain passages on Hebraism and Hellenism in this work and in Arnold is close enough to render mere coincidence improbable.

96. "All people are either Jews or Hellenes, people with drives that are ascetic, image-hating, and ravenous for spiritualization, or people of a nature that rejoices in life, is proud of display, and is realistic." Heine, 4:18 (*Ludwig Börne*). Cf. *Culture and Anarchy* (V, 163–68). For possible contributory influences on this dichotomy in Arnold, see Frederic E. Faverty, *Matthew Arnold the Ethnologist* (Evanston, Ill.: Northwestern University Press, 1951), chap. 6. For limitations on the possible influence of Renan, see Tesdorpf, pp. 174–75. John Stuart Mill's version of the dichotomy is analyzed by Edward Alexander in *Matthew Arnold and John Stuart Mill*, pp. 55–56.

97. "A quarrel which, old as the world, declares itself in all histories of the human race and stood out most glaringly in the duel that Judaic spiritualism carried on against the Hellenic splendor of life, a duel that has not yet been decided and that will perhaps never be fought to a finish: the little Nazarene hated the great Greek, who was, moreover, a Greek god." Heine, 4:17.

of Hebraism. Arnold's account of the Hebraic temper is, on the whole, more polite than Heine's, but it is conceptually equivalent. Heine defines spiritualism as the spirit's drive to dominate the flesh, and Arnold credits Hebraism with a single-minded opposition to fleshly sin.[98] The modern Hebraisers, Arnold says, wrongly believe themselves to possess a complete world view, "whereas what they really have is a law of conduct, a law of unexampled power for enabling them to war against the law of sin in their members and not to serve it in the lust thereof" (V, 177). For both Arnold and Heine, however, spiritualism is not a merely negative virtue. The discipline of renunciation associates itself for both with the development of the poetic faculties of feeling and imagination.

Heine describes himself as chiefly Hellenic in temper, but he believes that the primary problem of modern culture is the historic division of "soul" and "body." Like Arnold, too, he believes that a new spiritual basis must be fashioned through the unification of Hebraism and Hellenism. "Die Grundlage der menschlichen Gesellschaft wird einst eine bessere sein, und alle grossen Herzen Europas sind schmerzhaft beschäftigt, diese neue bessere Basis zu entdecken."[99] The new basis he hopes to discover comprehends the ideals of social progress but requires ultimately a spiritual resolution. "Die politische Revolution, die sich auf die Prinzipien des französischen Materialismus stützt, wird in den Pantheisten keine Gegner finden, sondern Gehülfen, aber Gehülfen, die ihre Überzeugungen aus einer tieferen Quelle, aus einer religiösen Synthese, geschöpft haben."[100] For Heine, as for Arnold, the new religious synthesis must be practiced not in the ceremonies and rituals of a church but in literature. Heine describes Goethe as a Greek who has assimilated something of the inwardness of Christian sentiment, but he finds the pattern for a cultural resolution more completely realized in the work of Shakespeare.

98. Heine, 2:484 (*Reisebilder*, "Die Stadt Lucca"); 3:517–18 and 533 (*Geschichte der Religion*).

99. "The foundation of human society will one day be a better one, and all the great hearts of Europe are painfully occupied in discovering this new, better basis." Heine, 3:472 (*Die romantische Schule*).

100. "The political revolution which is founded on the principles of French materialism will find no opponents in the pantheists, helpers rather, but helpers who have drawn their convictions from a deeper source, from a religious synthesis." Heine, 3:570 (*Geschichte der Religion*).

> Shakespeare ist zu gleicher Zeit Jude und Grieche, oder vielmehr beide Elemente, der Spiritualismus und die Kunst, haben sich in ihm versöhnungsvoll durchdrungen, und zu einem höheren Ganzen entfaltet.
>
> Ist vielleicht solche harmonische Vermischung der beiden Elemente die Aufgabe der ganzen europäischen Zivilisation? Wir sind noch sehr weit entfernt von einem solchen Resultate.[101]

Shakespeare unites the Hebraic moral consciousness with the Hellenic sensitivity to nature and art and so attains to a disinterested absorption in the life of humanity. Arnold assigns to Goethe, not Shakespeare, the foremost place in the creation of a new spiritual basis, but he agrees with Heine that in Shakespeare the two faculties of poetic interpretation, the moral and the naturalistic, "seem wonderfully to balance one another" (III, 33).

In defining "the whole task of our civilization" Arnold and Heine are at one. There is, however, a basic difference between their treatments of the cultural dichotomy. Heine believes that neither Hebraism nor Hellenism provides a model of human perfection, and Arnold, though he declares that neither is "the *law* of human development," nonetheless assigns to Hellenism the role of archetype for a complete humanity. Heine seeks a spiritual resolution that he regards as entirely new and original; Arnold seeks to reapproximate a spiritual synthesis that has, he claims, already been achieved once before. The actual body of ancient literature to which Arnold ascribes an adequate realization of the imaginative reason is small (consisting only of Simonides, Aeschylus, Pindar, and Sophocles), and Arnold hesitates to press the claim for perfection even in these writers. He concedes that, although this poetry represents "the most successful effort" ever made to realize the imaginative reason, "no doubt that effort was imperfect" (III, 230 and 231). Such as it is, however, this poetry provides him with at least some historical grounding for his cultural ideal. Heine, in contrast, treats all ancient literature as fundamentally one-sided. He grants to the ancients a unity of sensibility but maintains that this unity was bought at the price of a spiritual shallowness, a pre-

101. "Shakespeare is at once Jew and Greek, or rather, both elements, spiritualism and art, have in him interpenetrated one another, reconciled themselves, and evolved into a higher whole.

"Is perhaps such a harmonious blending of both elements the task of the whole European civilization? We are still very far distant from any such outcome." Heine, 4:47 (*Ludwig Börne*).

occupation with surface reality, and an unsympathetic egoism. Christianity first serves as a healthy reaction against the degenerate brutality of the late pagan world, but in developing its natural tendencies, it becomes a "sickness" that could be cured only by the "counter-poison" of Enlightenment materialism.[102] Though spiritually inadequate, the robust sensuality of the pagan world provides something of a pattern for health, and the first task of the modern world is "gesund zu werden."[103] At the same time, however, Heine believes that Christian spiritualism has created in men a wonderful richness of imagination, and he fears that this faculty will not survive in the new world of reason and utility. Heine regards his own generation as among the last that will comprehend anything from the old romantic past. "Und doch, welche süsse Träume haben wir träumen können! Unsere gesunden Nachkommen werden es kaum begreifen."[104] Heine figures himself as both a proponent and victim of neo-Hellenism. "Denn ach! ich gehöre ja selber zu dieser kranken alten Welt, und mit Recht sagt der Dichter: wenn man auch seiner Krücken spottet, so kann man darum doch nicht besser gehen. Ich bin der krankste von Euch allen und um so bedauernswürdiger, da ich weiss was Gesundheit ist."[105]

In Heine's account of cultural history, then, Hellenic *Lebensherrlichkeit* and Hebraic *Spiritualismus* serve as reactive corrections to the excesses of one another, but neither serves as an archetype (that is, origin and goal) of human perfection. The defects of each pole tend to be played off against the other and produce the ironic tonal reverberation that Arnold rebukes as "incessant mocking." Arnold does not himself escape the conflicts of cultural values expressed in Heine's irony, but Arnold will not allow his ambivalence ever to achieve a tonal synthesis. The conflict of Hebraism and Hellenism manifests itself in his alternating assertions of opposing viewpoints, but he resolutely keeps both

102. Heine, 3:557 (*Geschichte der Religion*).

103. . . . "to become healthy." Heine, 3:568 (*Geschichte der Religion*).

104. "And yet, what sweet dreams were we able to dream! Our healthy successors will scarcely comprehend it." Heine, 1:545 (*Aus den Memoiren des Herren von Schnabelewopski*).

105. "For alas! I myself belong indeed to this sick old world, and the poet rightly says: even if one mocks his crutches, for all that he can walk no better. I am the sickest of you all and all the more pitiable in that I know what health is." Heine, 3:593–94 (*Geschichte der Religion*).

sides of his idealism free of irreverence; he restricts the use of irony to ridiculing the opponents of both his Gods, the Hebraic and the Hellenic. Heine, in contrast, resolves his ironic suspension less often through veneration than through repugnance. In "Die Götter Griechenlands" he flatly avows his aversion for both the pagan and Christian divinities.

> Ich hab euch niemals geliebt, ihr Götter!
> Denn widerwärtig sind mir die Griechen,
> Und gar die Römer sind mir verhasst.
> Doch . . .
> . . . .
> . . . wenn ich bedenke, wie feig und windig
> Die Götter sind, die euch besiegten,
> Die neuen, herrschenden, tristen Götter,
> Die schadenfrohen im Schafspelz der Demut—
> O, da fasst mich ein düsterer Groll.[106]

Whereas Arnold finds in cultural history a dialectical progression toward a full humanity, Heine finds an alternation of opposing types of knavery. Heine does not always deny the better elements of both cultural types, but he does not, like Arnold, impose a teleological rationale on the shape of history.

Arnold's cultural idealism is not different in kind from that of Heine, but Arnold surpasses Heine in faith and hope. Heine's idealism, his commitment to a new spiritual basis and a new religious synthesis, has an air of desperation about it, and it struggles for survival against an equally strong impulse toward nihilistic hedonism. "Das Leben ist gar zu spasshaft süss; und die Welt ist so lieblich verworren; sie ist der Traum eines weinberauschten Gottes . . . aber es wird nicht lange dauern, und der Gott erwacht,

106. "I have never loved you, you gods!
For to me the Greeks are repulsive
And the Romans utterly odious.
Yet . . .
. . . .
. . . when I reflect, how timid and windy
Are the gods who conquered you,
The malicious ones in sheeps-clothing of humility—
Oh, then a gloomy rancor seizes me.
HEINE, 1:206–207

und reibt sich die verschlafenen Augen, und lächelt—und unsre Welt ist zerronnen in Nichts, ja, sie hat nie existiert."[107] Since Arnold requires of his idealism that it provide a sure foundation for happiness, the uncertainty of which Heine gives testimony poses itself as a threat. In "Heinrich Heine" Arnold responds to this threat by labeling it a moral failure, a defect of temperament that is associated, in some fashion, with personal vice. This defense is, however, only a stopgap. In order to assure himself that his own deliverance is intellectually secure, Arnold apparently feels that he must attribute Heine's spiritual unrest to an intellectual failure. Accordingly, in "Pagan and Mediaeval Religious Sentiment" Arnold arrogates to himself a superior critical perspective from which he may criticize the limitations of Heine's intellectual range. Arnold's tactic of relegating Heine to the neopaganism of the Enlightenment is so successful that in *Culture and Anarchy*, when he comes to explicate most fully the cultural theories he has derived from Heine, he can explicitly dissociate himself from Heine and disavow his indebtedness to him. Whereas in "Heinrich Heine" Arnold, borrowing from Heine's depiction of Goethe, had said that Heine combined the qualities of Hebraism and Hellenism, he now says that Heine, "and other writers of his sort," use Hebraism "just as a foil and contrast to Hellenism, and to make the superiority of Hellenism more manifest" (V, 164). In order to demonstrate the injustice of this remark we shall consider the way in which Arnold has prepared his case against Heine in "Pagan and Mediaeval" by adopting Heine's ideas and claiming them as his own.

Arnold's ostensible purpose in "Pagan and Mediaeval" is to contrast the pagan religion of sensual pleasure with the Christian religion of renunciation and "sorrow" and to judge of their relative adequacy to human needs. Arnold presents the conclusions of his essay as if they were empirical deductions from two hymns, one by Theocritus and one by Saint Francis. It seems more likely, however, that the conclusions were suggested to him, a priori, by

107. "Life is absolutely too amusingly sweet; and the world is so charmingly muddled; it is the dream of a wine-drunken god . . . but it will not last long, and the god awakes, and rubs his sleepy eyes, and smiles—and our world is dissolved into nothing, nay, it has never existed." Heine, 2:253 (*Reisebilder*, "Ideen").

Heine and that Arnold merely supplies his own examples.[108] In the *Reisebilder* Heine contrasts the happy *Festtagsgötter* of the Greeks with the Christian God of fleshly renunciation, and he anticipates Arnold's thesis that only a religion of sorrow can "be a comfort for the mass of mankind, under the pressure of calamity, to live by" (III, 229).

> Die Religion gewährte keine Freude mehr, sondern Trost. . . . War sie vielleicht nötig für die erkrankte und zertretene Menscheit? Wer seinen Gott leiden sieht, trägt leichter die eignen Schmerzen. . . . Das Mitleid ist die letzte Weihe der Liebe, vielleicht die Liebe selbst. Von allen Göttern, die jemals gelebt haben, ist daher Christus derjenige Gott, der am meisten geliebt worden.[109]

Arnold, too, identifies the dominant note of Christian sentiment as "love," and he avoids Heine's psychologistic explanation of this sentiment only by locating love in the "soul," which he does not define. In the Christian sensibility, he says, all experience is "transfigured by the power of a spiritual emotion, all brought under a law of supersensual love, having its seat in the soul" (III, 225).

Arnold not only fails to acknowledge the parallelism of his own ideas and those of Heine, he actively obscures this parallelism by denying to Heine any sympathetic participation in the Christian sensibility. Arnold follows Heine in defining the Renaissance as "in part, a return towards the pagan spirit," and like Heine, he locates "the grand reaction against the rule of the heart and imagination" in the eighteenth century. He departs from Heine, however, in depicting Heine himself as an unequivocal proponent of neopaganism.

108. David DeLaura, in *Hebrew and Hellene* (p. 183), notes that Arnold's idea of a religion of suffering may have been influenced by Goethe's "The Pedagogic Province" in *Wilhelm Meisters Wanderjahre* (*Jubiläums-Ausgabe*, 19:183). Goethe does identify Christianity as an extension of divinity to misery; his treatment of this issue is very brief and is part of a broader discussion of religious experience in general. He ultimately emphasizes as the goal of religion a reverence for the self. It seems unlikely that Arnold was particularly impressed by the *Wanderjahre*. In "A French Critic on Goethe," he quotes, without taking exception, Scherer's dismissal of the book as "a mere mass of symbols, hieroglyphics, sometimes even mystifications" (VIII, 268).

109. "Religion no longer accorded joy, but rather consolation. . . . Was it perhaps necessary for a humanity that was diseased and trampled down? Whoever sees his god suffer, bears his own pains more lightly. . . . Pity is the last consecration of love, perhaps it is love itself. Of all gods who have ever lived, therefore, Christ is the god who has been loved the most." Heine, 2:493 (*Reisebilder,* "Die Stadt Lucca").

> And this reaction has had no more brilliant champion than a man of the nineteenth . . . a man who, in his very last poem, divided the whole world into "barbarians and Greeks,"—Heinrich Heine. No man has reproached the Monte Alverno extreme in sentiment, the Christian extreme, the heart and imagination subjugating the senses and understanding, more bitterly than Heine; no man has extolled the Pompeii extreme, the pagan extreme, more rapturously.
>
> (III, 226–27)

Having factitiously established Heine as his opponent, Arnold sets out to defend Christianity by demonstrating the emotional inadequacy of a religion of pleasure. Since "poverty and suffering are the condition of the people, the multitude," the religion of pleasure, represented by Theocritus and Heine, can never be "popular" (III, 223). Heine himself suffered terribly in his last years, and he announced himself a convert to theism and the religion of renunciation. Arnold does not mention this, nor does he mention that in "Für die Mouche," the poem in which Heine divides the world into barbarians and Greeks, Heine represents this division as a conflict between "truth" and "beauty." This omission is not, however, very important, for Heine's "conversion" had little impact on his temperamental irreverence and his love of mockery. Arnold quotes a passage from the *Geständnisse* in which Heine pictures himself as the victim of the "Aristophanes of heaven," and he declares that Heine is virtually unique in his capacity to support himself "by a colossal irony . . . by covering himself and the universe with the red fire of this sinister mockery" (III, 229). By arguing on behalf of the suffering multitudes, Arnold attempts to create an impression of personal detachment. Nonetheless, if mockery brings no comfort to the millions, it also distresses Arnold himself, and he finds the fierce tenacity of Heine's ironic spirit unnerving.

Like Heine, Arnold locates the source of spiritualism in the suffering caused by the material and social conditions of humanity, but again like Heine, he argues that this retreat carries within itself the germ of a positive spiritual achievement. Arnold does not, however, admit this concession from Heine. He remarks that Heine reproaches medieval Christianity for having assigned the material world to the devil, and then as if arguing against Heine, Arnold declares that Christianity drew "from the spiritual world a source of joy so abundant that it ran over upon the material world and transfigured it" (III, 230). Contrary to Arnold's contention, Heine is by no means insensible to the "joy" of spiritual transfiguration. It is because of his susceptibility to the power of the spirit that he remains himself a member of "the old, sick world." "Um uns her verschwanden alle Herrlichkeiten der Welt, und wir fanden sie wieder in unserer inneren Seele—in unsere Seele flüchtete sich der Duft der zertretenen Rosen und der lieblichste Gesang der verscheuchten Nachtigallen."[110] Heine's attitude toward the medieval period is, like Arnold's own attitude, complex and ambivalent. The best commentary on Arnold's reduction of Heine's views to a narrow, antispiritualist sensualism may be found in Arnold's own essay on Heine.

> Heine, with a far profounder sense of the mystic and romantic charm of the Middle Age than Görres, or Brentano, or Arnim, Heine the chief romantic poet of Germany, is yet also much more than a romantic poet; he is a great modern poet, he is not conquered by the Middle Age, he has a talisman by which he can feel,—along with but above the power of the fascinating Middle Age itself,—the power of modern ideas.
>
> (III, 119)

When Arnold later revokes this judgment, he does not thereby render his own analysis of the mystic and romantic charm of the Middle Ages any the less dependent on Heine. After presenting the two hymns by Theocritus and Saint Francis, Arnold sums up the character of each in terms similar to those that Heine uses in *Die romantische Schule* to distinguish all classic and romantic art.

> Now, the poetry of Theocritus's hymn is poetry treating the world according to the demand of the senses; the poetry of St. Francis's hymn is poetry treating the world according to the demand of the heart and imagination. The first takes the world by its outward, sensible side; the second by its inward, symbolical side.
>
> (III, 225)

Heine also distinguishes classic and romantic poetry according to the different faculties they engage, but he goes beyond Arnold in that he supplies a rationale for this division by distinguishing the

110. "Around us all the splendors of the world disappeared, and we found them again in our inner souls—to our souls betook themselves the fragrance of the roses trodden underfoot and the loveliest song of the banished nightingales." Heine, 1:545 (*Schnabelewopski*).

two methods of poetry according to their philosophical assumptions and artistic purposes. He argues that the sensual objectivity of the ancient sensibility required an art of direct, realistic representation; conversely, because the Christian sensibility regards the sensual world as subsumed within a suprasensible network of spiritual relations, it requires an art of oblique, symbolic intimations.

> Die klassische Kunst hatte nur das Endliche darzustellen, und ihre Gestalten konnten identisch sein mit der Idee des Künstlers. Die romantische Kunst hatte das Unendliche und lauter spiritualistische Beziehungen darzustellen oder vielmehr anzudeuten, und sie nahm ihre Zuflucht zu einem System traditioneller Symbole, oder vielmehr zum Parabolischen. . . . Daher das Mystische, Rätselhafte, Wunderbare und Überschwengliche in den Kunstwerken des Mittelalters.[111]

Heine substantiates this thesis with a detailed series of comparisons between classic and romantic motifs. Arnold seems to have taken over Heine's leading ideas, but his theoretical formulations are not as precise as Heine's, and he bases his generalizations on only two examples.

Arnold may not have been fully conscious of the extent to which his ideas about the pagan and Christian forms of sensibility derived from Heine. However, when Arnold depicts Heine as simply and unequivocally a proponent of pagan sensualism, he appears to engage in intentional misrepresentation. The passage that Arnold quotes from the *Geschichte der Religion*, where Heine declares himself an adherent of the *Religion der Freude* (religion of joy), ends with Heine's statement that "I am a believer in progress, and I hold God to be a kind being who has intended man to be happy" (III, 227). Arnold shares this humane belief, as Heine intends it, but in the context of Arnold's essay it appears merely as a proclamation of hedonism.[112] Arnold does not quote or mention

111. "Classical art had only the finite to represent, and its forms could be identical with the conception of the artist. Romantic art had infinity and sheer spiritual relations to represent, or rather, to intimate, and it took refuge in a system of traditional symbols, or rather to the parabolic. . . . Hence the mystical, puzzling, marvelous and extravagant in the art works of the Middle Ages." Heine, 3:367.

112. Tesdorpf also notes the injustice of Arnold's judgment at this point. *Die Auseinandersetzung*, p. 124. She herself, however, maintains elsewhere (p. 158) that Heine's conception of Hellenism is primarily sensualistic and that Arnold, by overlooking this sensualism, distorts what he takes from Heine.

the passage that immediately follows this declaration. Heine concedes that his own willful optimism may be "eine törigte Hoffnung," for "die Menschheit ist vielleicht zu ewigem Elend bestimmt."[113] If this is the case, Heine says, then Christianity will still be necessary as a consolation to the masses and will at the same time continue to provide spiritual nourishment for the poetic imagination.

> Diese Religion war eine Wohltat für die leidende Menschheit während achtzehn Jahrhunderten, sie war providentiell, göttlich, heilig. . . . Ewiger Ruhm gebührt dem Symbol jenes leidenden Gottes. . . . Besonders der Dichter wird die schauerliche Erhabenheit dieses Symbols mit Ehrfurcht anerkennen.

Arnold himself echoes these remarks (VIII, 330), but the turn this passage takes next should give us some insight into the motives behind Arnold's misrepresentation of Heine. With perfect sincerity Heine begins from the point at which Arnold concludes his own treatment of this topic. The point that Heine reaches—a grim aesthetic fascination at the painful absurdity of cultural history—is for Arnold beyond the range of permissible experience.

> Der Mensch wird Gott; Gott wird reiner Geist! Ein ergiebiger, unversiegbar kostbarer Stoff für die Dichter ist das christliche Leben im Mittelalter. Nur durch das Christentum konnten auf dieser Erde sich Zustände bilden, die so kecke Kontraste, so bunte Schmerzen, und so abenteuerliche Schönheiten enthalten, dass man meinen sollte, dergleichen habe niemals in der Wirklichkeit existiert, und das alles sei ein kolossaler Fiebertraum, es sei der Fiebertraum eines wahnsinnigen Gottes.

Heine's imaginative license frightens Arnold, and he responds to the threat of Heine's vision by distorting and then dismissing it.

113. Optimism may be "a foolish hope," for "humanity is perhaps destined to eternal wretchedness."

"This religion was a blessing for suffering humanity throughout eighteen centuries; it was providential, divine, holy. . . . Eternal glory rightly belongs to the symbol of that suffering God. . . . Especially the poet will acknowledge with reverence the terrible sublimity of this symbol."

"Man becomes God; God becomes pure spirit! A fertile, inexhaustibly precious material for the poets is the Christian life in the Middle Age. Only through Christianity could there form themselves on this earth conditions which contain such bold contrasts, such bright sorrows, and such bizarre beauties that one should think such a thing has never existed in reality, and that all is a colossal fever-dream, the fever-dream of an insane god." Heine, 3:519.

In "Pagan and Mediaeval" Arnold accuses Heine of depicting God as a kind being who wants mankind to be happy. In Arnold's eyes Heine's real crime is the reverse of this; the real crime is that Heine dares to depict a God who is insane and to imagine a cultural history that may not be directed toward a realization of human happiness. Arnold had declared Milton's world view obsolete, but the spirit of Milton, the fear of God, manifests itself in Arnold's poem "Heine's Grave." The picture that Arnold draws of Heine at the beginning of the poem is an awkward but distinct imitation of the picture of Satan in book 1 of *Paradise Lost.* The only praise that Arnold grants to Heine is "not to have yielded to pain." In his "lasting pain" Satan sustains himself with the thought that he possesses "courage never to submit or yield."

> Darkened so, yet shone
> Above them all the archangel: but his face
> Deep scars of thunder had intrenched, and care
> Sat on his faded cheek, but under brows
> Of dauntless courage, and considerate pride
> Waiting revenge.
> (PARADISE LOST, BK. 1, LINES 599–604)

Arnold copies this image and joins it with an impressionistic rendering of other cataclysmic passages from book 1. The bathos is unintentional.

> No small boast, for a weak
> Son of mankind, to the earth
> Pinn'd by the thunder, to rear
> His bolt-scathed front to the stars;
> And, undaunted, retort
> 'Gainst thick-crashing, insane,
> Tyrannous tempests of bale,
> Arrowy lightnings of soul.

Arnold fuses the attitudes of Satan and Heine by his grouping of adjectives. Satan regards his defeat as the victory of "the tyranny of heaven," but the adjective *insane* is taken from Heine, not Satan. In "Heinrich Heine" Arnold commends Heine's bravery in purely human terms. "I have said he was not preeminently brave; but in the astonishing force of spirit with which he retained his activity of mind, even his gaiety, amid all his suffering, and went on composing with undiminished fire to the last, he was truly brave"

(III, 117). In "Heine's Grave" Arnold associates this bravery with a Satanic defiance of God and so turns it to Heine's discredit.

The purpose of Arnold's poem is to dissociate himself from the minions of hell, the "bitter spirits" to whom he consigns Heine's ghost at the beginning of the poem. Arnold feels that Heine, like Satan, inhabits the "regions of sorrow, doleful shades, where peace / And rest can never dwell" (*Paradise Lost,* bk. 1, lines 65–66). Arnold repudiates what he supposes to be Heine's "barren knowledge," the source of his "secret unrest," and he closes his poem with a prayer that "the Spirit of the world" will grant a different sort of life to Arnold himself.

May'st thou a mood more serene,
Happier, have utter'd in mine!
May'st thou the rapture of peace
Deep have embreathed at its core;
Made it a ray of thy thought,
Made it a beat of thy joy!

Arnold translates the Miltonic archetypes of good and evil into aesthetic terms of mood and tone. The good links itself in his mind with Lessing's conception of the affirmative religious function of poetry. In the "Epilogue to Lessing's Laocoön" Arnold celebrates "the charm which Homer, Shakespeare, teach," and in "Heine's Grave" he asserts that "charm is the glory which makes / Song of the poet divine." Led by his Miltonic theme, Arnold derives this "charm" from love as the primary good. "Love is the fountain of charm." The force of this thematic association requires of Arnold that he deny to Heine the power of love. He does not make this accusation directly, but he alludes to a passage in Eckermann's *Gespräche,* where Goethe was commonly, and mistakenly, thought to be referring to Heine.

But was it thou—I think
Surely it was!—that bard
Unnamed, who, Goethe said,
Had every other gift, but wanted love;
Love, without which the tongue
Even of angels sounds amiss?

The suggestion that Heine "wanted love" is not only false but also contrary to Arnold's own opinion. In his essay on Heine he mentions this remark by Goethe and takes the rare liberty of controverting Goethe's (supposed) opinion. "Goethe says that he was deficient in *love*; to me his weakness seems to be not so much a deficiency in love as a deficiency in self-respect, in true dignity of character" (III, 132). Milton's Satan wanted love and destroyed himself through pride, but the evil in Heine, for Arnold, is of a different character. Heine's sin is that he allows himself a vision of cosmic absurdity.

The Spirit of the world,
Beholding the absurdity of men—
Their vaunts, their feats—let a sardonic smile,
For one short moment, wander o'er his lips.
That smile was Heine!—for its earthly hour
The strange guest sparkled; now 'tis pass'd away.

The content that Arnold gives to this vision is of a rather mundane character. "*Hollow and dull are the great, / And artists envious, and the mob profane.*" This is the "barren knowledge" to which Arnold attempts to reduce Heine's message. "Cam'st thou from heaven, O child / Of light! but this to declare?" Heine declared, as Arnold well knows, a good deal more than this. Heine is not merely negative, nor merely "bitter." He is, above all, "strange," and Arnold cannot bring himself even to analyze in any very precise way the nature of this strangeness. He is satisfied to assure himself that, whatever it was, it lasted only a moment and has now "pass'd away."

If Arnold is successful in exorcising Heine's sense of absurdity from his own vision of cultural history, nonetheless, the main outlines of that vision remain dependent on Heine. In "Obermann Once More," published at the same time as "Heine's Grave," Senancour sums up the progress of Western culture in terms that Arnold has learned largely from Heine, and like Heine, he announces a new religion of joy.

Forward the gracious hours have fared,
And see! the sun is risen!

'He breaks the winter of the past;
A green, new earth appears.

. . . .

'The world's great order dawns in sheen,
After long darkness rude,
Divinelier imaged, clearer seen,
With happier zeal pursued.

Though still half-entrapped in the "old, sick world," Heine declares that "all mein Wort und Lied aus einer grossen, gottfreudigen Frühlingsidee emporblühte."[114] Arnold's announcement that joy is again possible for men implicitly depends on the power of his own cultural synthesis to provide an adequate idea of "the world's great order" and thus to fashion a deliverance from spiritual conflict. The critical effort culminating in *Culture and Anarchy* enables Arnold to propound a new religion of a progressive humanity, and in order to sustain his convictions Arnold denounces Heine's irony as profane. Without the influence of Heine's ideas, however, Arnold would not have been able to define his spiritual plight or to discover a resolution for it.

Arnold remains in many ways bound to both the neoclassicism of the English eighteenth century and to the Romanticism of the nineteenth century. He is nonetheless justified in regarding himself as the heir to the German critical tradition. In Lessing and Heine, Arnold finds an explicit recognition of cultural change and an effort to create a meaningful transition from the Christian past to the modern world. From Lessing, Arnold takes the idea of religion as a progressive revelation of permanent moral truth, and Lessing confirms for him the doctrine that literature must serve as the voice of religious affirmation. From Goethe, Arnold derives support for a religious naturalism to which he may relate the aesthetic and intellectual ideal of Hellenism. From Heine, Arnold adopts his basic cultural dichotomy and the ideal of a synthesis between its elements. By combining Heine's perception of spiritual division with Lessing's assumption of a purposeful cultural unity, Arnold gains for himself the "comprehension of this present and past" that serves for him as an intellectual deliverance. Finally, from all three of these writers Arnold derives the pattern for the kind of cultural criticism that constitutes the best part of his own work.

114. "All my word and song bloomed forth out of a great, happily devout, springtide-idea." Heine, 3:9 ("Vorrede zu Salon I").

Conclusion

As a critic Arnold has faults and blind spots that limit his usefulness. He remains nonetheless one of the great English critics, and there is much that we can learn from him. Perhaps the most serious defect in his critical vision is his failure ever to recognize the significance of prose fiction. He lived in an age when the novel had achieved an artistic distinction greater than that of most contemporary poetry, but for any adequate appreciation of prose narrative we must go to other critics. Arnold's love for poetry was sincere, and his taste was very fine, but it was narrowed by the virtual exclusion of comedy from the ranks of all higher literature. What Arnold requires of poetry, a complete comprehension and justification of all human experience, inevitably condemns most modern poetry as in some manner and degree "inadequate." We may be more willing than Arnold is to accept literature for what it actually does give us and to regard it as at all times a merely human form of utterance subject to the vagaries of circumstance and temperament. As an ideal of the highest possible excellence, however, Arnold's standard should help to keep us from being too easily satisfied with the sensational, the eccentric, and the base. Arnold's ideal for literature, like his ideal of cultural progress, may never be fully realized, but in an age when the majority of critical voices proclaim the supreme function of literature to be the realization and assertion of the Self, we would do well to keep Arnold's standards before us.

At the present time Arnold seems utopian in his belief that criticism can justify its existence by preparing a climate of ideas in which great literature can be written. Again, however, we would do well to remember that there can be a productive relation between the theory and practice of literature. In his analysis of the intrinsic value of criticism Arnold has formulated principles on which humane studies may still rely. Criticism, the disinterested endeavor to learn and propagate the best that has been thought and said, owes no obeisance to the partisans of the various types of utility. At the same time, as Arnold knew, criticism does not stop at the satisfaction of curiosity. Arnold's form of general, evaluative commentary should be supplemented by studies that are more specialized and scholarly, but the end of criticism is judgment. By trying to cover too much ground Arnold himself sometimes makes judgments that are superficial or imprecise, but he is not mistaken in his belief that criticism should be comparative, historical, and cultural. By applying these standards Arnold can make statements about literature that aim, however imperfectly, at being complete statements, that is, a criticism of life. It is only in this fashion that criticism can become "literature" and attain its own intrinsic justification.

Arnold derives a substantial part of his own commentary on literature and culture from both the English neoclassicists and the German cultural critics. The ability to use sources well, however, is a virtue, not a fault. Arnold selects wisely from his predecessors, even if he does not always acknowledge them, and he synthesizes his materials to construct an authentic critical system of his own. Arnold shares with the eighteenth century and with Goethe a concern for what is of permanent, fundamental, and universal significance in literature. He shares with the English and with Lessing a concern for unity in the historical progression of culture. He shares with Lessing and with Heine an intense recognition of historical change and a commitment to the modern spirit. He shares, finally, with all of these writers both a respect for the critical intelligence and a determination to preserve or construct a culture of high worth. Arnold turns to literature for solutions to the spiritual crisis of Western culture, and within our own world, which is more or less permanently in a state of spiritual crisis, his efforts should retain a place of interest. His solutions are not always satisfactory, but we may agree with him on the need for an intellectual deliverance, and we may agree as well that this deliverance cannot subsist by ideas alone; it must sustain itself through humane values.

Works Cited

Alexander, Edward. *Matthew Arnold and John Stuart Mill.* London: Routledge and Kegan Paul, 1965.

Allott, Kenneth A. "A Background for 'Empedocles on Etna.'" In *Essays and Studies 1968,* edited by Simeon Potter. London: John Murray, 1968. Reprinted in *Matthew Arnold: A Collection of Critical Essays,* edited by David J. DeLaura. Englewood Cliffs, N.J.: Prentice-Hall, 1973.

———. *Matthew Arnold.* London: Longmans, Green, 1962.

———. "Matthew Arnold's Reading-Lists in Three Early Diaries." *Victorian Studies* 2 (1959): 254–66.

Anderson, Warren D. *Matthew Arnold and the Classical Tradition.* 1965. Reprint. Ann Arbor: University of Michigan Press, 1971.

Arnold, Dr. Thomas. Appendix 1 of *The History of the Peloponnesian War,* by Thucydides. 3 vols. London: James Parker, 1874.

———. *Introductory Lectures on Modern History.* New York: D. Appleton, 1857.

Bonnerot, Louis. *Empedocles sur L'Etna.* Paris: Aubier, 1947.

Brown, E. K. "Matthew Arnold and the Eighteenth Century." *University of Toronto Quarterly* 9 (1940): 202–213.

———. *Matthew Arnold: A Study in Conflict.* Chicago: University of Chicago Press, 1944.

Bruford, W. H. "Goethe and Some Victorian Humanists." *Publications of the English Goethe Society* 18 (1949): 34–67.

Buckley, Vincent. *Poetry and Morality: Studies on the Criticism of Mat-*

thew Arnold, T. S. Eliot, and F. R. Leavis. London: Chatto and Windus, 1959.

Bush, Douglas. *Matthew Arnold: A Survey of His Poetry and Prose.* New York: Macmillan, 1971.

———. *Mythology and the Romantic Tradition in English Poetry.* 1937. Reprint. New York: Pageant, 1957.

Butler, Elsie M. "Heine in England and Matthew Arnold." *German Life and Letters* 9 (1956): 157–65.

Coulling, Sidney M. B. *Matthew Arnold and His Critics: A Study of His Controversies.* Athens, Ohio: Ohio University Press, 1974.

———. "Matthew Arnold's 1853 Preface: Its Origin and Aftermath." *Victorian Studies* 7 (1964): 233–63.

Culler, A. Dwight. *Imaginative Reason: The Poetry of Matthew Arnold.* New Haven, Conn.: Yale University Press, 1966.

Dale, Peter. *The Victorian Critic and the Idea of History: Carlyle, Arnold, Pater.* Cambridge, Mass.: Harvard University Press, 1977.

Davis, Arthur Kyle, Jr. *Matthew Arnold's Letters: A Descriptive Checklist.* Charlottesville: University of Virginia Press, 1968.

DeLaura, David J. "Arnold and Carlyle." *PMLA* 79 (1964): 104–129.

———. *Hebrew and Hellene in Victorian England: Newman, Arnold, and Pater.* Austin: University of Texas Press, 1969.

———, ed. *Matthew Arnold: A Collection of Critical Essays.* Englewood Cliffs, N.J.: Prentice-Hall, 1973.

Dryden, John. *The Poems of John Dryden.* Edited by James Kinsley. 4 vols. Oxford: Oxford University Press, 1958.

———. *The Works of John Dryden.* Edited by H. T. Swedenberg. Berkeley and Los Angeles: University of California Press, 1956–.

Dudley, Fred A. "Matthew Arnold and Science." *PMLA* 57 (1942): 275–94.

Ebel, Henry. "Matthew Arnold and Classical Culture." *Arion* 4 (1965): 188–220.

Eckermann, Johann Peter. *Gespräche mit Goethe in den letzten Jahren seines Lebens.* Edited by H. H. Houben. Wiesbaden: F. A. Brockhaus, 1959.

Eliot, T. S. "Arnold and Pater." In *Selected Essays.* 3d ed. London: Faber and Faber, 1951.

———. *The Use of Poetry and the Use of Criticism.* Cambridge, Mass.: Harvard University Press, 1933.

Farrell, John P. "Matthew Arnold's Tragic Vision." *PMLA* 85 (1970): 107–117.

Faverty, Frederic E. *Matthew Arnold the Ethnologist.* Evanston, Ill.: Northwestern University Press, 1951.

Fischer, Walter. "Matthew Arnold und Deutschland." *Germanisch-Romanische Monatsschrift* 4 (1954): 119–37.

Forbes, Duncan. *The Liberal Anglican Idea of History.* Cambridge: Cambridge University Press, 1952.

Forsyth, R. A. " 'The Buried Life'—The Contrasting Views of Arnold and Clough in the Context of Dr. Arnold's Historiography." *ELH* 35 (1968): 218–53.

Goethe, Johann Wolfgang von. *Goethes sämtliche Werke. Jubiläums-Ausgabe in 40 Bänden.* Edited by Eduard von der Hellen. 40 vols. Stuttgart: J. G. Cotta, 1902–1907.

Gottfried, Leon. *Matthew Arnold and the Romantics.* London: Routledge and Kegan Paul, 1963.

Heine, Heinrich. *Sämtliche Schriften.* Edited by Klaus Briegleb. 6 vols. in 7. Munich: Karl Hanser, 1968–76.

Holloway, John. *The Charted Mirror: Literary and Critical Essays.* London: Routledge and Kegan Paul, 1960.

———. *The Victorian Sage: Studies in Argument.* 1953. Reprint. London: Macmillan, 1962.

Hoopes, Robert. *Right Reason in the English Renaissance.* Cambridge, Mass.: Harvard University Press, 1962.

Houghton, Walter E. "Arnold's 'Empedocles on Etna.' " *Victorian Studies* 1 (1958): 311–36.

Johnson, E. D. H. *The Alien Vision of Victorian Poetry: Sources of the Poetic Imagination in Tennyson, Browning, and Arnold.* 1952. Reprint. Hamden, Conn.: Archon Books, 1963.

Johnson, Samuel. *The History of Rasselas, Prince of Abissinia.* Edited by Geoffrey Tillotson and Brian Jenkins. London: Oxford University Press, 1971.

———. *Johnson's Dictionary: A Modern Selection.* Edited by E. L. McAdam, Jr. and George Milne. New York: Random House, 1963.

———. *Lives of the English Poets.* Edited by George Birkbeck Hill. 3 vols. New York: Octagon, 1967.

———. *The Yale Edition of the Works of Samuel Johnson.* Edited by E. L. McAdam, Jr. with Donald and Mary Hyde. New Haven, Conn.: Yale University Press, 1958–.

Kermode, Frank. *Romantic Image.* 2d ed. London: Routledge and Kegan Paul, 1961.

Leavis, F. R. "Arnold as Critic." *Scrutiny* 7 (1938): 319–32. Reprinted in *A Selection from Scrutiny*, edited by F. R. Leavis. 2 vols. Cambridge: Cambridge University Press, 1968.

LeRoy, Gaylord C. *Perplexed Prophets: Six Nineteenth-Century British Authors*. Philadelphia: University of Pennsylvania Press, 1953.

Lessing, Gotthold Ephraim. *Sämtliche Schriften*. Edited by Karl Lachmann. 3d ed. by Franz Muncker. 23 vols. Stuttgart: G. J. Göschen, 1886–1924.

Liptzin, Solomon. *The English Legend of Heinrich Heine*. New York: Block, 1954.

Locke, John. *An Essay Concerning Human Understanding*. Edited by Alexander Campbell Fraser. 2 vols. New York: Dover, 1959.

Lowe, Robert Liddell. "Two Arnold Letters." *Modern Philology* 52 (1955): 262–64.

Lucas, F. L. "Matthew Arnold." In *Victorian Literature: Modern Essays in Criticism*, edited by Austin Wright. New York: Oxford University Press, 1961.

Madden, William. *Matthew Arnold: A Study of the Aesthetic Temperament in Victorian England*. Bloomington: Indiana University Press, 1967.

McCarthy, Patrick J. *Matthew Arnold and the Three Classes*. New York: Columbia University Press, 1964.

Miller, J. Hillis. *The Disappearance of God: Five Nineteenth-Century Writers*. Cambridge, Mass.: Harvard University Press, 1963.

Müller, Friedrich von. *Goethes Unterhaltungen mit dem Kanzler Friedrich von Müller*. Edited by C. A. H. Burkhardt. 3d ed. Stuttgart: J. G. Cotta, 1904.

Neiman, Fraser. "The Zeitgeist of Matthew Arnold." *PMLA* 72 (1957): 977–96.

Newman, Cardinal John Henry. *Apologia pro Vita Sua*. Edited by A. Dwight Culler. Boston: Houghton Mifflin, 1956.

Orrick, James Bentley. *Matthew Arnold and Goethe*. 1928. Reprint. London: Wm. Dawson and Sons, 1966.

Pater, Walter. *The Works of Walter Pater*. 10 vols. London: Macmillan, 1900.

Patrides, C. A. *The Cambridge Platonists*. London: E. Arnold, 1969.

Pope, Alexander. *The Poems of Alexander Pope*. Edited by John Butt. 11 vols. London: Methuen, 1961–69.

———. *Poetry and Prose of Alexander Pope*. Edited by Aubrey Williams. Boston: Houghton Mifflin, 1969.

Robbins, William. *The Ethical Idealism of Matthew Arnold.* London: William Heinemann, 1959.

Simpson, James. *Matthew Arnold and Goethe.* London: Modern Humanities Research Association, 1979.

Stanley, Arthur P. *Life and Correspondence of Thomas Arnold, D.D.* New York: Scribner, Armstrong, 1877.

Super, R. H. *The Time-Spirit of Matthew Arnold.* Ann Arbor: University of Michigan Press, 1970.

Swift, Jonathan. *Prose Works.* Edited by Herbert Davis. 14 vols. Oxford: Shakespeare Head Press, 1939.

Tesdorpf, Ilse-Maria. *Die Auseinandersetzung Matthew Arnolds mit Heinrich Heine.* Frankfurt: Athenäum, 1971.

Tillotson, Geoffrey. *Criticism and the Nineteenth Century.* London: Athlone Press, 1951.

Tillotson, Geoffrey and Tillotson, Kathleen. *Mid-Victorian Studies.* London: Athlone Press, 1965.

Tinker, C. B., and Lowry, H. F. *The Poetry of Matthew Arnold: A Commentary.* New York: Oxford University Press, 1940.

Trilling, Lionel. *Matthew Arnold.* 1939. Reprint. Cleveland, Ohio: World Publishing, 1955.

Warren, Alba H., Jr. *English Poetic Theory: 1825–1865.* Princeton, N.J.: Princeton University Press, 1950.

Wellek, René. *A History of Modern Criticism 1750–1950 in Five Volumes.* Vol. 4, *The Later Nineteenth Century.* New Haven, Conn.: Yale University Press, 1965.

White, Helen C. "Matthew Arnold and Goethe." *PMLA* 36 (1921): 436–53.

Whitridge, Arnold, ed. *Unpublished Letters of Matthew Arnold.* New Haven, Conn.: Yale University Press, 1923.

Willey, Basil. *Nineteenth Century Studies: Coleridge to Matthew Arnold.* New York: Columbia University Press, 1949.

Williams, Raymond. *Culture and Society: 1780–1950.* New York: Columbia University Press, 1960.

Wormley, Stanton L. *Heine in England.* Chapel Hill: University of North Carolina Press, 1943.

Wright, Charles D. "How Matthew Arnold Altered 'Goethe on Poetry.' " *Victorian Poetry* 5 (1967): 57–61.

———. "Matthew Arnold on Heine as 'Continuator of Goethe.' " *Studies in Philology* 65 (1968): 693–701.

Index